THOUGHT PROVOKING QUOTATIONS

THOUGHT PROVOKING QUOTATIONS

Collections
by
Dr. B. Rajaiah

PUBLICATIONS
KALPAZ PUBLICATIONS
DELHI-110052

Thought Provoking Quotations

Rs. 690

ISBN: 81-7835-313-2

Published in 2007 in India by
Kalpaz Publications
C-30, Satyawati Nagar,
Delhi-110052
Phone : 9212729499
E-mail: kalpaz@hotmail.com

Lasser TypeSetting by: Rudra Computer Graphics, Delhi
Printed at: Salasar Imaging System, Delhi

Contents

Preface

In this second attempt I have been able to rectify some of mistakes committed in the first book, it has been my Endeavour to include as many quotations as possible. The process of collection continues, because habits die hard. This book may cater to the needs of different people. The size of the quotations is relatively small compared to what ought to be written or collected.

All efforts have been made to make this work THOUGHT PROVOKING QUOTATIONS useful to scholars, teachers, and other common readers. The quotations in this book may address a myriad socio economic problems. It offers pass port to general knowledge development, and arouse people's concern to some of the deep rooted problems confronted in life the quotations by eminent men around the world put this book in international perspective this book meets the challenge of sustaining readers interest. This book is important in its own right with over 4300 quotations on social and psychological problems.

All readers are expected to be benefited by reading and using these quotations collected from various sources on different aspects of life and humanity. It is privilege to be able to write this book for young and old people in all countries. The book is of different kind attractive, informative, will continue to be a source of gems of wisdom and knowledge. The book provides an excellent opportunity to share ideas and you grow up and find it an interesting read.

I take this opportunity to express my thanks to all those people connected with this work directly and indirectly. I am greatly indebted to my family members Smt subhadra (my wife), . B. Leela (my daughter), B. Veeranna (my son), sidhartha, Harsha (grand sons), Deepthi, and Dinesh (grand children), and finally Dr. N. Lakshmi Bhavani (daughter in law), for allowing me to complete this work.

I express my thanks to Sri. Anil Garg for undertaking the work of publication.

Dr. B. Rajaiah

1. Walking briskly three or four times a day for 10 minutes at a time may provide the same benefits as walking continuously for 30 minutes.
2. The older you get, the harder it is to maintain your weight by simply restricting what you eat.
3. A fellow at Oxford UniversityWe want a woman chancellor not a womanising chancellor.
4. If a problem can be solved by giving Jaggery why give poison? — **Acharya Giriraj Kishore**
5. Suddenly fame descended on K. Chandrašhekar.
6. Her recent film made waves all over the world, a true story about female resistence.
7. A man's respect for law and order exists in precise relationship to the size of his pay check.

   — **Adam Clayton Powell Jr.**
8. We have to offer compensation without getting emotionally involved with the patient, if we do that, treatment would suffer.
9. People thought that nothing could be done about withering of muscles associated with ageing — **Dr. Meera**
10. Foods contain important components like fibre that you would get from a pill.
11. It is not really death it is dying that is problem.
12. People are looking for the magic bullet. It does not exist.
13. The impact of good or bad done to any one will be on neighbours and others in the society.

13a. If you pass gases through anus, take enema.

14. We have a Prime Minister (Manmohan Singh) who has great competence but no authority. — **Advani**
15. "We look for original creative thinkers". — **Williams**
16. We would often be sorry if our wishes were gratified.

   — **Aesop**

17. "The army took 50 percent of the harvest in tax and bought the other 50 percent for a pittance". — **Dr. Swaroop**

18. There is no country in the world where you can experience this amazing diversity of food, cultures and the people.

19. "My face was riddled with rapid fire double — checked kisses" — An African tourist in Swiss

20. Invention arises directly from idleness from laziness to save oneself trouble. — **Agatha Christe**

21. "Throw him one look you will get his attention. Men do not need much" — **Ms Sunitha**

22. Girls do not meet to eat they suffer alone.

23. I have forgotten 99 percent of what I learned in college.

— **Ahad Haam**

24. The less their ability the more their conceit

25. Music is her first love.

—**Ms Sunitha About Subba Lakshmi**

26. I could not converse for more than 5 minutes with any woman in the first meet.

27. I am caught in situation where I cannot see a future without him.

28. If she ever leaves me, I am going with her.

29. "I associate you with the mundane obligations of life. I want you to be part of my dreams".

30. Believe me, I never asked anyone to do anything for me.

— **Aishwarya Rai**

31. Nothing is natural that is not physically in existance

— **A B Sheridan**

32. I can write better than anybody who can write faster and I can write faster than anybody who can write better.

— **A.J. Liebling**

33. Freedom of the press should not be taken for granted. It is vital to government transparency and accountability of public officials.

34. A lot was expected from this budget 2005. — **Advani**

35. Sonia Gandhi – The Prime Minister's boss, Governors boss Chief election commissioner's boss, UPA boss, the communists boss, and congress boss – wants to boss over the supreme court.

— **Opposition Party Spokesman**

36. Sonia's Charishma did not work in Bihar. The Congress humiliation was complete with the party winning only 10 seats out of 243. —

37. Prime Minister Manmohan Singh an honest sincere leader of integrity is finding it difficult to get the support he requires with in the congress. —

38. We do not need 14 months inquiry producing 601 page report of the cost of $ 10 million to tell us that data on arms in Iraq was flawed. —

39. There is nothing wrong or shameful about pursuit of political power the main objective in politics, so no political party or leader can be faulted for relentless pursuit of power.

40. The Arab world was immune to winds of democracy.

41. You have to remove the fear from the minds of People.

— **A Kalam (President of India)**

42. You can prove she is an unfit wife, but you cannot prove she is an unfit mother. —

43. It is the collection of prejudices acquired by teen age of 18

— **Albert Einsten on Commonsense**

44. I have been accused of every death except the casualty list of the world war — **Al Capone US gangster**

45. Nothing is more dangerous than an idea when it is only one we have. — **Alain Chariter**

46. Man is the only creature that refuses to be what he is.

— **Albert Camus**

47. Do not walk behind me, I may not lead, do not walk infront of me, I may not follow. Just walk beside me.

48. The most beautiful experience we can have is the mystrious the emotion which stands at the cradle of true art and true science. — **Albert Einstein**

49. Our school books glorify war and hide its horrors. They inculcate hatred in the veins of children. I would teach peace rather than war. I would inculcate love rather than hate.

50. There is only one important question. Is the universe friendly?

51. Try not to become a man of success but rather to become a man of value.

52. The intellect has little to do on the road to discovery, there comes a leap in consciousness call it intuition or what you will and the solution comes to you and you do not know how or why.

53. If I had only known I would have been a lock smith.

54. If the facts do not fit the theory just change the facts.

55. The release of atomic energy has not created a new problem. It has merely made more urgent the necessity of solving an existing one.

56. Not everything that can be counted counts, and not everything that counts can be counted.

57. Imagination is more important than knowledge for knowledge is limited while imagination embraces the entire world.

58. I know not with what weapons world war III will be fought but world war IV will be fought with sticks and stones.

— **Einstein**

59. Anyone who has never made a mistake has never tried anything new.

60. The significant problems we face cannot be solved at the same level of thinking we were at when we created them.

61. The intuitive mind is a sacred gift and rational mind is a faithful servant. We have created a society that honours the servant and forgets the gift.

62. Great aspirants have always encountered violent opposition from mediocre minds.

63. In the middle of difficulty lies opportunity.

64. The secret to creativity is knowing how to hide your sources.

65. What we have done for ourselves dies with us. What we have done for others and the world remains and is immortal. — **Albert Pike**

66. The only ones among you who will be really happy are those who will have sought and found how to serve.

— **Albert Schweizzer**

67. An intellectual is a person who discovered something more interesting than sex. — **Aldous Huxley**

68. Experience is not what happens to you its what you do with what happens to you.

69. Perhaps the most valuable result of all education is the ability to make yourself do the thing you have to do when it ought to be done whether you like it or not.

70. Salmans fire burns in reverse. First the ash then the Diya.

— **Alec Smart**

71. It is possible to store the mind with million facts and still be entirely uneducated. — **Alee Bourne**

72. Happiness is like those places in fairy tales – we must fight in order to obtain it. — **Alexander Dumas**

73. Those who stand for nothing fall for anything.

— **Alexander Hanilton**

74. Writing a book has taught me more than reading a thousand books I could.

— **Alexandra Sanchez Gavito (Mexican Writer)**

75. Book reading can be exciting.

76. What we do today right now, will have an accumulated effect on all our tomorrows. — **Alexander Stoddard**

77. Drama is life with dull bits cut out. — **Alfrad Hitch Cock**

78. Every major horror of history was committed in the name of an altruistic motive. — **Alfred Knoff**

79. There are two ways in life. To believe everything or to doubt everything. Both ways save us from thinking.

— **Alfred Korzybski**

80. The happiness of a man in this life does not consist in the absence but in the mastery of his passions.

— **Alfred Lord Tennyson**

81. I have no heart to disappoint you.

82. I would like to hire only married people. they are less likely to go home early.

83. I can manage everybody but not the artist.

84. Inequality is natural but equality is to be practised if survival of mankind is to be ensured.

— **Amartyasen, Nobel Prize Winner**

85. Courage is not the absence of fear, but rather the judgement that something else is more important than fear.

86. The higher education system had not responded to innovation and failed to adopt itself to the requirements of present times.

87. You cannot beat our milk but you can whip our cream.

88. Begging is not a productive activity.

89. "My gut told me that something was wrong."

90. "We Arabs like people with strong minds"

91. My convictions and priorities do not buckle under pressure.

92. Seldom has the right triumphed over the wrong in my felt experience.

93. I stand alone.

94. To accomplish great things, we must dream as well as act. — **Anatole France**

95. Learning a foreign language, reading a challenging book, attending a lecture, the stimulating mental activities, will keep you mentally alert as you age. — **Angela Troyer**

96. How wonder it is that nobody need wait a single moment before thinking to improve the world. — **Anne Frank**

97. There will always be death and taxes, however death does not get worse every year. — **Anonymous**

98. There is a fine line between courage and craziness and one between wisdom and cowardice. The people who drew these lines never knew the difference.

99. We are told never to cross a bridge until we come to it, but this world is owned by men who have crossed the bridge in their imagination far ahead of the crowd.

100. In each of us are forces, speak to them and they will come forth.

101. We may all live under the same sky, but we do not see the same horizon.

102. The only way to make a dream come true is to wake up and live it.

103. To do carefully and constantly and kindly many little things is not a little thing.

104. Sometimes we put up walls not to block people out but to see. Who cares enough to break them down.

105. Excellence can be attained if you care more than others think is wise, risk more than others think is safe, dream more than others think is practical and expect more than others think is possible.

106. Life is not a race but a journey to be savoured each step of the way.

107. As a general rule, prosperity is what keeps us in debt.

108. It takes a steady hand to carry a full cup.

109. Better to understand little than misunderstand a lot.

110. Reach high for stars lie hidden in your soul, Dream deep for every dream precedes the goal.

111. Falling in love for me is a milestone in itself.

— **Anouksha Shankar**

112. I love so many things Music is one of them.

113. Relationships are really important to me.

114. I will be content with silence when images are inadequate.

— Ansel Adams

115. Bankim Chandra Chattopadhya composed the patriotic anthem– (1838 – 1894) 'Vande Mataram'.

— Anthem

116. People who lead a lonely existence always have something on their minds that they are eager to talk about.

— Anton Chekov

117. I believe leaving the children enough so they can do anything, but not enough so they can do nothing.

118. I battled the disease so long that I was tired

119. Foot ball is life.

120. To retain the smile from the child to the youth is to generate employment. It represents the aspirations and anxiety of nearly 5.40 million youth of our nation.

— A.P.J Abdul Kalaam

121. "Each affluent family should adopt one tsunami survivor (an orphan)". **— President of Indian Republic**

122. To those who have advocated looking high

I owe my sincere gratitude for.

They have granted me the opportunity.

To see some of the grandest views.

To those who have been my honest critics.

I owe my thanks for.

They have reminded me that.

I dare not forget to watch the trail.

For me right now time is standing still (Shock stricken)

123. I hear stories like this ten times a day, so many victims like this woman. It becomes hard in keep them all straight.

124. I do not share blame. I share credit.

125. Do not call him happy who has the most health but to him who has the fewest troubles. — **Appollodoms**

126. There is only one thing more painful than learning from experience and that is not learning from experience.

— **Archibald Mcleish**

127. A rapist should be flogged and humiliated in public and made to suffer a slow death.

128. It is the mark of an educated mind to be able to entertain a though without accepting it. — **Aristotle**

129. Dignity consists not in possessing honours, but in the consciousness that we deserve them.

130. We are what we repeatedly do. Excellence, then is not an act but a habit.

131. Man perfected by society is the best of all animals. He is the most terrible of all when he lives with law and without justice.

132. Anyone can become angry – that is easy. To be angry with the right person, to the right degree, at the right time, for the right purpose and in the right way – that is not easy.

133. Personal beauty is greater than any letter of introduction

135. 135.The roots of education are bitter, but the fruit is sweet.

134. Virtue is mean state between two vices one of excess and other of deficiency.

136. All human actions have one or more of these seven causes; chance, nature, compulsion, habit, reason, passion and desire.

137. Pleasure in the job puts perfection in the work.

138. We praise a man who feels angry on the right grounds and against the right persons and also in the right manner at the right moment and for the right length of time.

139. The moral virtues are produced in us not by nature not against nature.

140. The hardest victory is the victory over self.

141. Pessimism, when you get used to it is just agreable as optimism. — **Arnold Bennett**

142. The gain in self confidence of having accomplished a tiresome labour is immense.

143. When one is in a rut, one knows exactly where one is.

144. The original a discovery the more obvious it seems to be afterwards. — **Arthur Koestler**

145. Politicians should read science fiction not western and detective stories. — **Arthutc Clarke**

146. Genuinely talented students will get the right offers now.

147. "Have fun but do not get lost"

— **A senior fellow at the college**

148. You can help us to help you —

149. Exams or not I will not miss a cricket match.

— **Sidhartha**

150. India's epic struggle against colonial subjugation had certain features, which strike us as unique for their Universal and enduring appeal. — **Atal Bihari Vajpayee**

151. It would have been better if I had not joined politics. I want to write poetry. The poet in me is defeated, but not dead. — **Atal Bihari Vajpayee**

152. No organization can be allowed to inflame passions and spread hatred.

153. I am a woman by accident. — **Lakshmi**

154. Some people keep leaving and some people keep coming but the core remain stable and constant.

155. Cricketers are not going to war. —

156. It is a long journey but we have made a good beginning.

157. One may learn to walk on water, mesmerize a mad elephant, muzzle a tiger or lion, walk on fire and perform other feats, but yet the real feat would be to still the restless mind and understand one's real self.

158. The blacks in Argentina are a rare sight.

159. "I am not vegetarian because I love animals, I am a vegetarian because I hate plants".

160. I'd be willing to walk through fire, for the man I love but I am not willing to share a tooth brush. — **Charishma**

161. I leave my entire estate to my wife on the condition that she shall re marry, so there will be at least one man who regrets my death.

162. It is always better to have two men at the same time. One would do the cooking and other would do the cleaning.

163. Give me what I want, when I want it, and how I want it

164. Give me something I have always wanted since my childhood and wait for the love to shower on you.

165. Lose a habit of smoking to prove that you are a sacrifying man I ever wanted.

166. "whenever terrible things happen, I focus on the good things of life".

167. We women are never happy with our projection of ourselves.

168. I needed some one to look at one with admiring eyes to respect me.

169. My life is consumed by work and I lost my friends.

170. I have a feeling of a euphoric sense of rightness.

171. The mind works faster than hands.

172. It is little wonder that in any society where fear is rife, corruption in all forms becomes entrenched.

— **A.S. Suukyi**

173. He knows how to do every thing. He is able to do everything and he wishes to do every thing.

— About Bonaparte — Napoleon

174. My dad nags me so often I get annoyed.

175. Let us wake up and smell the coffee – Morality is passé (Out of date). — **Actress Riyasen**

176. Wrong on the whole pays better than right.

— Adeim antus in "The Republic"

177. More blood has been spilt over the cause of religion than over any other cause.

— After Gujarath riots (March 2002)

178. When a guy takes of this coat he is not going to fight. When a guy takes of his wrist watch out, he is going to fight. **— Al Mc Guire**

179. Our school books glorify war and hide its horrors. They inculcate hatred in the veins of children. I would teach peace rather than war. I would inculcate love rather than hate. **— Albert Einstein**

180. There is only one important question. Is the universe friendly?

181. The fairest thing we can experience is the mysterious. It is the fundamental emotion which stands at the cradle of true science. He who knows it not and can no longer wonder, no longer feel amazement, is as good as dead.

182. The ideals that have lighted my way, time after time, have given me new courage to face life cheerfully, have been kindness. Beauty and Truth.

183. Salman's fire burns in reverse, first the Ash, then the Diya.

— Alec Smart

184. A professional graphologist — Seven out of ten people are in the wrong profession. **— Allen Conway**

185. Freedom is often taken to be a remote virtue - not immediately relevant to the hungry masses.

— Amartyasen

186. The men and women of our armed forces have delivered a message now clear to every enemy of the United States. Even 7000 miles away, across oceans and continents, on mountains and in caves, you will not escape the justice of this nation.

— American President (George Bush)

187. You are eating diner with 20 billion dollars.

<u>3 C's to a patient :</u>

Consideration

Conversation and

Compassion

188. Adults' personalities are not set in stone.

189. A great debt I owe to this country India, my mother land, which I cannot repay for many lives.

— **Amita Bachchan**

190. Acting has been an effort to do a job correctly.

191. If the director approves then I know I have done correctly.

192. When I did something insignificant like growing a beard, it became a national calamity.

193. We are human, Jaya and I have been through a few hiccups. On some occasions we have been on different wave lengths. That is inevitable in every marriage.

194. I work for my children and I exist for them.

195. No one volunteers to pay back the government, but I did (ABC incurred losses to Rs. 80 or Rs. 90 crores)

196. Checks and balances are ineviatable in the daily conduct of every man (celebrity)

197. You may do what you like behind closed doors, but in the public you have to be cautious about your conduct.

198. "I flunked in physics at my B.Sc. Exam's"

— **Amita Bachchan**

199. Women pick distant men (in intimacy) and mourn their fate. — **Amy Bloom**

200. Intimate friends are almost as rare as intimate lovers.

— **Amytan**

201. You see what power is holding someone else's fear in your hand and showing it to them.

202. Believe those who are seeking truth. Doubt those who find it. — **Andre Gide**

203. Each new day is full of opportunities, full of possibilities, full of potential, make best of everyday, start today.

— **Annan**

204. If at first you do not succeed destroy all evidence that you tried. — **Anonymous**

205. Marriage is the three ring circus, Engagement ring, Wedding ring and Suffering. — **Anonymous**

206. Only in America, can a pizza get to your house faster than an ambulance.

207. Nothing is understood by the intellect which is not first perceived by the senses. — **Aristotle**

208. A lot of good things have come out of dreaming.

— **Arthur Miler**

209. India's epic struggle against colonial subjugation had certain features, which strike us as unique for their universal and enduring appeal. — **Atal Bihari Vajpayee**

210. The coalition politics prevent the government to bring forth legislation to reserve one third seats for women in Loksabha.

211. I am not Prime Minister courtesy Congress, despite its opposition people want me and I will remain Prime Minister till they want. — **A.B. Vajpayee**

212. The change of regime will help build a new Bihar.

213. We have not come here to form the government, we are here to ensure that the government does its work.

[Sonia, in election rally in Bihar]

214. Tsunami should not make us doubt the benevolence of God

215. "When an influential person has been put out of the way, a grand and heroic deed has been done.

— **August Babel**

216. We were in the same bed but we were like strangers

217. We do not want any one to get involved in our personal lives. — **Ayn Rand**

218. Happiness is that state of consciousness which proceeds from achievement of one's values.

219. The truth is not for all men but only for those who seek it.

220. Guys always consider me hot property — **Shilpa**

221. My best friend ran away with my friend, I really miss him.

222. We talk of emancipation but we feel sad when a man can not support us.

223. Bank Debit Tax, introduced in India w.e.f. 1-4-2005, Rs. 10 (ten rupees) have to be paid on every Rs. 10,000 with drawn from the Bank, (The rate of tax 0.1 percent). BDT is prevalent in Argentina (0.60 percent) Bolivia (0.30 percent), Brazil (0.38 percent), Colombia (0.4 percent), Peru (0.10 percent) Venezela (0.5 percent)

— **Chidamrum on Bank Debit Tax**

224. Great ability develops and reveals itself increasingly with every new assignment. — **Baltasar Gracian**

225. Jacqueline Kennedy was 39, when she married Aristotle Onassis. The Greek shipping tyucoon, in his sixties, in October 1968.

226. Virtue enlightened can be as calculating as vice.

— **Balzac**

227. The power to command frequently comes from failure to think. — **Barbara Tuchman**

228. In the rush to cure all the ills to which humans are heir, liberty is often an innocent bystander and accidental casualty. — **Barry Gold Water**

229. Good judgement comes from experience and experience comes from bad judgement. — **Barry Lepatner**

230. It would be nice to have the body of 25 years

— **"Barbara"**

231. Celebrate work. Work is a celebration that's we do for a living. — **Basava**

232. Lord Basaveshwara says that he does not want positions of Brahma, Vishnu, or Rudra, but he wants to stay on earth serving the servants of God. — **Basaveshwara**

233. No matter how big or soft or warm your bed is, you still have to get out for activities — **Bauer**

234. Aid is not sufficient for development.

235. Foreign aid is more likely to inhibit economic advancement than to promote it because it tends to prop up anti development policies or activities

236. I take great inspiration from the fact that the prophet's wife was a working woman. — **Benazir Bhutto**

237. Genius with out education is like silver in the mine.

— **Benjamin**

238. It is easier to be critical than correct.

— **Benjimin Desraeli**

239. Great services are not cancelled by one act or by one single error. — **Benjamin Desraeli**

240. All power is a trust that we are accountable for its exercise that from the people and for the people all springs and all must exist.

241. Action may not bring happiness, but there is no happiness with out action.

242. What we anticipate seldom occurs, but what we least expect generally happens.

243. There is no kind of dishonesty into which other wise good people frequently fall than that of defrauding the government. — **Benjamin Francklin**

244. Remember not only to say the right thing in the right place, but for more difficult to leave unsaid the wrong thing at the tempting moment.

245. Pay what you owe and you will know what is your own.

246. Either you write things worth reading or do things worth the writing.

247. We live in enchanted times with our spirits right.

— Ben Okri

248. The first step to getting things you want out of life is this – Decide what you want. **— Ben Stein**

249. It is my dream. Let us wait and see. **— Bentla**

250. The dawn of knowledge is usually the false dawn.

— Bernord De Voto

251. Reasonable people adapt themselves to the world unreason-able people attempt to adapt the world to themselves. All progress depends on unreasonable people. **— Bernard Shaw**

252. Everyone seems to know XYZ everything, but nobody knows the ABC of anything.

253. The greatest problem with communication is the illusion that it has been accomplished once and for all.

254. Take the utmost trouble to find the right thing to say and then say it with utmost levity.

255. Almost everything that distinguishes the modern world from earlier centuries is attributable to science, which achieved its most spectacular triumphs in the seventeenth century.

— Bertrand Russell

256. No one can be respectable without being wicked.

257. We know very little and yet it is astonishing that we know so much, and still more astonishing that so little knowledge can give us so much power.

258. No one gossips about other people's secret virtues.

259. The time you enjoy waiting is not wasted time.

260. It is a waste of energy to be angry with a man who behaves badly, just as it is to be angry with a car that would not go.

261. It has been said that man is a rational animal. All my life I have been searching for evidence which could support this.

262. Mathematics possess not only truth, but supreme beauty, beauty, cold austere like that of sculpture.

263. Do not fear to be eccentric in opinion for every opinion now accepted was once eccentric.

264. A critic is one who leaves no turn unstoned.

265. Government can exist with out law, but law cannot exist with out government.

266. Education is what survives , what has been learnt, has been forgotten. **— B.F. Skinner**

267. I am old, but my music is not

— Bharat Ratnam, Ustad Bismilla Khan

268. It is better to die for an idea that will live than to live for an idea that will die. **— Biko**

269. When a man is in love or in debt, some one else has the advantage. **— Bill Balance**

270. "I want to study the philosophy of Gandhi. It is so relevant in the present day world. **— Bill Clinton**

271. "I cannot go out and do the samething over and over and over again. **— Bill cosby**

272. I do not know the key to success, but the key to failure is trying to please every body.

273. If you can find humour in anything even poverty you can survive it.

274. Sulking about your mistakes only leads to future ones.

— Bill Cosby

275. A real patriot is the fellow who gets a parking ticket and rejoices that the system works. **— Bill Vaughan**

276. I have reached the age where competence is turn on.

— Billy Joel

277. They say sex is sin, but if there was no sex we would not have been born. Sex is the word by which the world grows.

— Bipasha Basu (the actress)

278. Man has tried to live in the space and succeeded. He has

tried to live under water and succeeded. It is only in between he is struggling. — **Bishen Singh Bedi**

279. The only way to deal with the social democratic was to drive them to deeds of desperation and pursue them in to the street and there shoot them down. — **Bismarck**

280. The heart has it's reason of which reason knows nothing.

— **Blaise Pascal**

281. Blaise Pascal compared human beings to thinking reeds that even modest wind can bend destroy.

282. Man is equally incapable of seeing nothingness from which he emerges and the infinity in which he is engulfed.

283. BMI The weight of body (in kilogrammes) is divided by the square of your height (in meters) gives you Body Mass Index. If the resultant quotient is 18.5 or less it is under weight. If the value is 18.5 to 24.9 then it is average if it is 25-29.9 it is over weight.

Value	Result
18.5 or less	Under weight
18.5 — 24.9	Average
25 — 29.9	Over weight

The formula can be written as follows

$$BMI = \frac{\text{Weight (in kgs) of the body}}{(\text{Height in mts})^2}$$

284. It would be unfair to have baby and not able to give enough time.

285. The discipline you learn and character you build from setting and achieving a goal can be more valuable than the achievement of the goal itself. — **Bo Bennett**

286. Game theory is a mathematical theory dealing with models of conflict and cooperation. — **"Borel"**

287. The factual is enough to embrace the whole truth life always spills over the rim of every cup. — **Boris Pasternak**

288. Only two things can stop the government from doing anything and money and politics.

— Brandley Whit Ford

289. People who ask our advice almost never take it. Yet we should never refuse to give it upon request for it often helps us to see our own way more clearly. **— Brendan Francis**

290. To truly punish a man do not take away what he already has, simply not give him what he desires most.

— Brendan Polotrack

291. We have had to conclude that council consensus is not possible. **— British ambassador Jeterny**

292. Winning not losing triggers violence at sports event.

— British Medical Journal

293. Money and success do not buy us class. —

294. "I am perceived as this sophiticated debonair, a distant person. This macho guy" **— Britney Spears**

295. "I do not have a licence to kill, but I love vodka martinis which are delicious after a long day"

— Brosnan, who Played Jamesbond

296. Conceit is God's gift. **— Bruce HartonBruce wills**

297. The violence in films generates violence in real life.

298. I believe in taking care of the needy, the elderly.

299. When Bruce Wills was on the stage, he stopped stuttering as he went out of the stage, he started it again. "This is a miracle I have got to investigate it".

300. Romance dies hard.

301. We are taught the mythology of romance from the books we read, films we see and songs we enjoy.

302. Love and marriage is like a garden that needs to be tended everyday.

303. There is fear for his love, joy for his fortune,honour for his valour, and death for his ambition. **— Brutus**

304. Never in this world can hatred stilled by hatred, it will be stilled only by non-hatred. This is the law of eternal.

— Buddha

305. Ultimately there is only victory or defeat.

306. The conquest of self is the greatest triumph that any man can achieve.

307. To live a pure unselfish life, one must count nothing, nothing as one's in the midst of abundance.

308. Even death is not to be feared by one who lived wisely.

309. Every one has one time in their lives when they are down or tempted. **— Buddhit women**

310. Not every one is so kind.

311. Seize opportunity by the beard, for it is bald behind.

— Bulgarian Proverb

312. The observer in the southern hemisphere cannot see the pole star. The pole star will be exactly over the head of the observer, at the north pole and pole star will be at the horizon at the equator. **— Buzan**

313. When you train the muscles of memory you are simultaneously training the muscles of creativity, general thinking, survival and problem solving.

314. All that we know is, nothing can be known. **— Byron**

315. You – and – me – against the – world humour can be a big help . **— Carrere — an Expert Family Consultant**

316. It is the improvement of individual character that goes to make the national character **— C. Rajagopalachari**

317. Men are masters of their own fates. **— Caesar**

318. A good action is never lost. It is a treasure laid up and guarded for the doer's need. **— Caldron**

319. War was a time when everything stopped dead and when everything went on hold. **— Captain John Miller**

320. A man who does not trust himself can never truly trust anyone else. **— Cardinal De Retz**

321. A man would do nothing if he waited until he could it well. — **Cardinal New Man**

322. Everything that irritates us about others can lead us to an understanding of ourselves. — **Carl Gustav Jung**

323. Your vision will become clear only you can look into your own heart, who looks outside dreams who looks inside awakes. — **Carl Jung**

324. As far as we discern the sole purpose of human existence is to kindle a light of meaning in the darkness of mere being.

325. The afternoon of life must also have a significance of its own and cannot be merely a painful appendage to life's morning.

326. Absence of evidence is not evidence of absence. — **Carl Sagan**

327. Life is an onion, you pull it off one layer at a time, and some times you weep. — **Carl Sand Buru**

328. "Miss Loren you are the most beautiful woman I have ever seen". — **Carolyn Ponti**

329. "I met people who had nothing, but were so happy". — **Carolyn Thomas**

330. Every day I am reminded how short life is and that very few things are worth getting worked up about

331. Time management is doing fewer things of greater importance rather than doing more in less time.

332. After the fist sampling of something sinful, it becomes easier to sin again. — **Casanova**

333. Life is like a pudding, it takes both the salt and sugar to make a really good one — **Catherine**

334. We must be grateful when fortune smiles, resigned when she turns away.

335. If I turn up at a premiere with my breasts hanging out I am doing it for a reason — I am promoting my work

336. I praise loudly, I blame softly. — **Catherine II**

337 For marriage to be a success every woman and every man should have her and his bathroom. "The end".

— **Catherine Zeta**

338. Buy not what you want, but what you have need of, what you do not want is dear at a farthing. — **Cato**

339. Grasp the subject, the words will follow.

— **Cato the Elder**

340. There are two kinds, of people. Those who say to God "Thy will be done". Those to whom God says "Have it your way" — **C.B. Lewis**

341. All that is eternal is out of date.

342. Every one says forgiveness is a lovely idea, until they have something to forgive.

343. God whispers in our pleasures but shouts in our pain. Pain is God's megaphone to rouse a dulled world.

344. Examinations formidable even to the best prepared, for the greatest fool can ask more than the wisest man can answer. — **C. C. Colion**

345. We have to marry our soft power and economic power.

— **Chairman Bajaj Auto**

346. Conscience is a dreadful thing. — **Charles Dickens**

347. Reflect on your present blessings of which every one has many, not on past misfortunes of which every one has some

348. All causes are essentially mental and whosoever comes into daily contact with a high order of thinking must take on some of it. — **Charles Fill More**

349. The world hates change but it is the only thing that has brought progress. — **Charles Kettering**

350. If you want to be miserable, think about yourself, about what you want, what you like what respect people ought to pay you, and what people think of you.

— **Charles Kingsley**

351. Making the simple complicated is common place, making the complicated simple very simple that's creativity.

— **Charles Mingus**

352. Books are the quietest and most constant of friends, they are the most accessible and wisest of counsellers and most patient of teachers. — **Charles W. Eliot**

353. Although the world is full of suffering its also full of overcoming of it. — **Charlie Chaplin**

354. A day without laughter is a day wasted. — **Hellen Keller**

355. A woman should give her lover his way and not cross him in anything. — **Charmian in Cleopatra**

356. By going through the Gita, party leaders will think and work self-lessly. — **Chandrababu Naidu**

357. It is not the strongest of the species that survive nor most intelligent, but the one most responsive to change.

— **Charles Darwin**

358. No man really becomes a fool until he stops asking questions. — **Charles steinmetz**

359. When you stop comparing what is right here now with what your wish were you can begin to enjoy it.

— **Cheri Huber**

360. I do not deliver. Delivery is in the hands of ministries state governments and panchayats.

— **Chidambaram, Finance Minister**

361. Beware of the wrath of a quietman. — **Chinese Proveb**

362. Capitalism is like an Island surrounded by a sea of Poverty

— **Chomsky**

363. When something does not work, you respond by doing more of it. — **Christen**

364. I do not get angry because it would not do any good.

— **Christopher Reeve**

365. My ignorance is my best asset.

366. We all have a little voice inside us that will guide us.

367. If you aspire to the highest place, it is no grace to stop at the second or even at the third place — **Cicero**

368. Natural ability without education has more often raised a man to glory and virtue than education without natural ability.

369. A true gentle man is one who is never un intentionally rude.

370. There is no grief which time does not lessen and soften.

371. The events of each era shape a generation's way of talking.

— **Claire Raines**

372. Courage is the ladder on which all other virtues mount

— **Clare Booth Luce**

373. The first half of our lives is ruined byour children and the second half by our children. — **Clarence Darrow**

374. History repeats itself that is one thing that is wrong with history.

375. The most human thing we can do is to comfort the afflicted and afflict the comfortable.

376. No medicine can hold a lover for ever. — **Cleopatra**

377. Honour and safety for a defeated kind / queen do not go together.

378. If you find him in mirth, tell him I am sick, if he is sad, tell him I am dancing". — **Cleopatra**

379. Honour and safety for a woman do not go together.

380. Pride sullies the noblest character. — **Cleudeances**

381. The more we study the work of Faraday, one of the greatest scientific discoverers of all time, with the perspective of time, the more we are impressed by his unrivalled genius as an experimental and a natural philosopher.

— **C.N. Rao**

382. Unto dust thou shall return the day you stop representing the street.

383. The U.S. has the sovereign right to take military action.

— **Colin Powel Secretary State of U.S.**

384. Wisdom is what is left after we have run out of personal opinions. — **Collen hightown**

385. Jamadagni ordered his son Parusaram to behead his mother Renuka. The son obeyed his father. Jamadagni was pleased and asked his son to fulfil any of his promised desire Parusaram prayed his father to give life to his mother. So Renuka relived for long.

386. You ask credit, I do not give, you get mad. You ask credit, I give credit, you do not pay. I get mad. Better you get mad. — **Confucious**

387. Men of virtue love mountains and men of learning love sea.

388. Our glory is not in never falling, but in rising every time we fall.

389. Where ever you go, you go with your heart.

390. To see what is right and not to do it is want of courage or of principle.

391. I hear and I forget, I see, I remember, I do and I understand.

392. He who speaks without modesty will find it difficult to make his words good.

393. According to the constitution, the apex court rulings are law of the land.

394. Reconciliation should be accompanied by Justice otherwise it will not last while we all hope for peace it should not be peace at any cost but peace based on principle of justice. — **Corazon Aquino**

395. When we have strong emotion, we are liable to fool ourselves — **Corl Sagan**

396. Life is too important to take seriously. — **Corxy Siegel**

397. The stars are thick skinned devoid of any sense of civic duty or responsibility to the nation and have no IQ at all.

— **Criminal lawyer**

398. To want to be what one can be is purpose in life.

— Cyntha Oziak

399. There are three kinds of people who never amount to much. Those can not do what they are told and those who can not do what they are told and those who can do nothing else. **— Cyrus Curtis**

400. The only kind of dignity which is genuine is that which is not diminished by the indifference of others.

— Dag Hammar — SK joeld

401. "Stand for your own rights, your own values but at the same time be a good friend." **— Dalai Lama**

402. The communist authoritarian system sooner or later will have to change.

403. You have political leadership through elections.

404. Sexual desire and sexual attachment are enjoyable but they act as a basis to anger, hatred and jealousy

405. Persons creating suffering are creating new karma, and they have to face long term negative consequences.

406. Reducing anger does not mean we give in, we carry on our struggle for justice, and for our rights.

407. Buddha in his previous lives, killed one person to save 499 lives, violence is not in action but violence in motivation.

Buddha thought that if that one person was allowed to continue, 499 people will be killed. So it would be sin to allow that one person.

408. Parents should provide every occasion for genuine human affection for the child.

409. I do not believe in God. I do not believe in the creator. But I have respect.

410. We must respect other religions. To try to convert them is counter productive and creates a lot of problems.

411. More contact with other traditions helps to reduce this extreme fundamentalist sort of attitude. For example,

Muslims in India are more open than Muslims in Arab countries who are isolated and not exposed to other religions.

412. "What is the meaning of this life?".

Ans. So long as space remains so long sentient beings suffering remains, I will remain in order to help, in order to serve...

413. The feeling of "I am important" creates arrogance and exploitation.

414. If your life creates problems or suffering to others, then there is no meaning in your existence.

415. If you provide some happiness, some comfort to others then your life becomes meaningful.

416. A woman likes better known faithful than remain faithful.

417. You can make more friends in two months by becoming interested in other people. — **Dale Carnegie**

418. The ability to speak well is the short cut to distinction.

419. You are a bureaucrat if

a You know your exact retirement date, even though it is more than five years away.

b You believe that the more employees rule, there are the fewer employee problems. — **Dale Dautenv**

420. He who would leap high must take a long run.

— **Danish Proverb**

421. A perfect parent is a person with excellent child rearing theories and no actual children. — **Dave barry**

422. There is no need to go to the World Bank every day and ask for loans. There are tonnes of money in the country.

— **Dave Gowda, former P.M.**

423. While it is important to win, it is imperative to compete.

— **Dave Weinbaum**

424. Anyone who does not believe in miracles is not a realist.

— **David Ben Gurion**

425. The chemicals in some foods lead to swelling of blood vessels causing you headache. — **David Buchhotz**

426. Do you know what the greatest test is ? Do you still get excited about what you do when you get up in the morning ? — **David Halberstam**

427. Beauty in exists in the mind which contemplates them.

— **David Hume**

428. The privilege to work is a gift, the power to work is a blessing, the love of work is success.

— **David O Mekay**

429. Progress depends on people knowing they will be able to profit from their ideas. — **Deborah Niville**

430. The Supreme Court ruled that a child born out of illegitimate relationship between a high caste man and SC or ST woman would be categorised under the higher caste, kids retain biological father's caste.

— **Deccan Chronicle 29-1-2005**

431. The annual income of Tirumala for 2005 –06 (estimates) Rs. 675 Crores, vatican's income $ 174 millions. (870 crores) the average daily pilgrims at Tirumala 50,000.

— **Deccan Chronicle 4-3-2005**

432. The ground water levels have fallen by 5 mts in the state.

— **Deccan Chronicle 6-3-2005**

433. The pictures have a very old wine story line, the hero falls in love with a sexy vamp girl friend. — **Deepa Gablot**

434. Denial is often the response to the most painful realities.

— **Denial**

435. If it takes lot of words to say what you have in mind, give it more thought. — **Dennis Roth**

436. Property law is not a silver bullet, but silver it is a missing link.

437. In many countries, the gray economy is much larger than the official sector.

438. There are many statistics on who is living on $1 or $2 a day, but there are no statistics on who is outside the law.

439. The ILD has estimated that the poor in developing countries own $ 9.3 trillion in assets. — **De soto**

440. Everything comes if a man only wants. — **Desraeli**

441. You should be courageous enough to lose money

442. Flops do not break me.

443. Some one above the earth scripted our life story.

444. To succeed you have to single mindedly pursue a dream.

445. I kept knocking on doors never losing hope.

446. Some times natural elements favour you.

447. You need to be cold-blooded for politics

448. Chivalry kindness, and good manners, are never out dated.

449. I do not smoke, drink, or eat meat. — **Dev Anand**

450. By strength of will we cut off our intutive knowledge from admitted consciousness. This causes a state of dread or apprehension, which makes the blow ten times worse. What it does fall. — **D.H. Lawrence**

451. Try to find your deepest issue in every confusion and abide by that.

452. The only justice is to follow the sincere intuition of the soul angry or gentle. Anger is just and pity is just but judgment is never just.

453. 5"I found royal life an extraordinary burden, boring and increasingly irritable" — **Diana**

454. No woman has ever put me so much in the shade before.

— **Di Maggio**

455. The earlier you get slapped in the face the better it is for you, because, life is not a bed of roses. — **Dimple Kapadia**

456. I have never wanted to direct the work of other. I was always afraid to waste their time. I don't mid wasting my own time, but I don't want to waste the time of others.

— **Dirac**

457. Human beings have the ability to learn from the experience of others and they have also disinclination to do so.

— D.N. Adams

458. The activities like puzzle solving, cross words filling, reading, News papers, will reduce the risk of heart diseases by 47 percent for over 60 age group. **— Dr Swaroop**

459. The pleasure of pure sleep just gets heightened by the drugs.

460. The more faithfully you listen you listen to the voice within you, the better you will hear what is sounding outside.

— Dog Hammerskjold

461. The men snub the boys and order them about the car men snub the sweepers the artisans snub the unskilled labourers, the foremen drive and bully both the labourers and artisans the artisans find fault with the foremen, the chief engeneers drop on the assistants, the departmental managers worry the chiefs.

462. The U.S. will maintain global hegemony permanently and that any challenge will be blocked by force.

— Donald Rumsfeld — Defence Secretary

463. It is enough for me to know that you are young to love.

— Don Bosco

464. The Surprising thing about young fools is how many survive to become old fools. **— Dong Larson**

465. " A large man Marched upto our table and babbled something in arabic" **— Don Pinnock**

466. It is more important to understand other people than to have them understand you. **— Dorothy**

467. The cure for boredom is curiosity. There is no cure far curiosity. **— Dorothy Parker**

468. If you want to know what God thinks of money look at the people he gave it to.

469. Anyone who is capable of getting himself made president, should on no account be allowed to do the job.

— **Douglas Adams**

470. There are some people who live in a dream world and there are some who face reality and there are those who turn one into the other. — **Douglas Everette**

471. Keep a smile on your face till 10 O' clock and it will stay there all day. — **Douglas Fair Bank**

472. Love is like measles all the worse when it comes late in life. — **Dougles Jerrold**

473. It is essential for India and Pakistan to place all their eggs in one incubator and watch the eggs nurture so that no one kicks it over. — **Dr APJ Abjul Kalam**

To Pakistan President-17-4-05

474. I really learned it all from my mother.

— **Dr. Benjaminspock**

475. Family is very important for your happiness and growth

— **Dr. Blosoom**

476. It is better to suffer wrong than to do it. — **Dr. Johnson**

477. "I have seen miracles happen to men and women in all walks of life all over the world" — **Dr. Joseph Murphy**

478. When fear knocks at the door of your mind or when worry anxiety and doubt cross your mind, behold your vision and goal.

479. Solution lies within the problem.

480. When you really have an intense desire there is a way out— victory and triumph are assured.

481. You are as young as you are.

482. The joys of old age are greater than those of youth.

483. Money is not evil.

484. Regular physical activity is probably as close to a magic bullet as we will come in modern medicine.

— **Dr. Jo Ann manson**

485. Sex is a simple biological reaction to stimuli with no moral, spiritual or psychological dimension. — **Dr. Kinsey**

486. Mao did not brush his teeth. — **Dr. Li Zhswi**

487. All men biologically programmed to breed.
— **Dr. Nick Neave**

488. In villages, altruism is normal, the other stuff— as part of human nature – greed, selfishness, and dishonesty – is abnormal. — **Dr. Paul Farmer**

489. Spiritual life offers us strength and solace in the hour of need and sorrow. It is the conviction that love and justice are at the heart of Universe and man will rise to perfection
— **Dr. S. Radha Krishnan**

490. What is life without challenges? — **Dr.Kanwel Vilku**

491. You can have anything you want if you will give up the belief that you cannot have it. — **Dr. Robert Anthony**

492. The mother is the best person to deal with the child.
— **Dr. Sujata Raman**

493. All great men have been great dreamers.
— **Dreson Swelt Marden**

494. Most troubles come because we go half way to meet them.
— **Duc de Levis**

495. I am a man of principles and one of my first principles is flexibility. — **Durkson**

496. "I know what is dharma, but my mind does not prompt me to do it. I know what is not dharma, but my mind provokes me to do it. The inner self makes me do all these things,"
— **Duryodhana**

497. What counts is not the size of the dog in the fight – it's the size of the fight in the dog. — **Dwight Deisen Hower**

498. People are always copying our ideas.
(a). Sale of royal yacht Britannia.

(b) Opening of Bucking palace to the public.

(c) Queen paying taxes. — **Dyson**

499. Only when he no longer knows what he is doing does the painter do good things. — **Edgar Degas**

500. There are two ways of spreading light to be the candle or the mirror that reflects it. — **Edith Wharton**

501. Rudyard Kipling is our first authority on the second rate.

— **E.M. Forester**

502. Reconciliation may imply concession on the one part or on the other. — **Edmund Burke**

503. If Conciliation fails, force remains, if force fails, no further hope of conciliation.

504. No passion so effectively robs the mind of all its power of acting and reasoning as fear.

505. It is better to have enough ideas for some of them to be wrong than to be always right by having no ideas at all.

— **Edward De Bono**

506. The author himself is the best judge of his own performance, none has so deeply meditated on the subject. None is so sincerely interested in the event.

— **Edward Gibbon**

507. As far as the laws of mathematics refer to reality they are not certain, and as far as they are certain they do not refer to reality. — **Einstein**

508. You gain strength, courage and confidence by every experience in which you really stop to look fear in the face.

— **Eleanor Roose Velt**

509. Beautiful young people are accidents of nature but beautiful old people are works of art.

510. You will be damned if you do anything, and damned if you do not do anything.

511. Half the work done in this world is to make things appear what they are not. — **Elias Root Beadle**

512. In a great romance each person plans a part, the other really likes. **— Elizabeth Ashley**

513. Learn to get in touch with the silence within yourself and know that everything in this life has a purpose.

— Elizabeth Kubler Ross

514. It is life that weighs us down it's the way we carry it.

— Elizabeth potier

515. "You have health, leisure and intelligence. Elizabeth, why do not you devote these qualities to the service of suffering women".

516. A man may fall many times, but he would not be failure until he says that someone pushed him.

— Elmer G. Letterman

517. It is who you are makes people look, up to you.

— Elvispresley

518. A friend is one before whom I may think aloud.

— Emerson

519. The things that are taught in schools and colleges cannot be considered education but the means of education.

520. There are two kinds of scholars those who love ideas, those who hate them. **— Emile Chartier**

521. Success is counted sweetest by those who never succeed.

— Emily Dickinson

522. The artist is nothing without the gift, but the gift is nothing without work. **— Emile Rola**

523. No one has yet realised the wealth of sympathy, kindness and generosity hidden in the soul of a child. The aim of education should be to unlock that treasure.

— Emma Goldmans

524. Pure soul is one which has right judgment.

— Epicurtus

525. Death does not concern us because as long as we exist death is not here, when it does come we no longer exist.

— Epicurus

526. Wealth consists not in having great possessions but having a few wants.

527. Absolute faith corrupts as absolutely as power.

— Eric Hoffer

528. Do not go through life make an effort to grow through life.

— Erle Butterworths

529. By introducing the young to great literature, we open to them the possibilities that lie within the human spirit — enable them to see visions and dream dreams.

— Eric Anderson

530. Everyone has a talent but rare is the courage to follow the talent to the place it leads. **— Erica Jong**

531. The disadvantageous peace is better than most just war.

— Errassmus

532. The China's share in the world trade increased from 1 percent in 1979 to 5 percent in 2003. **— Eswar Prasad**

533. I expect to pass through this world but once, any good thing therefore that I can do or any kindness that I can show to any fellow creature let me do it now.

— Etinne De Grellet

534. Waste not fresh tears over old griefs. **— Euripides**

535. The rich are very different from you and me.

— F. Scot Fitzger ald

536. The test of first rate intelligence is the ability to hold two opposed ideas in the mind at the same time and still retain the ability to function.

537. Never confuse a single defeat with a final defeat.

538. Books are like food. Some books are to be tasted, some

books are to be swallowed whole, and a few books need to be thoroughly chewed and digested.

— **Francis Bacon**

539. Success consists in being successful not in having potential for success. — **Fernando Pessoa**

540. The doors we open and close each day decide the lives we live. — **Flora Whittemore**

541. For better study :

S, Q, 3R, technique.

(a) Survey

(b) Question

(c) Read

(d) Recall

(e) Review.

542. Movie acting is not brain surgery. — **Ford**

543. The human beings are reduced to scrabbling like a pack of rats. — **Foreign tourist on (Indian poor)**

544. The human beings are reduced to scrubbing like a pack of cards.

545. Natural abilities are like natural plants they need pruning by study. — **Fracis Bacon**

546. He that can not see well let him go softly.

547. In taking revenge a man is but equal to his enemy but in passing it over he is his superior.

548. The job of the artist is to deepen the mystery.

549. The greatest hope for maintaining equilibrium in the face of any simulation rests within ourselves.

— **Francis J. Braceland**

550. The glory of great men should always be measured by the means they have used to acquire it.

— **Francois De La Roche Foucauld**

551. A process cannot be understood by stopping it. Understanding must move with the flow of the process must gain it and flow with it. — **Frank Herbert**

552. All human situations have their inconveniences.

— **Franklin**

553. It's common sense to take a method and try it, if it fails admit it frankly and try another, But above all try something.

— **Franklin D. Roosevelt**

554. Experience is that marvelous thing that enables you to recognize a mistake when you made it again.

— **Franklin P. Jones**

555. Spilling your guts is just exactly as charming as it sounds.

— **Fran Leeowitz**

556. Television is the triumph of machine over people.

— **Fred Allen**

557. One must still have chaos in oneself to be able to give birth to a dancing star. — **Friedrich Nictzsche**

558. The level of civilisation in a society may be determined by entering its prisons. — **Fydor Dostoyevsky**

559. A feeble romantic convention is that the initiative in sex business must always come from the man.

— **G.B. Shaw**

560. The talented, energetic people retain their self respect through shameful misconduct, they do not lose the respect of others, because their talents benefit and interest everybody while their vices affect only a few.

561. It is dangerous to be sincere unless you are also stupid.

562. I often quote myself. It adds to spice to my conversation.

563. A life spent in making mistakes is not only more honourable, but also more useful than life spent doing nothing.

564. We are all weak about women. Morality consists of suspecting other people of being legally married.

565. People go to the theatre not to see the play, but the person acting.

566. Those who can do, those who cannot teach, those who cannot teach — teach teachers.

Teaching needs (3) qualities.

1. Knowledge is first.
2. Ability to teach communication skill.
3. Aptitude.

567. If history repeats itself and unexpected always happens, then man must be in capable of learning from experience.

568. I can forgive Alfred Nobel for having invented dynamite. But a fiend in human form could have invented the Nobel Prize.

569. The Indian have principles but not interests.

— G.C. Mehtha

570. If any one desires to probe into his religious scriptures, he should full well know those of other religions.

— G.K. Chesterton

571. An adventure is only an inconvenience rightly considered. An inconvenience is an adventure wrongly considered.

572. The object of opening the mind as of opening the mouth is to close it again on something solid.

573. Any argument interrupts a good discussion.

574. Hang me if found guilty.

— Gajapathi Raju., DC – 1-2-2005

575. I do not feel obliged to believe that the same God who has endowed us with sense, reason, and intellect has intend us to forego their use. **— Galileo Galilei**

576. I have been put to confusion and driven to despair of ever explaining something for which I could not account, but which my senses told me could not be true.

577. You can not teach a ma anything, you can only help him find it within himself.

578. Not all my sons are harmful to you and you should not have killed all my sons. One or two might be left to look after the old parents. — **Gandhari to Dharmraj**

579. Co operation is a duty as long as Government protects your honour and non¾co operation is an equal duty when government instead of protecting robs of your honour.

— **Gandhi**

580. Three types of persons

(a) You live for yourself, do not live for others ___Selfish, First Category

(b) You live for yourself and you live for others ____ Second category

(c) You do not live for yourself. You live for others ___ Third Category.

581. Non-cooperation is a protest against an unwilling participation in evil.

582. Simplicity means a singleness of purpose sincerity and honesty.

583. In true democracy every man and woman is taught to think for himself or herself.

584. I cannot appreciate the tremedous attachment to property.

585. I would favour the use of the most elaborate machinery if thereby India's pauperism and resulting idleness be avoided.

586. Honest disagreement is often a sign of progress.

587. Careers like rockets do not always take off on schedule. The key is to keep working on the engines.

— **Gary Sinse**

588. My prayers have been aswered. — **Gen. K.M. Cariappa**

589. Prosperity depends more on wanting what you have than having what you want. — **Geoffrey Abert**

590. Do not do to others what you want others to do to you – Their tastes may be different.

— **George Bernard Shaw**

591. No question is so difficult to answer as that to which the answer is obvious.

592. Common sense is instinct enough of it is genius.

593. A man's feet should be planted in his country, but his eyes should survey the world.

594. You see things and say why ? But I dream things that never were, and I say "why not".

595. Only the idle have the time for thinking whether they are happy or not. The formula for being happy is to keep busy.

596. If all economists were laid end to end they would not reach a conclusion.

597. The power of accurate observation is commonly called cynicism by those who have not got it.

598. Nine out of ten things I did were failures. I did not want to be a failure, so I did ten times more work.

599. Patriotism is your conviction that your country is superior to all other countries just because you happen to be born in it.

600. In any conflict, your fate will depend on your actions. Do not destroy oil fields, a source of wealth. Do not obey any command to use weapons of mass destruction, and war crimes will be punishable. It would be no defence to say I was just following orders. — **George Bush**

601. "I appointed him, he disappointed me"

602. I will not get into any discussion about when military hostilities may or may not begin.

603. Saddam will disarm himself or will be disarmed by force.

604. All the decades of deceit and cruelty have now reached an end Saddam Hussain will leave the country or face the war.

605. The United Nations Security Council has not lived upto its responsibilities, so we rise to ours.

606. In a free Iraq (after Saddam), there will be no more wars of aggression, no more poison, no more excutions of

dissidents, no more torture, chambers, and rape rooms, the tyrant will be gone soon. The day of your liberation is near

607. The men and women of our armed forces have delivered a message now clear to every enemy of the united states. .even 7000 miles away across oceans and continents on mountains and in caves you will not escape justice of this nation. **— Bush**

608. No one deserves to be a slave.

609. On funeral day 8-4-05 Throughout the West John Paul's witness reminded us of our obligation to build a culture of life in which the strong protect the weak.

610. Opportunity is a haughty goddess who wastes no time with those who are unprepared. **— George S.Clason**

611. Creativity can solve almost any problem.

— George Lois

612. A man travels all over the world in search of what he needs and returns home to find it. **— George Moore**

613. Never tell people how to do things. Tell them what to do and they will surprise you with their ingenuity

— George S. Patton

614. When you do the common things in life in an uncommon way, you will command the attention of the world.

— George Washington Carver

615. Recognition is the greatest motivator.

— Gerard Eakedale

616. To change and to change for better are two different things.

— German Proverbs

617. Everybody knows that if you are too careful, you become so occupied in being careful, that you are sure to stumble over something. **— Gertrude Stein**

(Pope John Paul 11 died on Saturday night 2-4-2005.

618. This Pope will have a place in history not just for attracting

the great masses but for his views on the sanctity of all human life. — **Gilbert K. Chesterton**

619. Education is simply the soul of society as it passes from one generation to another. — **GM. Trevelyan**

620. Education has produced a vast population able to read but unable to distinguish what is worth reading.

— **Goerge Bush, President of U.S**

621. There can be no two ways looking at the context and setting.

622. Good conduct is heaven and evil conduct is hell. God is infinite but men is limited. The marvel of marvel is that man becomes God.

623. God is one, you call him by different names.

624. From God we receive and to God we offer. — **Goethe**

625. What you can do or think you can do it. For boldness has magic power and genius in it.

626. When we treat man as he is we make him worse than he is. When we treat him as if he already were what he potentially could be we make him what he should be.

627. When ideas fail, its words that come in very handy.

628. We should neither admit any element that is not directly experienced nor exclude any element that is directly experienced.

629. We should not confine ourselves to the waking state to explore the reality.

630. Be a whole or Join a whole.

631. There is nothing more frightening than active ignorance.

632. Behaviour is mirror in which every one displays his image

633. Too many people miss silver lining because they are expecting gold.

634. Viewed from the summit of reason all life looks like malignant disease and the world like a mad house.

635. One ought, everyday to hear a song, read a fine poem and to speak a few reasonable words.

636. A useless life is an early death.

637. Correction does much but encouragement does more. Encouragement after censure is the sun after a shower.

638. Those who attack us should not be surprised if they are hit seven folds in response.

— **Gold Meir, PM, Israel**

639. Those who do not know how to weep with their whole heart do not know how to laugh either.

640. Everything flows, everything changes.. If there were no changes, we would not have anything to talk about.

— **Gorbachev**

641. Our timeless rhythms –rhythms which are part of our lives – our open spaces, our joys our celebrations – rhythms that belong to our pulsation's our bodies – rhythms that are universal, and yet specifically our own, — rhythm, that will emanate from our dreams and go forth to generate a participatory movement in the bodies of men and women. The soviet people known the world over for their love of music and dance.

642. We should look at hand writing before issuing gun or driving licenses. — **Graphologists (BIG)s**

643. For a great man, the inner man and the outer man are the same. He is an integrated man – his heart and mind leading to the same goal. He is an immortal and universal man.

644. Grief is the agony of an instant the indulgence of grief is the blunder of life.

645. Miltary intelligence is a contradiction in terms.

— **Groucho Marx**

646. The crucial factor, even more than lack of opportunities – is the lack of will to seize them as they arise, a tendency to

strive for nothing other than to preserve their customary low levels of living. — **Gunner Myrdal**

647. The ignorance of the affluent middle class with regard to the poverty of millions is still intact.

— **Gunter Gras Nobel Laureate**

648. If I am not for myself who will be for me ? If I am only for myself what am I ? And if not now – when ?. — **Halli**

649. Much of moral indignation is jealousy with a halo.

— **H.G. Wells**

650. Our character is what we do when we think no one is looking. — **H. Jackson – Brain Jr.**

651. The average man does not want to be free. He simply wants to be safe. — **H.L. Menchen**

652. We must respect other fellow's religion only in the sense and to the extent, that we respect his theory that his wife is beautiful and his children are smart.

653. For the last few years there has been accusations against the judiciary we are thinking of making judiciary accountable. — **H R Bharadwaj, Union Law Minister**

654. Ministers should not attend marriages where dowry is given or a child marriage is being performed.

655. Force can be used as the very very last resort.

— **H.W. flower**

656. Time is the life of soul. — **H.W. Long fellow**

657. It has become very common to have an affair

658. Some cardinal rules for having an affair.

(a) Do not bring it close to stable relationship.

(b) Try public phones, never call from home land lines or personal cell phones.

(c) Never from lover's home or his house.

(d) There are always fears of tell tale marks for an affair.

(e) Never tell it to people.

(f) Never make false promises of marriage.

(g) Never get careless, pregnancy will kill an affair.

(h) Have an affair with a woman who has more to lose than yourself. — **H.Sen Guptha**

659. Saddam has a great ability to hide his intentions may be his greatest skill — **Hamid**

660. The pope's funeral brings enemies together – it is the last miracle of Pope John Paul

661. The true secret of giving advice is, after you have honestly given it, to be perfectly indifferent, whether it is taken or not, and never insist in trying to set right.

— **Hannah Whitall Smith**

662. The greatest truths are the simplest and so are the greatest men. — **Hare**

663. I have no time to waste on games. — **Hari Prasad**

664. Nobody is totally incorruptible. — **Harlow**

665. We must be willing to fight and to loose sometimes, if you want to lead.

666. Democracy is based upon the conviction that there are extra ordinary possibilities in ordinary people.

— **Harry Emerson**

667. The two most abundant things in the universe are Hydrogen and stupidity — **Hartan Ellison**

668. A country is not a company.

— **Harvard Business Review**

669. My early choice in life was either to be a piano player in a whore house or a politician. — **Harry Truman**

670. What we call progress is exchange of one nuisance for another nuisance. — **Havelock Elliss**

671. A swim for 30 minutes a day burns 250-350 calories.

— **Health**

672. Food affects our body and moods.

673. Faith is the substance of things hoped for, the evidence of things not seen. —**Hebrews**

674. "If you learn more about theory of music, it does not prevent you from being carried away by the beauty of musical notes" — **Helen Fisher**

675. "The mystery never goes away. I have studied love but never learnt how to fall in love and make it last".

676. Silence would teach man the joys of sound.

677. Of all the senses, sight must be the most delightful.

678. There is no king who has not had a slave among his ancestors and no slave who has not had a king among his.

679. Character cannot be developed in ease and quiet. Only through experience of trial and suffering can the soul be strengthened ambition inspired and success achieved.

680. Keep your face to the sunshine and you cannot see the shadow.

681. A great tragedy is when people have right but no vision.

682. Life is a daring adventure or nothing.

683. The best and most beautiful things in the world cannot be seen or touched they must be felt with the heart.

684. Optimism is the faith leading to achievement without hope, nothing can be done. — **Hellen Keller**

685. The film industry is a place where a hit is more important than talent. — **Hema Malini**

686. A teacher affects eternity. — **Henry Brooks Adams**

687. Nothing in education is so astonishing as the amount of ignorance it accumulates in the form of inert facts.

688. Heaven is under our feet as well as over our heads.

— **Henry David Thoreace**

689. Live your beliefs and you can turn the world around.

690. Dreams are the touchstone of our character.

691. The good and the brave are never in majority.

692. Beware of all enterprises that need new clothes.

693. An idealist is a person who helps others to be prosperous.
— Henry David Thoreau

694. Obstacles are those frightful things that you see when take your eyes off your goal. — **Henry Ford**

695. There is not a person anywhere who is not capable doing more than he thinks he can.

696. The man who insists upon seeing with perfect clearness before he decides never decides. Accept life and you must accept regret. — **Henri Frederic Amiel**

697. Three things in human life are important. The first is to be kind. The second to be kind. The third is to be kind.

— **Henry James**

698. The nice thing about being a celebrity is that when you bore people they think it's their fault.

— **Henry Kissinger**

699. A person without a sense of humour is like a wagon without springs, jolted by every pebble on the road.

— **Henryward Beecher**

700. You cannot step twice into the same river for, other waters are continually flowing on. — **Herallitus**

701. Youth would be an ideal state if it came a little later in life.
— **Herbert Henry Asquith**

702. A positive attitude may not solve all your problems, but it will annoy enough people to make it worth the effort.

— **Herm Albright**

703. People with courage and character always seem sinister to the rest. — **Hermannltess**

704. Anyone who stops learning is old, whether at twenty or eighty. Anyone who keeps learning stays young. The greatest thing in life is to keep your mind young.
— **Hery Ford**

705. Right thinking is in all things the most important factor.

— **Hesoid**

706. Social cohesion is worth any price. — **Hitler**

707. God does not ask me for any money.

708. I do not want sex to be just sex.

709. Young man's minds are always changeable, but when an old man is concerned in a matter he looks both before and after. — **Homer**

710. The world is a tragedy to those who feel, but a comedy to those who think. — **Horace Welpole**

711. Do not worry about people stealing your ideas. If your ideas are good, you will have to run them down peoples throats. — **Howard Akin**

712. If you truly believe the magic will happen. It happened with me.

713. Once you cross the line with confidence it gets easier

714. If I accept defeat and cut myself off my dreams, then I would soon be 50, and never would have been an actor

715. I treated my own back I found a way of strengthing my back and it reinforced my belief that miracles can happen.

716. Whatever I have done has been a leap of faith, It is very important to believe. It is tough, but once you cross the line with confidence it gets easier

717. It is easy to over act — **Hrithik**

718. In Love Lab (US) language 'kitchen sinking' means, the husband dumps everything on the wife, bringing up grips from the past.

719. Sometimes, the fights between wife and husband wander all over the map never resolve anything.

720. The couple should not air past experiences in their fightings.

721. We judge ourselves by what we feel capable of doing. While others judge us what we have already done.

— **H.W.Long fellow**

722. If you are going to sin, sin against God, and the bureacracy, God will forgive you, but the beauracracy would not.

— **Hyman G. Rickover**

723. "I did not know I had it in me"? — **I.A.R. Wylie**

724. I had enjoyed myself most when I had been at my best.

725. I can never write without having some personal experience.

— **Indira Goswami, Jnanapeeth awardee 2002**

726. India is notorious for blowing its chances not only in cricket.

727. There is much that divides us, but there is more that unites us. — **Indira Gandhi**

728. There are two kinds of people those who work and those who take the credit. Try to be in the first group, there is less competition there.

729. Education is a liberating force, and in our age it is also democratising force cutting across the barriers of caste and class, smoothing out in equalities imposed by birth and other circumstances.

730. You must learn to be still in the midst of activity.

731. There is no foretelling where it will lead. I cannot avoid the responsibility or my duty to safeguard the safety of my country.

732. The public sector investment should yield adequate returns.

733. Happiness is good health and bad memory.

734. Be yourself. The world worships the original.

— **Ingrid Bergman**

735. Democracy does not guarantee equality of conditions, it only guarantees equality of opportunity — **Irving Kristol**

736. What was destroyed in 20 days can not be built in 20 years.

— **Amartysen on Iraqi War**

737. What one has not experienced, one will never understand in print. — **Isadora Duncan**

738. Life is pleasant, death is peaceful. It's the transition that troublesome. **— Issac Asimov**

739. The human beings belong to various blocks –national, social, political, religious (Regional). The way of thinking and attitude are conditioned by the block they belong to.

— J.B. Priestly

740. In a democracy, a bullock-cart-driver is as much a citizen as the Prime Minister, it is an insult to deny him (hullock – cat – driver) the use of a public road.

— J.C. Kumarappa

741. The highest appreciation is not to utter words but live by them. **— J.F. Kennedy**

742. You have to take chances for peace just as you have to take chances in war. **— J. Frank Dorie**

743. Originality does not consist in saying what none has ever said, before, but saying exactly what you think yourself.

— J.F. Stephen

744. Understanding like friendship is two way affair in which both sides have to play their part. **— J.K. Galbraith**

745. Man is superior and woman is inferior, Man rules and woman is the ruled.

746. Knowledge is the only instrument of production that is not subject to diminishing returns. **— J.M. Clark**

747. This was a terrible occasion in which so many innocents were slaughtered for which I feel shame and sorrow.

— Jack Straw [US] in Visitors book at Jalian Wala Bagh Memorial

748. It is a rash man who reaches a conclusion before he gets to it. **— Jacob Levin**

749. I am sixty two now (1991) and I have been in the public eye for more than 30 years.

750. I feel as though I have turned into a public property.

751. What does the way I wear my hair have to do with my husband's ability to serve as president.

752. I want people to know about how the rest of the world lives. — **Jacqueline Kennedy**

753. De soto is the most interesting intellectual writing on development — **Jagdish Bhagwathi**

754. I never asked for the post of patron in chief to be given to me, never manoeured for it and tried to be neutral when I was being elected. — **Jagmohan Dalmia**

755. There is no problem in showing programmes certified 'A' or adult by the Central Board of Film Certification after 10 pm. — **Jaipal Reddy, Information and Broadcastng Minister**

756. You cannot dream yourself into a character you must hammer and forge yourselves one.

— **James A Froade**

757. Work joyfully and peacefully knowing that right thoughts and right efforts inevitably bring about right results.

— **James Allen**

758. Not everything that is feared can be changed, but nothing can be changed until it is feared. — **James Baldwin**

759. A pound of pluck is worth a ton of luck.— **James A Garfield**

760. Do just once what others say, you cannot do and you will never pay attention to their limitations again.

— **James Cook**

761. Life is a long lesson in humility. — **James & M. Barrie**

762. Some people are ready to change and others are not.

— **James Gord on MD**

763. An acre of performance is worth the whole world of promise. — **James Howell**

764. Mistakes are portals of discovery. — **James Joyee**

765. Every life is many days day after day. We walk through ourselves meeting robber, ghosts, giants, old men, young men wives and widows, brothers-in-law, But always meeting ourselves.

766. Profit is not a right but a reward for good management.

— **James L. Hayes**

767. Education has twin objectives Education for living and education for making a living. — **James Mason Wood**

768. The foolish person keeps happiness in the distance, the wise person grows it under his feet.— **James Oppenheim**

769. In creating the only hard thing is to begin, a grass blade is no easier to make than an oak.

— **James Russel Lowell**

770. All human beings should try to learn before they die, what they are running from and to and why.— **James Thurber**

771. There are three Ks to bring about social change in India Kanoon (law), Karma (deeds), Katal (murder)

— **Jaya Prakash Narayan**

772. The only true wisdom is in knowing. — **Jim Rohn**

773. There was something about the appearance of the people that told you; Here you are in a place of safety.

— **John Webster on Malta**

774. It is the state which is a violator of human rights in maximum cases in the country.

— **J.S. Verma, Chairman NHRC**

775. The distance between genius and insanity is measured by success. — **James Bond**

776. Heaven is an American salary Chinese cook, an English house and Japanese wife, Hell is defined having a Chines salary, an English cook a Japanese house and an American wife. — **James H. Kabbler III**

777. Our relatively peril – free lives set humans apart from animals. In civilized life it has become possible to pass from the grave without ever having had a pang of genuine fear. — **James, Philosopher**

778. Those who do not complain are never priced.

779. Vanity and pride are different things, though the words are

often used synonymously. A person may be proud without being vain. Pride relates more to our opinion of ourselves, vanity to what we would have others think of us.

— Jane Austen

780. We all have a better guide in ourselves if we would attend to it, than any other person can be.

781. Genius only means an infinite capacity for taking pains.

— Jane Hopkins

782. May be the greatest challenge now is to find a way to keep independence while also committing ourselves to the ties that bind people, families, and ultimately societies together.

— Jane O'Reilly

783. Religion may be alright when applied to ethics, and morals, but if it enters the political sphere it has a minus effect on morals. **— Jawaharlal Nehru**

784. Lord Basaveshwara set model for others, human beings. by following the foot steps of such master, a devoted man of God, is bound to realize the delights of spiritual experience. **— Jaya Chamaraja Wadiyar**

785. The supreme court ruled that they cannot have nativity scene in Washington because they could not find three wise men and a virgin. **— Jay Leno**

786. Everyone believes very easily whatever they fear or desire.

— Jean De La fontaine

787. It is a choice not chance that determines your destiny.

— Jean Nidetch

788. Friends are the family you choose. **— Jennifer Aniston**

789. Love does not cost a thing. **— Jennifer Lopez**

790. There are all these ideals about what is perfect and what is beautiful, and what is smart but the most appealing thing is me, is nobody else.

791. Once in a while you get shown the light in the strangest of places if you look at it right. **— Jerry Garcia**

792. Anything is not 100 percent right or wrong.

— **Jet Li, a Chinese popular producer.**

793. You cannot change the public perception by force.

794. Good guy kills bad guy in films

795. Violence is not only solution.

796. We are used to watching heroes using violence to stop violence.

797. You can not always be at the top.

798. Your physical body is given to you by your parents, but there is something innate that comes from your past life. These innate abilities allow you to be distinuished in what you do.

799. Chinese people do not know what American people think and vice versa.

800. Li was martial artist at the age of 11.

801. If man and woman can understand each other, it would be a wonderful world.

802. To clap you need both hand.s

803. If you know how to die, you know how to enjoy life.

804. Long, unproductive meetings are the bare of present civil life.

805. "Just do not be a bum" advice given by my teacher.

— **Jim Belushi**

806. Christmas is a holiday that persecutes the lonely frayed and the rejected. — **Jimmy Cannon**

807. The worst thing in your life may contain seeds of the best, when you can see crisis as an opportunity your life becomes not easier, but more satisfied. — **Joe Kogel**

808. If people are free in any meaningful sense of word, that means they are at liberty to foul up their lives as much as make something grand of them. That is gamble we take. That is the risk of liberty. — **Joel Miller**

809. The only thing you take with you when you are gone is what you have not annuled. — **John Ahston**

810. A plan is a list of actions arranged in whatever sequence is thought likely to achieve an objective. — **John Arganti**

811. An atheist is a man who has no invisible means of support. — **John Buchan**

812. The lure of the distant and the difficult is deceptive. The great opportunity is where you are. — **John Burroughs**

813. I do not understand why people are frightened of new ideas. I am frightened of the old ones. — **John Cage**

814. The self is not something ready made, but something in continuous formation through choice of action.

— **John Dewey**

815. The willingness to accept responsibility for one's own life is the source from which self respect springs.

— **Joan Dideon**

816. God never made his work for man to mend.

— **John Dryden**

817. Be nice to people on your way up because you meet them on way down. — **John Durante**

818. One's existence as a self conscious being has to be attributed to super natural spiritual creation.

— **John Eccles (Nobel Prize Winner)**

819. If a free society cannot help the many who are poor it cannot save the few who are rich. — **John F Kennedy**

820. Forgive your enemies but never forget their names.

821. We stand for freedom. That is our conviction for ourselves. That is our only commitment to others. — **Bush**

822. He who has done his best for his own time has lived for all times. — **Johann Von Schiller**

823. It is not necessary to advertise food to hungry people, fuel to cold people, a house to the homeless.

— **John K. Galbraith**

824. Idealism increases in direct proportion to one's distance from the problem. — **John Gals Worthy**

825. It is not giving children more that spoils them. It is giving them more to avoid confrontation. — **John Grey**

826. The universe is not only stranger than we suppose, but stranger than we can suppose. — **John Haldane**

827. The true test of character is not how much we know how to do, but how we behave when we do not know what to do. — **John Holy**

828. A thing of beauty is a joy for ever its loveliness increases it will never pass into nothingness — **John Keats**

829. Life is what happens to you while you are busy making other plans. — **John Lennon**

830. New ideas are always suspected, and usually opposed with out any other reason but because they are not already common. — **John Locke**

831. In the province of the mind, what one believes to be true, either true or becomes true. — **John Lilly**

832. All Prime Ministers face intolerable problems.

— **John Major, P.M. England**

833. Where there is no hope in the future there is no power in the present. — **John Maxwell**

834. Maturity begins to grow when you can sense your concern for others outweighing your concern for yourself.

— **John Menaughton**

835. A timid person is frightened before a danger, a coward during the time, a courageous person afterwards.

— **John Paul Richter**

836. Patience and perseverance have a magical effect before which difficulties disappear and obstacles vanish.

— **John Quency Adams**

837. The highest reward for man's toil is not what he gets for it, but what he becomes by it. — **John Ruskin**

838. As we age, our bodies become less efficient at absorbing nutrients (multi vitamin tablets with minerals).— **Johnson**

839. 1Boswell asked "But what do you think of supporting a cause which you know to be bad ?" Johnson gave a classic reply "Sir you do not know it to be good or bad till the judge determines it. An argument which does not convince you may convince the judge to whom you urge it. If it does convince him. Why then Sir, you are wrong and he is right".

840. Everyone is a scoundrel unless proved otherwise.

— **Johnson**

841. Against criticism a man can neither protest nor defend himself, he must act in spite of it and then it will gradually yield to him. — **Johann Wolfgangvon Goethe**

842. So divinely is the world organised that every one of us, in our place and time is to balance with everything else.

— **Johann WV Goathe**

843. Eventlessness has no posts to drape duration on – from nothing to nothing is no time at all. — **John Stein Beek**

844. Be kind. Remember everyone you meet is fighting a hard battle. — **John Watson**

845. Ability may get you to the top but it takes character to keep you on the top. — **John Wooden**

846. A man should never be ashamed of saying that he had been in the worng, It means that he is wiser today than what he was yesterday. — **Jonathan Swift**

847. Neither are any wars so famous and bloody or of so long continuance, as those occasioned by difference in opinion, especially if it be in things indifferent.

848. They say fingers were made before forks, and hands before knives.

849. Poor nations are hungry, and rich nations are proud and pride and hunger will ever be at variance.

850. It is only imperfection that complains of what is imperfect.

The more perfect we are the more gentle and quiet we become towards the defects of others.

— **Joseph Addison**

851. Knowledge is that which next to virtue truly raises one person above another.

852. I write in English, think in French and dream in Polish.

— **Joseph Conrad**

853. Life is a Social Process.

854. Defeat never comes to men until he admits it.

— **Josephus Daniels**

855. The snob's error is to put good taste before good heart.

— **Joseph Epstein**

856. If you go in for arguments take care of temper. Your logic if you have any, will take care of itself.

— **Joseph Farrell**

857. An animal that cannot detect danger cannot stay alive.

— **Joseph Le Doux**

858. Silence is one of the hardest arguments to refute.

— **Josh Billings**

859. One of the greatest victories you can gain over some one is to beat him at politeness.

860. As a professional journalist, he gets to meet people so many people, all kinds every kind, who talk to him let him wonder through their lives, even making out milestones for him to examine and comment on, some people leave an indelible imprint on the mind of journalist writer.

861. Any one who is bored on his own is boring in company.

— **Jozsef Egry**

862. The ultimate measure of a mán is where he stands at times of challenge and controversy. — **Jr. M.L Kin**

863. It is hard to make New Year's resolutions when you are already perfectly behaved. — **Judith Martin**

864. You can tell the health of a marriage by the number of teeth marks on the body. **— Judith Sills**

865. "I have never regretted making the choice I made that morning, or I will never regret the choice I make every morning". **— Judy Muller**

866. Profectionism runs in my blood.

867. Sometimes I have to deal with the deedlines or daughters.

868. Radio is a perfect career for me. Off the air by noon, a long liquid lunch, home to greet kids, have a few drinks while making dinner, then off to bed ready to start all over again at 3 a.m. the next day.

869. The 12-step recovery groups seem silly with their bumper sticker philosophy.

870. Laziness is nothing more than the habit of resting before you zet tired. **— Jules Renard**

871. Men willingly believe what they wish. **— Julius Caesar**

872. There is a holy mistaken zeal in politics as well as in religion. By persuading others we convince ourselves. **— Junius**

873. Encouraging a common man particularly in the rural areas to resort to most dangerous vices cannot be justified. **— Justice L, Narsimha Reddy, H.C.**

874. The protection of the rights of the individuals is our primary concern and the laws are based on the supreme value of the human personality. **— Justice Shah**

875. Always be a first rate version of yourself instead of a second rate version of somebody else. **— Judy Garland**

876. We were forced to extend support to the congress led UPA government to save the country from the barbaric and uncivilised rule of the BJP. **— Jyothi Basu**

877. "We want to have good number so that we can have control over the situation, we do not want to sacrifice our movement **— K. Chandrasekhar Rao (TRS Leader)**

878. I am not worried what people think of me. My mission is clear and I will reach my goal.

— **K Jana Reddy (Home Minster A.P.)**

879. I am not scared of death. Death is inevitable and one has to face it boldly. Let it come fast for me.— **Kabir (in Hindi)**

880. Friendship and love like a thread once broken cannot be joined, if joined, tie remains.

881. If a teacher is indeed wise he does not bid you enter the of his wisdom, but rather leads you to the threshold of your own mind. — **Kahlil Gibran**

882. Keep me away from wisdom which does not cry, the philosophy which does not laugh, and the greatness which does not bow before children.

883. We cannot allow our collective conscience to be quelled by writing off cheques alone. — **Kamal Hasan**

884. Look to this day For it is life, the very life of life
In its brief course
Lie all the varieties and realities of your existence
The bliss of growth
The glory of action
The splender of achievements
For yesterday is but a dream
And tomorrow is only a vision
But today well lived makes yesterday a dream of happiness
And every tomorrow a vision of hope
Look well therefore to this day
Such is the salutation to the Dawn. — **Kalidasa**

885. Women change their destinies and not wait for society men and laws to change

— **Kanchan Choudhary Bhattacharya (Women DIG)**

886. I am open to doing every kind of role (even backless in recent film). — **Kareena Kapoor**

887. To love is to receive a glimpse of heaven. — **Karen Sunde**

888. Being on the tight rope is living, everything else is waiting.

— Karl Wallenda

889. I never feel tired. I feel great –never better. — **Kate**

890. "I have spent twenty five years learning to be invisible in all the proper places".

—Katharine Hepburn a Proud and Independent Woman

891. Regret is an appalling waste of energy. You cannot build on it its only good for wallowing in.— **Katherine MansfielD**

892. You cannot step twice into the same river for other waters are continually flowing in.

893. The conflict between social conformity and individual liberty is permanent unresolvable and necessary.

— Kathreen Norris

894. Laila Rauss, an Indian 29 year old actress who refused $ 250000 offer from play boy for a naked shoot. I am not afraid of being seen in bed room scenes. It seemed that I was breaking the mould, India is where the Kamasuthra is from. — **Kaushik Basu, Editor**

895. Begging was one of the means of support. — **Kautilya**

896. We can destroy ourselves by cynicism and disillusion just as effectively as by bombs — **Kenneth Clark**

897. There has not been much progress in substantive issues. There has been progress on people to people contact and means of communications. — **Khurshid M. Kasauri on Indo Pak ties [DC – 24-2-2005]**

898. I have learned something from everyone, and what man is there who has not learned something from all.

— Knut Humsun

899. There can be no acceptance of those who would seek to justify the deliberate taking of innocent civilian life regardless of cause or grievance.

— Kofi Annan Secretary General United Nations (Nobel Prize for Peace 2001)

900. It is good to have a player like Sania in our tournament.
— **Krishna Bhupathi**

901. The U.S. has condemned the terrorism but has not stopped giving aid to Pakistan. — **Krishna Reddy**

902. I have two daughters appreciation and misunderstanding.
— **Kuppu Swamy**

903. It is better to burn out than fade away. — **Kurt Cobain**

904. To be pink of health and youth sums up paradise. Heaven could be the company of pretty girls. — **Kushwant Singh**

905. Fear strikes when we are most comfortable, comfort occurs, when we are fearful. — **Kyle Joseph Pereie**

906. Walk away from them until you are stronger, all your problems will be there, when you get back, but you will be better able to cope. — **Lady Bird Johnson**

907. There is more self – love than love in jealousy.
— **LA Roche Faucald**

908. This paswan is a pendulum who is neither this side nor that side. It oscilates from here to there and back without sticking to one place. — **Lalu Prasad**

909. If knowledge is power, why do not more people aspire to it. — **Laszlo Feleki**

910. This sort of calamity shakes our faith in every law of nature.
— **Lata**

911. Imagination is the highest kite one can fly.
— **Lauren Becall**

912. Equal opportunity means everyone will have fair chance at being incompetent. — **Laurence J. Peter**

913. An economist is an expert who will know tomorrow why the things predicted yesterday did not happen today.

914. You cannot build a reputation on what you intend to do.
— **Lazsmith**

915. We cannot score a decisive victory against terrorism unless a special law of this kind [POTO] is enacted.

916. It is easy to instigate people for instataneous political gain.

917. We cannot deny the underlying truth of India shining. We are witnessing a new and rising India.

918. The Jharkhand Governor has murdered democracy. He is a supari (contract) Killer acting at the beset of the U.P.A.

— **L.K. Advani**

919. In Indian conditions if a choice had to be made one would opt for higher growth and more employment even if it meant putting up with higher prices. — **L.K. Jha**

920. Continuous effort not strength or intelligence is the key to unlocking our potential. — **Lean Cardes**

921. You understand people better if you look at them as if they were children. For most men never mature, they simply grow taller. — **Leo Rosten**

922. Motivation is everything. You can do the work of two people but you cannot be two people. Instead you have to inspire the next to inspire the next guy down the line and get him to inspire his people. — **Lee Lacocca**

923. To solve big problems you have to be willing to do unpopular things.

924. The Gita taught me detachment. — **Leela Seth**

925. A sense of self esteem is important for women.

926. Balancing home and work is nothing exceptional.

927. It is important to have a family, but it is also important to have a sense of self esteem from work.

928. It is important to have interests of your own.

929. I am a great believer in transparency and transparency in everything — transparency in life, and action, in the govt. in judiciary, administration etc., is very important

930. The children in the family are part of entire decision making process.

931. Reputation is an important aspect of life.

932. I do not have any regrets though there are some unpleasant experiences in life.

933. You are what you are

934. The virtue of our people must be courage, valour, fearlessness in struggle, readiness to fight together as one people against the enemies of our country. — **Lenin**

935. When you reach for the stars you may not get one but you would not come up with a handful of mud water.

— **Leo Burnett**

936. The purpose of life is not to be happy, to be useful to be responsible. It is above all to matter to stand for something, to have made some difference that you lived at all.

— **Leo Rosten**

937. When you are content to be simply yourself and don't compare or compete everybody will respect you.

— **Leo Tzll**

938. He who knows does not speak. He who speaks does not know.

939. Every man however old he may be has an exaggerated interest in viewing sexual object. — **Leo – Tolstory**

940. I can deceive, but how can I deceive myself?

941. The religious restrictions on smoking, drinking and pre marital or extra marital sex, etc. lead to some positive health effects. — **Levin**

942. All participants in peace talks must submit to the tyranny of meaninglessness. — **Lewis Carroll**

943. Sometimes I have believed as many as six impossible things before breakfast.

944. The trouble with being in the rat race is that even if you win you are still a rat. — **Lily Tomlain**

945. Let us have faith that right makes might and in that faith,

let us to the end dare to do our duty as we consider it. — **Lincoln**

946. That is the risk you take, if you change. The people you have been involved with would like the new you. But other people who do will come along. — **Lisa Auther**

947. Even the most enlightened people are after one thing that is sex. — **Lisa wolfe**

948. Reputation is what other people know about you. Honour is what you know about yourself. — **Lois Me Master Bujold**

949. In great attempts, it is glorious even to fall — **Longinus**

950. A woman is half full of cold, half full of fire. — **Lorca**

951. To be able to look back upon one's past life with satisfaction is to live twice. — **Lord Acton**

952. Justice is not cloistered virtue, she must be allowed to suffer the scrutiny, even through outspoken comments of ordinary men. — **Lord Atkin**

953. Education makes a people easy to lead, but difficult to drive, easy to govern but difficult to enslave. — **Lord Brougham**

954. The law is the true embodiment of everything that is excellent. It has no kind of fault or flaw. — **Lord Chancellor**

955. I lived long enough to find out that one may be very angry and very wrong. — **Lord Eldon (Lord Chancellor)**

956. I do not let my mouth say nothing my head cannot stand. — **Louis Armstrong**

957. The bane of common humanity is that what is urgent takes priority over what is important, so that what is important will be attended only when it becomes urgent, which may be too late. — **Louis Halle**

958. In the field of observation chance favours only the prepared mind. — **Louis Pasteur**

959. Our minds go fatter than our hands and speed is very bad for writing. **— Lovett**

960. Things do not fall apart, things hold **— Lucille Clifton**

961. Lines connect in thin ways that last and lives become generations made out of pictures and words just kept.

962. A large part of mankind is angry with the sinners and not with the sins. **— Lucious Annaeus Seneca**

963. The mystical is not how the world is, but that it is.

— Ludwig Wittgestein

964. Learn to laugh at your troubles and you will never run out of things to laugh at. **— Lyn Karol**

965. The sri Venkateshwar a Temple Tirumala has surpassed the vatican in terms of income and pilgrims to become the richest religious institution in the world.

— M. Satyanarayana Rao[the minister for Endownments. AP]

966. India has the world's largest stocks of food grains (60 m. tons) and the world's largest number of hungry people.

— M. Swaminathan

967. The dismissal of the government in Goa is a midnight murder of democracy. **— M. Venkaiah Naidu**

968. There are (3) types of people. Those who dispute, the disputed land. Those who dispute undisputed land, those who dispute government going to court. (on Ayodhya dispute)

969. Success and failure are merely incidental –they don't contribute to real satisfaction. **— M.C. Chagia**

970. We feel bad, if a woman we love, a daughter we care for is kidnapped.

971. My work is not about sex gymnastics. It is about sex aesthetics.

972. Eroticism has been part and parcel of our culture.
— M.F. Hussain [Famous Painter]

973. Nothing contributes so much to tranquilizing the mind as a steady purpose – a paint on which the soul may fix its intellectual eye.

974. A speaker keeps getting rewards from his party that gave him the job. A speaker is poor mathematian and forgets how to count. — **MJ Akhar Journalist**

975. We are not afraid of POTO, but we are afraid of its misuse.

976. Never refuse any advance of friendship for if nine out of ten bring you nothing, one alone may repay you.

— **Madame De Tencis**

977. You are never too old to become younger. — **Mae West**

978. After training in archery, Kauravas and pandavas participated in " archery contest" Arjuna introduced himself as a disciple of Dronacharya while other archers introduced themselves as sons of Pandu Raju. — **Maha Bharatha**

979. For God— Fearing men, all religions are good and equal.

— **Mahatma Gandhi**

980. Always aim at complete harmony of thought and word and deed. Always aim at purifying your thoughts and everything will be well.

981. Freedom is not worth having, if it does not include the freedom to make mistakes.

982. Every accomplishment big or little has its stages - drudgery and triumph, a beginning, a struggle and a victory.

983. Suffering is circumstantial it either stops or we die.

— **Maite Proenea**

984. Weddings and funeral are inevitable events – like accidents. I am tired of being called pretty.

— **Manisha Koirala**

985. Education's purpose is to replace an empty mind with an open one. — **Malcom Forbes**

986. If is so much easier to suggest solutions when you do not know too much about the problem.

987. Disaster comes by way of mouth. — **Mao**

988. Revolution is not a tea party.

989. War can only be abolished through war and in order to get rid of the gun, it is necessary to take up the gun.

— Mao Zedong – (1893 – 1976) Mao Tse – Tung.

990. The emperors in china believed that more sex partners they had, the longer they would live – They had thousands of concubines. — **[Mao followed those Emperors.]**

991. India's real challenges are at home.

— Manmohan Singh (P.M.)

992. Political politics was needed at the time of Independence movement Today what is needed for India is developmental politics.

993. A door has been opened **– Manmohan Singh P.M [after inaugural Bus Service to Muzaffarabad on 7-4-05]**

994. Kindness in giving creates love. — **Mao Zedong**

995. I did not write half cf what I saw -

996. In Persian village zardanadan people had gold teeth

997. In dal village, people had tattoos of tigers, elephants and adages they said tattoos identify you.

998. The robbers make the whole day dark by their enchantment then they kill the old and the young they take and sell them for serfs and for slaves. (in his book The description of the world. – on travel 9700 kms)

999. People there dined on raw flesh including that of fowl, sheep, oxen, and buffalo (Chinese continued this tradition on special occasions (in his book, 1254-1324 at 70 Yrs.)

— Marco Polo

1000. It is not death a man should fear, but he should fear never beginning to live. — **Mareny Airelius**

1001. An eye for an eye only leads to more blindness.

— Margaret Atwood

1002. Being rich is having money, being wealthy is having time.

— **Margaret Bonnano**

1003. At such times when we can do nothing we can still love with out expecting any reward or change or gratitude.

— **Margaret Jell Costa (Translation from portugese)**

1004. We remain determined to pursue the policies for growth stability employment and prosperity. — **Margaret Thatcher**

1005. Thanks to all those who voted for me and those who voted against me.

1006. Standing in the middle of the road is very dangerous, you get knocked down by the traffic from both sides.

1007. Speak not against anyone whose burden you have not weighed youself. — **Marian Bradley**

1008. An act of Justice closes the book on misdeed, an act of vengeance writes one of its own. — **Marilyn**

1009. Other side of every fear is freedom. — **Marilyn Ferguson**

1010. Kindness is a language which the deaf can hear and the blind can read. — **Mark Twain**

1011. Any one who can think of only one way to spell a word obviously lacks imagination.

1012. Always do right. This will gratify some people and astonish the rest.

1013. All you need in this life is ignorance and confidence then success is sure.

1014. In religion and politics people's beliefs and convictions are gotten at second hand and without examination.

1015. Never tell the truth to people who are not worthy of it.

1016. You cannot depend on your eyes when your imagination is out of focus.

1017. Let us be thankful for the fools, but for them, the rest of us could succeed.

1018. Be careful about reading health books. You may die of misprint.

1019. When angry count to four, when very angry swear.

1020. The man who does not read good books has no advantage over the man who cannot read them.

1021. Let us so live life that when we die even the under taker will be sorry.

1022. Broad, whole some charitable views of men and things cannot be acquired by vegetating in one little corner of earth all one's lifetime.

1023. God made the idiot for practice, and then he made the school board.

1024. It is better to deserve honours and not have them than have honours and not deserve them.

1025. Grief can take care of itself, but to get the full value of a joy you must have somebody to divide with.

1026. The more sensitive you are the more certain you are to be brutalised, develop scabs. Never evolve. Never allow yourself to feel everything because you always feel too much. — **Marlon Branco**

1027. You know, the first time a man beats you up, it makes you angry when it happens a second time you would have to be crazy to stay. — **Marilyn Manroe**

1028. People consistently need advice on how to express their love how to deal with betrayal and how to find their life partner. — **Marinella Fedrigoli**

1029. If everything seems to be under control. You are just not going fast enough.

— **Mario Andretti** [1983-1969, Creator of Aikido.]

1030. We promise to discover new things, places, and people together to view our life together as a work of fate.

— **Marriage Contract**

1031. Good will is the only asset that competition cannot under sell or destroy. — **Marshal Field**

1032. Every one has the power for greatness not for fame, but greatness is determined by service. — **Martin Luther King**

1033. An angry man is not an intellectual. He makes a career out of being angry and has therefore not time left to learn. But to be apathetic is equally self destructive.

—**Marshall McLuhan quoted by Mrs. Indira Gandhi**

1034. I do not necessarily agree with everything I say.

1035. If you have made mistakes, even serious ones there is always another chance for you. What we call failure is not the falling down, but staying down. — **Mary, Pickford**

1036. Our scientific power has outrun our spiritual power. We have guided missiles and misguided men.

1037. We must accept finite disappointment. But never lose infinite hope. — **Martin Luther King**

1038. Any progress is precarious and the solution of one problem brings us face to face with another problem.

1039. The law cannot make love me, but it can stop him from lynching me. I think that is important.

1040. Our lives begin to end the day we become silent about the things that matter.

1041. Forgiveness is not an occasional act, it is permanent attitude.

1042. Sitting is an occupational hazard in many jobs.

— **Matt Todman**

1043. I do not care if people are interested in me or not, I have no desire to impart knowledge. I have no feeling to others, and I do not feel the need to correct them if they are wrong.

— **Maugham**

1044. I find men unaccountable. I am more inclined to expect them to do ill than to do good.

1045. Money is the sixth sense.

1046. Money, the possession of which is like the possession of sixth sense.

1047. Stress makes you stupid. — **Mc Ewen**

1048. Simple decision to stick together no matter what makes an enduring relationship.

1049. Success and failure are merely incidental they do not contribute to real satisfaction. — **MC Chagla**

1050. There are all these ideals about what is perfect and what is beautiful, and what is smart, but the most appealing thing is that which is me nobody else. — **ME**

1051. Do not load yourself with hate, it is heavier than you think.

— **Medame De Sevigne**

1052. Being alone is okay for some time. — **Meg Ryan**

1053. We need anything that is going to enliven spirit.

1054. Men are much more myopic and much more directional.

1055. I kick - start the day by reading the news paper

— **Megha Chatterjee**

1056. What goes around comes around.

1057. Despite capitalism's triumph over communism, the market system is in deep trouble as long as so much of the world remains poor.

1058. Tens of millions of poor entrepreneurs across the third world have been excluded from the system of bureaucracy and red tape.

1059. The main problem of development is not that the poor in the third world lack capital, but that many lack the legal title to assets they already hold.

1060. The poor in the third world have houses but not titles, crops but not deeds, businesses but not statutes of incorporation.

— **Mernando de sato**

1061. Even God lends a hand to honest boldness.

— **Menander**

1062. I can not give you a sure fire — formula for success, but I can give you a formula for failure try to please everybody all the time.

— **Merbert Bayard Swope**

1063. No matter what we do in life. No matter how high we climb the ladder of success, we will ultimately be remembered for we helped others less fortunate than our selves .

— **Mex Freed**

1064. One problem with gazing too frequently into past is that we may turn around to find the future has run out.

— **Michael Cibenko**

1065. There is no conversation more boring than the one where everybody agrees. — **Michel De Montaigne**

1066. Nothing fixes a thing so intensely in the memory as the wish to forget it.

1067. It will take time and effort to bring these efforts to fruition, but the risks are immediate.

— **Michel Camdessus M.D. for IMF.**

1068. I have failed over and over again in my life that is why I succeed. — **Michael Jordan**

1069. Fear is that little dark room where negatives are developed

— **Michael Prichard**

1070. It is not miserable to be blind, it is only miserable not to be able to endure blindness. — **Milton**

1071. Indian woman is undoubtedly the strongest of women on the globe. — **Miss India-2005**

1072. If you don't know what to do with many of the papers piled on your desk, stick a dozen colleagues.

— **Molcolm Forbes**

1073. There are three ways to get something done. Do it your self, Employ some one, or Forbid your children to do it.

— **Monta Crane**

1074. I have always observed that in this world, to succeed one should appear like a fool but bewise. — **Montes Quiel**

1075. Kind words can be short and easy to speak but their echoes are endless. — **Mother Teresa**

1076. I know God will not give me anything I cannot handle. I just with that he did not trust me so much.

1077. It comes from my heart as such you will win.

— Motilal Nehru

1078. Go on working my dear boy, as you have been, good solid steady work doing interrupted with a fair amount of recreating, amusement and otherwise you will shine out as one of the leading lights of your time.

— Motilal Nehru to his son Jawaharlal Nehru

1079. The inner environment of biological health, full creativity and mental development and outer environment of culture stimulus and beauty shared affection and civil liberty.

— Mrs. Barbara Ward the British Economist

1080. It is better to have a devil you know than one you do not know. **— Mr. Nixon**

1081. We cannot expect to make everyone our friend, but we can try to make every one our enemy.

1082. The diplomatic window has been closed as a result of the UN's failure to enforce its own resolution for Saddam to disarm. **— Mr. Fleischer**

1083. Developed countries lend to developing countries but maintain trade barrier which prevent them from acquiring the means to repay.

— Mr. Frank D Crean, Governor for Australia

1084. There might be differences in ideology between ourselves and our friends in opposition on the question of economic goods. We have to work together and take the country forward. **— Mr. Rajiv Gandhi**

1085. The manager in the public sector is denied the minimum degree of autonomy and freedom to take decisions.

— Mr. Tata

1086. The wives and mothers of those Americans who will fight us will weep blood, not tears. **—Mr Uday Son of Saddam**

1087. The corruption is the most infallible symptom of constitutions liberty. **—Mulk Raj Anand (Gibbon)**

1088. What will happen will happen but look at the bright side

— **Murphy's Law**

1089. Economics is the only field for having divergent views

— **Myrdal and Hayek**

1090. The governments over looked minorities whether in India or Abroad. — **Nadira, W/o Naipal, Nobel Laureate**

1091. I believe that whole wedding thing was over rated. But Soumya my husband is a kind of man I would like to grow old with. — **Nandita Das – Actress**

1092. The moral right should not be greater than a power created entirely by force — **Napoleon**

1093. It is the large number which defeats the small.

1094. He knows how to do everything, he is able to do everything and he wishes to do everything

— **about — Napoleon Bonaparte**

1095. Glory is fleeting, but obscurity is for ever.

1096. Ability is of little account without opportunity.

1097. I fear three News papers more than a hundred thousand baynotes.

1098. It requires more courage to suffer than to die.

1099. In politics stupidity is not a handicap.

— **Napoleon Bonaparte**

1100. History is the version of past events that people decided to agree upon.

1101. Gujarath has emerged victorious in Bihar polls.

— **Narendra Modi**

1102. Self esteem is the reputation we acquire with ourselves.

— **Nathaniel Branden**

1103. "We believe in freedom with passion that only those who have been denied of it can understand. We believe in equality because many in our country were so long deprived of it. We believe in the worth of human being for that is the foundation of our democracy and our work for development. That is the frame of our national programme.

1104. No one will be able to seize power in India on the basis of Exclusivist Philosophy. — **Natwar Singh**

1105. The biggest tragedy in the time of a job boom in India is an acute scarcity of the right people for the good jobs.

— **Navneeth Dhawan**

1106. In social service, you make friends, and you have benefit of feeling useful and needed. — **Neena Chapell**

1107. The essence of teaching of Mahatma was fearlessness and truth and action allied to these, always keeping welfare of the masses in view. — **Nehru**

1108. People who lived through the Freedom struggle still bear its scars.

1109. "You can tell the condition of nation by looking at the status of its women".

1110. Either follow me or leave me.

1111. In a large organisation confusions and tensions are inevitable.

1112. After the death of Narsimha Rao, the family was soaked in sorrow.

1113. India is struggling to overcome problems of backwardness, stunted development and legacy of colonialism.

1114. All societies of the past perpetrated and perpetuated social injustice without meeting any significant resistance from those who were victimized by the social system.

— **Neibuhr**

1115. I love living. I have some problems with life, but living is the best thing they have come up with so far.— **Neil simon**

1116. There is nothing like returning to a place that remains unchanged to find the ways in which you yourself have altered. — **Nelson Mandela**

1117. Death is nothing but to live defeated and inglorious is to die daily. — **Nepoleon Bonaparte**

1118. If I had to choose religion, the sun as the universal giver of life would be my god.

1119. Wherever I found a living creature, there I found the will to power. **— NIETSCHE**

1120. After reversals, U-turns, and retreats Kashmir has gone far beyond our reach today.

—Nawaz Sharif, Pak Prime Minister

1121. The raped woman becomes transformed through suffering into right angle. **—Nightingale**

1122. Guns on either side do not solve crisis. What is needed today is the courage to call for peace the courage that made Gandhi into the Mahatma **—Nikhil Cakravarthy**

1123. When violence succeeds on its own terms, it increases the likelihood of further resort to violence

—Noam Chomsky

1124. "Accept only clear and distinct ideas, break each problem into as many parts as necessary to solve it. Work from simple to complex. Always check for mistakes."

1125. There are plenty of people around the world who have endured freedom.

1126. In a democracy you have to control people's minds, but you cannot control them by force.

1127. The intellectuals are both main architects and main victims of democracy.

1128. Violence is a powerful instrument of control, but dilemmas of dominance are formidable.

1129. We are all designed for a specific purpose we all have something for which each of us alone is responsible. **— Noemi Stephan**

1130. Any kiddie in school can love like fool but hating is an art **— Ogden Nash**

1131. Wisdom makes but a slow defense against trouble though at best sure one. **— Oliver Gold Smith**

1132. I find the great thing in this world is not so much where we stand as in what direction we are moving.

1133. A moment's insight is sometimes worth a life's experience.

1134. We are staying under one roof but everything is not perfect.

1135. "ek nukte ne hamein mehrum mujrim kardiya

kyonki hum du'a likhte rahe aur vo dagha padte rahe."

From confidante to wrong doer, one single dot did bring one down, one betrayal she did read, for every blessing I wrote. — **Oliver Wandell Holmes**

1136. South Korea is beginning to be recognised as second Japan.

1137. After several meetings, I could pick up my courage.

1138. My husband insured his life for Rs.— one lakh but I would have spent one thousand to get him recovered from illness.

1139. Most of the time my husband comes home from work after the children have gone to bed.

1140. Every time I saw him, my blood boiled, my heart pounded and I would get so tense that I literally felt sick.

1141. (jealousy on seeing my wife's paramour)

1142. Among my most prized possessions are words that I have never spoken. — **Orson Rega Card**

1143. "Books are well written or badly written that is all".

— **Oscar Wilde**

1144. The artist is the creator of beautiful things.

1145. People who find beautiful meanings in beautiful things are the cultivated lot and the artist has no ethical sympathies.

1146. Man is a rational animal who always loves his temper when he is called upon to act in accordance with the dictates of reason.

1147. He proved to be both. "Somehow or other, I will be famous and if not famous I will be notorious".

1148. Relations are simply a tedious pack of people who have not got the remotest knowledge of how to live, not smallest instinct about when to die.

1149. Being idle is very hard work because everyone is against you.

1150. One can survive everything nowadays except death and live down everything except a good reputation.

1151. Life imitates art far more than art imitates life.

1152. To love oneself is the beginning of a life long romance.

1153. Good Looks are a snare that every sensible person would like to be caught in. — **Oscar Wilde**

1154. Experience is the name everyone gives to his mistake.

1155. Moderation is a fatal thing. Nothing succeeds like success.

1156. Consistency is the last refuse of the unimaginative.

1157. Selfishness is asking others to live as one wishes to live.

1158. A fool learns from his experience. A wise person learns from the experience of others. — **Ottovon Bismark**

1159. Laws are like sausages, it is better not to see them being made.

1160. Faith always implies the disbelief of a lesser fact in favour of greater. — **OW. Homes**

1161. The human mind treats a new idea the same way the body treats a strange protein, it rejects it. — **P B Medawar**

1162. Terrorism means any act involving the use of violence, is against American citizens or property whether or not such violence is provoked by the United State's Governments own policies or actions and act injuring the collective ego and belittles the image of the United States as a super power. — **P.K. Dorai Swamy**

1163. Every child is an artist. The problem is how to remain an artist once he grows up. — **Pablo Picasso**

1164. Every act of creation is first an act of destruction.

1165. Money is not always best remedy to all our problems

— **Padmini B. Patel**

1166. Beware of the advice from those who stand to gain from your decision. — **Panchatantra**

1167. Jacqueline Kennedy was 39, when she married Aristotle Onassis (in his sixties) the Greek shipping tycoon in October 1968. — **Partner Selection**

1168. Force and not opinion is the queen of the world but it is the opinion that uses force. — **Pascal**

1169. "You make the same mistake in composition as the pupil next to you"? teacher said.

1170. "What do you have to say about that?" asked the teacher.

1171. "We both have the same teacher" replied the boy.

— **Passport to Excellence**

1172. There is no down side to winning. — **Pat Conroy**

1173. Sexual revolution means mutual respect. feminism means empowering ideas of identity. — **Patrick Neate**

1174. When we walk to the edge of all the light we have to take the step in to the darkness of the unknown. Then one of the two things will happen. There will be something solid to stand on or we will be taught to fly.

— **Patrick Overtone, (Novelist)**

1175. Trouble about common sense is that it can often let you down. — **Paul Davies**

1176. It was a sort of act of faith with us that any equation which describe fundamental laws of nature must have great mathematical beauty in them. It was very profitable relation to hold and can be considered as the basis of much of our success. — **Paul Dirac**

1177. One must not Judge a man's worth from his poorer work, one must always judge him by the best he has done.

1178. It is more important to have beauty in one's equation than to have them fit experiment — it seems that if it is working from the point of view of getting beauty in one's equation and if one has really sound insight one is on sure line of progress

1179. Parents and children should never be thought of as functional equals. — **Paul Krup**

1180. When you find peace within yourself, you become the kind of person with others.

1181. Ironie as it may sound I am a strong believer in democracy.

— **Pervez Musharaff**

1182. If we fail we will have weakened moderates and strengthened extremists because the extremists do not think that a political solution is possible while moderates say we will resolve it politically. The whole world should understand this. — **Musharaff**

1183. The value of marriages is not that adults produce children, but that children produce adults. — **Peter De Varies**

1184. Life in a famous family has its advantages and disadvantages. — **Peter Hillary**

1185. People in Asia put the country above anything else, while an American hero puts the country last.

1186. Life with out vanity is almost impossible.

—**Peter Principle**

1187. Every individual tends to rise to his own level of incompetence.

1188. Corruption and inequality make people cynical about democracy. — **Peter Stoyanov (President Bulgaria)**

1189. Prayer for world peace 1978. —Prayer:

1190. Let us pray for the power to be kind, strength to be forgiving, endurance to accept, power to love and overcome hatred, pray for inspiration and power to fullfill the destny for which we are created. —**(modified)**

1191. Leaders inspire. They are not assigned leadership. They command it. — **Phil Maccraw**

1192. People have vast potential. They can do extra ordinary things if they have the confidence or take risks, yet most people do not. They sit in front of the telly and treat as if it goes on for ever. — **Philip Adamas**

1193. Reality is that which when you stop believing in it does not go away. — **Philip K. Bach**

1194. A man who is good for anything ought not to calculate the chance of living and dying, he ought to consider whether in doing anything he is doing right or wrong. — **Plato**

1195. Everything that deceives may be said to enchant.

1196. My government is running in accordance with the common Minimum programme and 80 % of the pledges made in the congress manifesto have been incorporated in the CMP. — **P.M. Manmohan Singh**

1197. It is not the tragedy of Goa, alone. It is the tragedy of all 28 states of India. — **Political Comment**

1198. "I do what I love to do and I do it with joy"

— **Prabudha Das Gupta**

1199. Wars bring disaster and misery. India has already experienced wars with pakistan in 1965, 1971 and then Kargil which brought no fruit. Now two nations want peace.

— **Pranab Mukharjee**

1200. It is not correct to say any political party suggested scaring down of the Republic Day celebrations. This is an observance of achievement of the nation.

1201. What you get married for if you do not want children?

— **Preparing Question**

1202. The earth takes millions of years to go round the Milky Way galaxy. What is the life time of one man compared to them? But what sets man apart is the reasoning power?

— **President Abdul Kalam**

1203. Dream Dream, Dream for dreams turn into thoughts and thoughts result in action.

1204. Power in India can only flow from the ballot box, never from the barrel of a gun. — **Abdul Kalam**

1205. I am not a tree. I am bush. — **President Bush**

1206. Bullets will not stop the bus to Muzaffarabad.

— Manmohan Singh

1207. The supreme court declared that Chief Minister and Leader of opposition are public servants.

1208. The desire for safety stands against every enterprise.

— Publius Cornelius Tacitus

1209. Where did we go wrong? **— Queen Elizabeth – II**

1210. You can not write poetry on the compete.

— Quentin Tarantwo

1211. Feminists are "Women" trying to be men, I suppose "men" trying to be women are "humanists". **— R. Brooke**

1212. I read news papers to get some ideas.

1213. I do not think about time I carry on till my work is finished.z

1214. I have served the Times of India for 54 years (2004)

(The longest service by any standard)

1215. The politicians have been providing me with my bread and butter.

1216. Nehru called me for ten minutes but our meeting went on for an hour.

1217. The power is in keeping one's mouth shut.

1218. I failed in school because I was weak in mathemantics.

1219. Never copy. Draw from real life.

1220. I have never been as happy since the day I met you -"A lover" **— R.K. Laxman**

1221. I have no disappointments in my life. **— Bohm-poet**

1222. Marx and Engels were men of thought while Lenin and Stalin were men of action. **— R.R. Diwakar**

1223. It is hep not to be married. I am not interested in being hep.

1224. Education is more than filling a child with facts. It starts with, posing questions.

1225. It is better to be known by six people for something you are proud of than 60 million for something you are not.

1226. Passion makes the world go round. Love just makes it a safer place.

1227. The mind is the limit. As long as the mind can envision something, you can do it.

1228. When you relinquish the desire to control your future you can have more happiness.

1229. A great marriage is not when perfect coupie comes together. It is when an imperfect couple learns to enjoy their differences.

1230. The first step to getting the things you want is this. Decide what you want.

1231. When the heart speaks, the mind finds it indecent to interfere.

1232. It is very strange that the years teach us experience that the shorter our time, the greater our capacity for waiting.

1233. It's a shallow life that does not give a person a few scars.

1234. It would be great if people got angry at some one for doing something they have done themselves.

1235. It takes a lot of courage to show your dream to some one else.

1236. An ego – trip is something that never gets you any where.

1237. Character – the willingness to accept responsibility for one's own life – is the source from which self-respect springs.

1238. Change is not merely necessary to life. It is life.

1239. Discipline without freedom is tyranny, freedom without discipline is chaos.

1240. Doing the best at this moment puts you in the best place for the next moment.

1241. Change is what keeps us fresh and innovative, what keeps us from getting stale, what keeps you young.

1242. Memories are not perishable.

1243. There is no cure for the common birthday despite all advances in medicine.

1244. You cannot exist with out humor, you have to be able to laugh at yourself, otherwise you suffer.

1245. Behind every successful man is a woman, behind her is his wife. (RD).

1246. No subject is too private for good.

— Milton Fried man (Nobel prize winning economist)

1247. If a government were put in charge of the Sahara Desert, within five years they would have a shortage of sand.

1248. I would like to attack the tyranny of love and see if life could offer other values than the inevitable Man–woman relationship. **— R.K. Narayan**

1249. Man is driven to seek further titillation and sexual activity in a futile never ending cycle.

1250. I found in the life around me plenty of material for writing.

1251. The world is not waiting to read your stuff. People have better things to do. You must work hard and by your sheer persistence draw their attention to yourself – so you must write, write and write.

1252. I had to pass through a phase of impossible love sickness. The blind urge to love goes to fantastic lengths. The one sided love can know no bounds, Physical, racial, or age or distance, one reads significance in every glance by a young girl, and gets a feeling of enrichment. **— R.K. Narayan**

1253. Blessed is he whose fame does not outshine his truth.

1254. Where the world is not broken up into fragments by narrow domestic walls. **— Rabindranath Tagore**

1255. Trees are the earth's endless effort to speak to the listening heaven.

1256. I dreamt that life was a joy, I awoke and saw that life was service. I found that service was a joy.

1257. When a full blown crisis hits, it would be heartless to turn away. — **Rahul Bose**

1258. Adjournments of the both houses of parliament costed nation Rs. 52 crores (2004). — Rahul Gandhi

1259. The opposition first kill democracy and then they try to save it.

1260. Repeated adjournments of parliament are a waste of time and money.

1261. You have a point of view as the opposition and we have a point of view at the government.

— **Rahul Gandhi [on Jharkhand issue DC 3-3-2005]**

1262. The forces which seek to undermine the independence are always on look out for opportunities to work out their nefarious designs. — **Rajiv Gandhi**

1263. Let us of four attachment to being right and suddenly your mind is more open you are able to benefit from the unique viewpoint of others without being crippled by your own judgment. — **Ralph Marston**

1264. What lies behind us and what lies before us are tiny matters compared to what lies within us.

— **Ralph Waldo Emerson**

1265. The great man is he who in the midst of the crowd keep with perfect sweetness the independence of solitude.

1266. The reward of a thing well done is to have done it.

1267. All life is an experiment. More experiments you make the better.

1268. Do not be too timed.

1269. If we find a man of rare intellect we should ask him what books he reads.

1270. No great man ever complains of want of opportunity.

1271. Meditate till you know that you are not meditation.

— **Ramana Maharishi**

1272. Human beings have basic instincts like power, fear and sex . Sex is the most powerful. — **Ramgopal Varma**

1273. We (LJP) want form minus RJD and minus BJP government. It will take some time, but it will definitely be formed. — **Ram Vilas Paswan – [On Jharkhand]**

1274. I will join hands neither with communal BJP nor the corrupt and casteist RJP.

1275. Come what may I will not help the government for the mess in Bihar.

1276. Turbulence is life force. It is opportunity. Let us love turbulence and use it for a change. — **Ramsay Clark**

1277. Whenever there is a calamity all we do is sit before the T.V and cry. — **Rani Mukherjee**

1278. Love can wait, but work cannot wait.

1279. "Work is the passion of my life"

— **Rasipuram Krishna Swamy Laxman**

1280. Many Germans refuse to go out of their own country because they regard their parents as friends.

1281. I do not know why people do not come out in the open and confront this menace of terror.

1282. So many lives have been lost in one sweep. We all must come forward to do our best. — **Raveena Tandon**

1283. Spirituality is the food of every human being not selected few. — **Ravi Shankar**

1284. It is not good enough to have a good mind, the main thing is to use it well. — **Rene Descartes**

1285. What a caterpillar calls the end of the world the master calls butterfly. — **Richard Bach**

1286. You are never given a wish without also being given the power to make it come true.

1287. Adventures happen to those incapable of planning an expedition. — **Richard Evans Schultes**

1288. The first principle is that you must fool yourself and you are the nearest person to fool. — **Richard Feynman**

1289. For a successful technology reality must take precedence over public relation for nature cannot be fooled.

1290. My basic instinct is to go into my room, shut the door and cry in privacy. — **Richard Gere**

1291. When you are in love, it is the most glorious two and a half minutes of your life. — **Richard Lewis**

1292. Bureaucracy can be understood as a structural and organisational expression of the related process of secularisation and disenchantment of the world and rationalisation. — **Richard L Rubenstein**

1293. The man who views the world at 50 the same as he did at 30 has wasted 20 years of his life. — **Richard Moss**

1294. There is not enough darkness in all the world to put out the light of even one small candle. — **Robert Alden**

1295. Envy can be a positive motivator Let it inspire you to work better for what you want. — **Robert Bringle**

1296. A minute's success pays the failure of years.

— **Robert Browns**

1297. If you limit your choices only to what seems possible or reasonable you disconnect yourself from what you truly want and all that is left is compromise. — **Robert Fritz**

1298. The world is full of willing people, some willing to work the rest are willing to let them.

1299. Education is the ability to listen to almost anything without losing your temper or yourself confidence.

— **Robert Frost**

1300. We dance round in a ring and suppose. But the secret sits in the middle and knows.

1301. I am against a homogenised society because I want the cream to rise.

1302. The reason that worry kills more people than work, because there are people who worry more than work.

1303. I can sum up everything I have learned from life – It goes on.

1304. Love is an irresistible desire to be irresistibly desired.

1305. Cherish your own emotions and never undervalue them.
— **Robert Henri**

1306. There is but one art to omit. — **Robert Louis Stevenson**

1307. I know that you believe you understand what you think I said, but I am not sure you realize that what you heard is not what I meant — **Robert Mecloskey**

1308. Those who dare to fail miserably can achieve greatly.
— **Robert F. Kennedy**

1309. The greatest test of courage on earth is to bear defeat without losing heart. — **Robert G. Ingersoll**

1310. Courage without conscience is a wild beast.

1311. General principles should not be based on exceptional cases. — **Robert J. Sawyer**

1312. Politics is perhaps the only profession for which no preparation is thought necessary.
— **Robert Louis Stevenson**

1313. Keep your fears to yourself, but share your courage with others. — **Robert L. Stevenson**

1314. She sips her water — **Rohit**

1315. Facts are stupid things — **Ronald Reagon**

1316. There are no limits of human intelligence imagination and wonder.

1317. The best executive is the one who has sense enough to pick good men to do what he wants to be done and self restraint enough to keep from meddling with them about how they do it. — **Roosevelt**

1318. Science and every day life cannot and should not be separated. Science for me gives a partial explanation of life. In so far as it goes, it is based on fact, experience and experiment. — **"Rosalind Franklin"**

1319. A leader takes people where they want to go. A great leader takes people where they do not necessarily want to go, but ought to be. — **Rosalyn Carter**

1320. Repentance is not so much remorse for what we have done as the fear of consequences. — **Rouchefouclard**

1321. Here to us that are here

1322. You that are there

1323. And rest of us everywhere — **Rudyard Kipling (Toasting)**

1324. You have to have confidence in your ability and then be tough enough to follow through.

1325. A man's reach should exceed his grasp.

1326. Trust but verify.

1327. When people say that cannot be done, my mind responded, by thinking it would be interesting, exciting, and fulfilling to prove that it can be done.

— **Rudy Giuliani (New York Mayor)**

1328. "We are going to have to invent a way to get through this (people were jumping from the tower 100 story building)".

1329. If the people of Britain could get through months of bombing during world war-II, we can get through a day or two of this.

1330. We are just as good as people were.

1331. "I am here and I am okay, and city is here the city is okay".

1332. Churchill told his people, during the World War-II, that he had nothing to offer but blood, sweat and tears.

1333. I had to balance being honest and being hopeful.

1334. It is hard for me to think of myself as a greatman.

1335. I think too much pressure is put on kids to be perfect.

1336. "My father constantly put tremendous pressure on me about being honest about everything"

1337. People who live in freedom are stronger than terrorists.

1338. Hitler did tremendous damage, but he did not win.

1339. We are right, terrorists are wrong. It does not mean all our ideas are right or we are always right.

1340. You do not know just as you do not know what you might do.

1341. Why did one man live and another die? When you contemplate those questions-the mysteries of life-it humbles you.

1342. God has a plan, even when you do not understand it fully. You can either do good or bad, you have choice

1343. Can I ever know you or You know me? — **S. Teasdale**

1344. True religion should bring about a transformation and change of outlook and create a sense of Universal brother hood. — **S. Radha Krishnan (President of India)**

1345. 1No ruler had the interest of the common man at heart. This made it easy for the British to conqueror the country.

— **S. Radha Krishnan**

1346. To find the exact answer, one must first ask the exact question. — **S. Tobian Webster**

1347. Defections have invariably been one of the many banes afflicting the polity of the states. — **S. Viswam**

1348. I have been doing what my conscience has directed me to. Why an award? — **S.R. Sankaran**

1349. I am happy as long as I know. I gave off my best on a cricket field. I would rather Judge myself in my own eyes.

— **Sachin Tendulkar**

1350. I am not interested in what people think to day – but in what they will think of me in 500 years. — **Saddam**

1351. Ultimately, guilt or innocence does not matter because there is no law or value beyond the tyrant's will.

1352. The American people are weak.

1353. Iraq does not choose its Path on the orders of a foreigner and does not choose its leaders according to decrees from Washington.

1354. Saddam is most wanted to be admired, remembered and revered.

1355. "How can you prevent people from expressing their feelings towards me?" — **Sad**

1356. Saddam's plan was to capture American soldiers, and tie them to their tanks. "The Americans will never fire on their own soldiers"

1357. "I enjoy being an actor" (Popular producer — USA)

— Sadra Bullock

1358. I know what I have, I know what I am, I know I am great

1359. Man has no reason to philosophise except with a view to happiness. **— Saint Augustine**

1360. Face is the mirror of mind and eyes without speaking confess the secrets of the heart. **— Saint Jerome**

1361. Somewhere on this globe, every ten seconds there is a woman giving birth to a child. She must be found and stopped. **— Sam**

1362. Cruel to be kind. **— Sampradaya Chudamani**

1363. The Iraqis could expect nothing more than swift defeat

1364. You can do very little with faith, but you can do nothing without it. **— Samuel Butler**

1365. Life is the art of drawing sufficient conclusions from insufficient premises.

1366. The true, strong and sound mind is the mind that can embrace equally great things and small.

— Samuel Johnson

1367. Wine makes a man pleased with himself.

1368. Gratitude is a fruit of great cultivation you do not find it in gross people.

1369. Happier to be sometimes cheated than not to trust.

1370. Few things are impossible to diligence and skill, great works are performed by not strength but perseverance.

1371. The worst is better than none, and the best cannot be expected to go quite true.

1372. Great works are performed not by strength but by perseverance.

1373. You got to do what you got to do, Now I know once was not a fluke. I can beat the top.

1374. Success is not everything in life.

1375. I pray five times a day. — **Sania Mirza**

1376. The most beautiful thing on this dark earth is the person you love. — **Sappha**

1377. "I have more time to appreciate what is around me instead of go-go-going all day". — **Sarah Scott**

1378. In spiritual super market you get instant nirvana.

1379. Two foes of human happiness are pain and boredom. — **Schopen Haver**

1380. Freedom is for honest people. No man who is not himself honest can be free— he is his own trap. — **Sciential Ron Hubbard**

1381. Creativity is allowing oneself to make mistakes, Art is knowing which comes to keep. — **Scott Adems**

1382. It is a great challenge to be better than your opportunities. — **Search Jessica Parker**

1383. Each step towards peace, could be bringing India and Pakistan closer to war. — **Secretary of State**

1384. It is the first time perhaps, that's the Prime Minister (Manmohan Singh) is not allowed to exert the authority endowed by the constitution. — **Seema Mustafa**

1385. It is better to know useless things than to know nothing. — **Seneca**

1386. For greed all nature is too little.

1387. While fate permits, live happily, life spends on hurried step and winged days, the wheel of the head long year is turned 8 year old. — **Septuagenarian**

1388. It is next to impossible for some one to beat me. — **Serena Williams**

1389. It is excellent to have a giant's strength but tyrannous to use it like a giant. — **Disappointed Romeo Shakespear**

1390. Gone are the days when of all he surveyed.
The husband was the master and was obeyed
Now it is the Lady of the house the wife.
Who holds you in thrall all your life.
For every disappointed Romeo.
It is becoming quite a fashion.
To kill himself or his Lady Love.
In a fit of raging passion.
Logic leads me to think.
It is dangerous to fall in love.
You never know when your beloved.
Will dispatch you above.

— **Shankar's Weekly 13-12-1972**

1391. The pictures churned out of shankar's dream factory are meant to star on the box office, and the collections exceed over Rs. 100 crores in 11 years.

1392. There is so much to achieve, but there is no time to relax.

— **Sheetal Malhur**

1393. I would close my eyes and take a few good, long deep breaths. In a minute or two, the mind gets clam and peace.

— **Shelly wahle**

1394. Life is like a game of chess in which there are an infinite number of moves possible. The choice is open, but the move contains in itself all future moves. One is free to choose, but what follows is the result of one's choice – from consequences of action there is never any escape.

— **Shelly Smith**

1395. It is time for show holics during Diwali. — **Shoaholics**

1396. The thread that ties flowers together, becomes fragrant as well — **Shobhana**

1397. Women need not tell their partners every detail of their past relationships, because these things have a nasty habit of boomeranging. — **Shoba De**

1398. Marriage is the single most perplexing institution in the world. It has been there through centuries, the world has not come up with a better alternative. It has survived.

1399. The consumerist culture is turning women into sex objects.

— **Shome Sen**

1400. I believe in goodness of life. — **Shraddha Nigam**

1401. Do not cross this field unless you can do it in 9.9 seconds. The bull can do it in 10 seconds. — **Sign board**

1402. When you are in tension recite Hanuman Chalisa.

— **Sindura**

1403. Houses are built to live in not to look on, therefore let use be preferred before uniformity, except where both may be had.

1404. The most elementary qualification demanded of a minister is honesty and incorruptibility. It is however necessary not only that he should possess these qualifications but also that he should appear to possess them.

— **Sir Ivor Jennings**

1405. To every action there is always an opposite and equal reaction. — **Sir Isac Newton**

1406. We carry with us the wonders we seek with out us.

— **Sir Thomas Browne**

1407. The willow which bends to the tempest often escapes better than the Oak which resists it. — **Sir Walter Scott**

1408. Hate and mistrust are the children of blindness.

— **Sir William Walton**

1409. The power man has grown in every sphere except over himself. — **Sir Winston Churchill**

1410. Men occasionally stumble over the truth, but most of them pick themselves up and hurry off as if nothing has happened.

1411. It is a mistake to try to look too far ahead. The chain of destiny can only be grasped one link at a time.

1412. Solitary trees, if they grow at all, grow strong.

1413. We are not the lap dogs or pet dogs or of anybody. We are the watch dogs of Indian people and that is the role we play as far as this job is concerned. — **Sitaram Yechuri**

1414. Women keep on dying in their homes and harassed husbands go scot free.

1415. The shortest and surest way to live with honor in the world is to be in reality what we would appear to be.

— **Socrates**

1416. Do not run through life so fast that you forget not only where you have been, but where you are going you know nothing.

1417. People work hard to gather wealth, but little care they take of the children to whom they must one day relinquish all.

1418. Violence can only be concealed by a lie and the lie can only be maintained by violence. — **Solzhenitsyn**

1419. After marriage I got freedom. Earlier mom used to call up asking me when I would be home. Now she is cool.

— **Sonali Bindre**

1420. "Becoming Prime minister is not my priority"

1421. I am an Indian. I do not resent when they (BJP) talk about my foreign origin. It makes me laugh.

1422. I lost two beloved members of my family to extremists I am fully aware of the problems extremism and violence will create in society. — Sonia Gandhi

1423. The doors for talks with extremists, are always open.

1424. Whenever there is a catastrophe of any kind everyone has got together. All of us government, individuals, and civil society have to come together.

1425. Rather fail with honour than succeed with fraud.

— **Sophocles**

1426. Whoever gossips to you will gossip of you.

— **Spanish proverb**

1427. The legislatures should not cross Laxman Rekha, similarly we feel all organs of the constitution should not cross the limits. — **Somnath Chatterjee (Speakers meet)**

1428. He who loves God cannot want that God should love him in return. He does not expect return, reward or recompense. — **Spinuza**

1429. Peace is a virtue, a state of mind, a disposition for benevolence, confidence and justice. — **Spinuza**

1430. People know what is genuine, because, heart knows. The head cannot relate to spirituality.

1431. The companionship of the holy and the wise is one of the main elements of spiritual progress.

— **Sri Rama Krishna**

1432. First you know where you are and what you are. Then you will know, who is God and where he is.

— **Sri Ramana Maharishi**

1433. Resentment is like taking poison and hoping the other person dies. — **St. Augustine**

1434. People at all levels should be ready to bear levies in support of our army, all working people must be roused to defend our freedom, our honour, our country. — **Stalin**

1435. The economic policies of a democratic country very often seriously conflict with their own objectives and this is likely to persist. — **Stanley Please**

1436. We are not human beings on spiritual journey, we are spiritual beings on human journey

— **Stephen Covey**

1437. The esence of radiant beauty is the mixture of youth, vibrance, ever freshness and elegance.

1438. Sometimes you refer many books more than 100 to get the right word in the right context.

1439. You decide what you value most, build your life around core values then get rid of the clutter that does not contribute to your goals. — **Stikemen**

1440. The human brain is a most unusual instrument of elegant and yet unknown capacity. — **Stuart Saton**

1441. Life was never meant to be a struggle. Just a gentle progression from one point to another, much like walking through a valley on a sunny day. — **Stuart Willde**

1442. Great achievements are often born out of small beginnings — **Subhash Chandra Bose**

1443. Opportunities multiply as they are seized (selected).

— **Sun tiu**

1444. Pension is not a charity. — **Supreme court**

1445. The benefit payable to a pensioner cannot be equated to any other commercial transaction .

1446. When an employee breaches such discipline resulting in his dismissal, the labour court cannot take a contrary view and award lesser punishment.

1447. If what is stated in the petition is true, filed by Munda, then it is (Jharkhand Governor's act – on Syed Sabti Rai-) a total fraud on the Indian Constitution.

— **Supreme Court Bench**

1448. My Guru instilled in me the passion for dance and unquestioning surrender to the art. — **Surupa Sen**

1449. Dance is like jealous husband, it is difficult to make another commitment.

1450. When you have water and fire you have space

1451. Dance is my life — **Susan Sarandom**

1452. There is a tendency to treat married people as a couple.

1453. Sometimes people do go out of control.

— **Sushmita Sen**

1454. I do not cry because people misbehave with me I cried because I was talking about something very close to me. I do not regret because it is an emotion like laughing.

1455. I live by own rules and I do not care about comments made by people

1456. Working to help others makes me happy.

1457. No one should be charitable at own cost.

1458. Weapons have no place in a democracy. Nothing can be achieved through violent means. History has proved this.

— **Sushil Kumar Shinde Governor (A.P.)**

1459. People know where they want to be, but do not know why they can not get there — **Suzy**

1460. Help and not fight, Assimilation and not destruction, Harmony and peace and not Dissension.

— **Swami Vivekananda**

1461. Think positive and masterfully, with confidence and faith, and life becomes more secure, richer in achievement and experience.

1462. The real artists never insult their audience.

— **Swathi Somanath**

1463. ·Maturity begins when we are content to feel we are right about something with out feeling the necessity to prove some one else is wrong. — **Sydney J. Harris**

1464. I am not repenting my decision. I invited because I was convinced about his number. I did nothing wrong.

— **Syed Sabty Rai (Jharkhand Governor)**

1465. To do two things at once is to do neither. — **Syrus**

1466. It is my upbringing I can never tom my ahievement

— **Tabu**

1467. Half of the harm done in this world is due to people who want to feel important. — **T.S.Eliot**

1468. Only those who risk going too far can possibly find out how far one can go.

1469. And the way up is the way down, the way forward is the back.

1470. We do not know very much of the future except that from generation to generation the same things happen again and again.

1471. Marriage two people who know that they do not understand each other, breeding children whom they do not understand and who will never understand them.

1472. Television permits several million people to laugh at the same time and still feel lonely.

1473. Implication of the Girglani Commission recommendations was the only solution to check the demand for separate Telangana. **— T. Veerabhadram CPM, Leader**

1474. There is the greatest practical benefit in making a few failures early in life. **— T.H. Huxley**

1475. Whoever destroys a single life destroys the entire world, who ever saves a single life, saves the entire world.

— Talmud

1476. We do not see things as they are, we see things as we are.

1477. I do not pass any student either Students Pass and fail themselves.

1478. Self-reverence, self-knowledge, self-control—alone lead us to sovereign power. **— Tennyson**

1479. There is a demand in these days for men who make wrong appear right. **— Terence**

1480. It is true wisdom to know how to alter one's mind when occasion demands it.

1481. If those who were responsible for the protection of the late prime Minister had done, what they ought to have done, what ought not to have happened would not have happened. **— Thakkar Commission**

1482. He is my ex-flame.

1483. The Queen lost much her inherited privileges.

1484. Let's see what I did wrong yesterday.

— The Duke of Edinburgh (Queen's Husband)

1485. "I, Philip Duke of Edinburgh do become your liegeman of life and limb and of earthly worship and faith and truth, I will bear unto you, to live and die against all manner of folks". — **The Duke**

1486. The framers of our constitution tried to put in checks and balances to protect minorities, have done master job of understanding what it takes to preserve integrity of our nation of nations, but have not foreseen, how it could be rendered impotent overnight by entrenched personal prejudices. — **The Hindu**

1487. The president has become a lame duck.

— **Advani The Leader of Opposition**

1488. Confrontation is part of human nature it can be used to reconcile yourself with your neighbour and with the world.

1489. I am terrified sometimes of making a promise and then perhaps living to regret it". — **Prince Charles**

1490. "I have had Diana for an hour — and she cried nonstop".

— **Queen Elizabeth II**

1491. "Your thoughts and prayers are with me. I have been aware all the time that my people spread over all the corners of the world, are united to support me in the task to which I have now been dedicated with such solemnity".

— **Queen Elizabeth [on the first Christmas Evening]**

1492. "I ask you to pray for me, pray that God may give me wisdom and strength to carry out the solemn promises I shall be making and that I may faithfully serve Him and you all the days of my life."

1493. "My father spoke to his people in all parts of the world. Today I am doing this to you, who are now my people.

— **Queen after Coronation**

1494. The public may have some role in democracy.

1495. God bless the roots. Body and soul are one.

— **Theodore Roe Thike**

1496. By changing what man knows about the world, he changes the world he knows, and by changing the world in which he lives, he changes himself, here lies a danger and hope, a danger because random chages of the biological nature are likely to produce deterioration rather than improvement, a hope because changes resulting from knowledge can also be directed by knowledge.

— **Theodosius Dodzhansky**

1497. Opportunity is missed by most people because it is dressed in overalls and looks like work. — **Thomas Alva Edison**

1498. Time is really the only capital that any human being has and the one thing that he cannot afford to lose.

1499. There is a way to do it better find it.

1500. In the court of science there is no obligation to obey an unjust law. — **Thomas Aquinum**

1501. Confession is good for the soul, but it is bad for the reputation. — **Thomas Denter**

1502. Our greatest weakness lies in giving up, The most certain way to succeed is to try just one more time.

— **Thomas Edison**

1503. He does not believe that does not live according to his beliefs — **Thomas Fuller**

1504. Wilful waste brings woeful want

1505. A man who qualifies himself well for his calling never fails of employment. — **Thomas Jefferson**

1506. The art of life is the art of avoiding pain and he is the best pilot who steers clearest of rocks and shoals with which it is beset.

1507. Now is the dwelling place of God himself.

— **Thomas Kelly**

1508. Boredom is the feeling that everything is a waste of time, serenity that nothing is. — **Thomas**

1509. Large nations do what they wish, while small nations accept what they must. — **Thucydides — Maxim**

1510. Mystery is a resource like coal or gold and its preservation is a fine thing. — **Tim Cahi**

1511. When people have to obey other people's orders, equality is out of question. — **Tiruvalluvar**

1512. All happy families resemble one another and each unhappy in its own way. — **Tolstoy**

1513. Fiction has to make sense. — **Tomclaney**

1514. I am saddened — this President failed so miserably at diplomacy that we are forced to war. — **Tom Daschie**

1515. Accept failure as a normal part of living. — **Tom Hobson**

1516. Happy marriages begin when we marry the ones we love, and they blossom when we love the ones we marry.

— **Tom Mullen**

1517. Under promise: over deliver — **Tom patens**

1518. There are many things worth living for, there are a few things worth dying for, but there is nothing worth killing for.

— **Tom Robbins**

1519. "The Queen was the people's princess and that is how she will stay" — **Tony Blair (of the Queen)**

1520. He is pretty quick, a bit wild as well. He will be quite exciting. Bitterness imprisons life, love releases it.
– Henry Emerson. — **Trevor Carlin**

1521. Any one desiring a quiet life had done badly to be born in twentieth century. — **Trotsky**

1522. It is amazing what you can accomplish if you do not care who gets the credit. — **Truman**

1523. The ideal man would be some one who is older and dominating. — **Udita Goswami**

1524. Be always green like the pine tree, flexible like bamboo beautiful as the lotus and elegant as the lily.

— **Ueshiba**

1525. My father was a communist. I do not hate any one not even congress. — **Uma Bharathi**

1526. The day July, 4, we survive, is our Independence Day.

— **Jefferson U.S. President**

1527. We wil invade Iraq without meaningless seal of UN security council, whether or not Saddam Hussain and his family leave the country. — **U.S. Spokesman**

1528. I wish I had more time to enjoy the splendor of Himalayas

1529. The NDA believes that the legislature and judiciary are supreme in their own fields both must subserve the purpose and goals enshrined in the constitution.

— **V.K. Malhotra**

1530. Truth is not simply what you thionk it is, it is also the circumstances in which it is said, and to whom why and how it is said. — **Vaclav Havel**

1531. Hope is not the conviction that something will turnout well but the certainity that something makes sense regardless of how it turnsout.

1532. Art is not a mirror to reflect the world, but a hammer with which to shape it. — **Valdimir Mayakonsky**

1533. I feel I have seen the light and shade in my personal life.

— **Vanessa Mae**

1534. No matter how compelling or elegant it is, a theory of physics must be subjected to experimental verification or it differs little from medivial verification theology.

1535. There is nothing like a dream to create the future. Utopia today flesh and blood tomorrow. — **Victor Hugo**

1536. Self-employment is the best choice and best status in life.

— **Vidura**

1537. My body burns with a forbidden passion. — **Vijayan**

1538. Leaders are like eagles, they do not flock. you find them one at a time. — **Vince Lambardi**

1539. In the end we shall have had enough of cynicism skepticism, humbug and we shall want to live more musically. — **Vincent Van [GOGH]**

1540. For most of history Anonymous was a woman.

— **Virginia Woolf**

1541. I can not stand her coming late all the time — **Vishal**

1542. We do not know whether we are living or dead.

— **Vivekananda**

1543. Have you anything to give? If you have, then give. It is the question of giving and taking and listening.

1544. Not any one of the prophets is born to rule the world for ever.

1545. We do not know what is the meaning of our lives, we cannot realize it we do not know whether we are living or dead.

1546. I could not turn my back on this (Tsunami hit village.)

— **Vivek Oberoi**

1547. Love truth and pardon error. — **Voltaire**

1548. Chance is a word void of sense. Nothing can exist without a cause.

1549. When it is a question of money, every one is of the same religion.

1550. Appreciation is a wonderful thing. It makes what is excellent in others belong to us as well.

1551. It is like, asking a man whom we have invited to dinner to prepare foods at his expense. — **V.P. Singh**

1552. A constitution is not intended to be a static document. In a developing country its provisions must lend themselves to meeting the changing needs and requirements of the society. — **V.V. Giri**

1553. When thinking would not care fear, action will.

— **W. Clement Stone**

1554. If you cannot describe what you are doing as a process, you do not know what you are doing.

— **W. Edwards Deming**

1555. Tradition is a guide and not a jailer.

— **W. Somerset Maugham**

1556. It is funny thing about life if you refuse to accept anything but the best, you often get it.

1557. When you choose your friends, do not be short changed by choosing personality over character.

1558. The most useful thing about a principle is that it can always be scarificed to expediency.

1559. Dying is very dull dreary affair, and my advice to you is to have nothing what ever to do with it.

1560. Not I, nor any one else can travel that road for you, you must travel it yourself. — **Walt Whitman**

1561. Re examine all you have been told. Dismiss what insults your soul.

1562. Institutions fix the confines of and impose from upon the activities of human beings. — **Walton Hamilton**

1563. Never ask barber if you need a hair cut.

— **Warren Buffett**

1564. When all men think alike, no one thinks very much.

— **Water Lipp Man**

1565. Man is simply the most formidable of all the beasts of prey, and in deed the only one that preys systematically on its own species.

1566. No one knows the precise point at which anger becomes dangerous.

1567. The final test of a leader is that he leaves behind him in other men the conviction and the will to carry on.

1568. I strongly believe that if we join hands together, we will certainly be able to set a new trial in the IT business world, when the day comes it will signify the coming of the Asian century of IT industry.

— **Wen Jiabad, the chenepromier 10-4-2005**

1569. Never cry over the spilt milk because it may have been poisoned. — **We Fields**

1570. A parrot talks much but feels little. — **Wilbur Wright**

1571. Every one is ignorant on different subjects.

— **Will Rogers**

1572. What makes a human being ? A human being is the imperfections. **— Will smith**

1573. When we seek to discover the best in others we somehow bring out the best in ourselves.

— William Arthur Ward

1574. When the doors of perception are cleansed everything appears as it truly is infinite. **— William Blacke**

1575. It is easier to forgive an enemy than to forgive a friend.

1576. Think like a wise man but communicate in the language of the people. **— William Butler Yeats**

1577. Forget past mistakes forget failures, forget everything except that you are going to do now and do it.

— William Durant

1578. Plenty of people miss their share of happiness. Not because they never found it, but because they did not stop to enjoy it. **— William Feather**

1579. Some people are making such thorough preparation for rainy days that they are not enjoying today's sunshine.

1580. Man is the only animal that laughs and weeps and knows the difference between what things are and what they ought to be. **— William Hazlitt**

1581. The art of being wise is the art of knowing what is to overlook. **— William James**

1582. Be not afraid of life. Believe that life is worth living and that belief will help create the fact.

1583. A human being can alter his life by altering the attitudes of mind.

1584. Human beings by changing the inner attitude of their minds, can change the outer aspects of their lives.

1585. True silence is the rest of the mind and is to the spirit what sleep is to body nourishment and refreshment.

— William Penn

1586. A good listener is not only popular everywhere, but after a while he or she gets to know something.

— **Wilson Mizner**

1587. You have freedom of choice, but not freedom from choice

— **Windell Tones**

1588. Man will occasionally stumble over truth, but usually manages to pick himself up walk over or around it and carry on.

1589. The power will go into the hands of rascals, rogues and free booters. They are men of straw, they will fight among themselves. — **Winston Churchill**

1590. Courage is what it takes to stand up and speak, courage is also what it takes to sit down and listen.

1591. Construction has to be slow, long, laborious but destruction can be done in one day by senseless action.

1592. To improve is to change to be perfect is to change often.

1593. When I am abroad, I make it rule never to criticise or attack the government of my own country. I make up for the lost time when I come home.

1594. Some men change their party for the sake of principles, others their principles for the sake of their party.

1595. Success is the ability to go from one failure to another with no loss of enthusiasm.

1596. An appeaser is one who feeds a crocodile hoping it will not eat him last.

1597. Truth is incontrovertible. Panic may resent it. Ignorance may decide it. Malice may distort it. But there it is.

1598. Never give in, never give in, never, never, never, never – in anything great or small large or petty – never give in except to convictions of honour and good sense.

1599. The inherent vice of capitalism is the unequal sharing of blessings. The inherent virtue of socialism is the equal sharing of miseries. — **Wonder of the World**

1600. The pyramids of Egypt.

1601. The hanging Gardens of Babylon.

1602. The Statue of Godeus (Jupiter) at Olympia.

1603. The trimph of Goddess Diana.

1604. The Tomb of Masolns Halicarnassus.

1605. The Colossus of Rhodes.

1606. The Light House of pharios at Alexandria.

1607. I not only use all the brain I have but, all I can borrow.

— **WoodrowWilson**

1608. I am astounded by People who want to know the Universe when it is hard enough to find your way around Chinatown.

1609. Sexuality immediately doubles your chance for a date on a Saturday Night. — **Woody Allen**

1610. To see a world in a Grain of sand

And a Heaven in a Wild Flower

Hold Infinity in the palm of your hand

And Eternity in an hour — **Wordsworth**

1611. The poor people face a chronic shortage of income, a sense of voicelessness and powerlessness and high level of economic insecurity. — **World Bank-2000**

1612. Horse sense is the thing a horse has which keeps it from betting on people. — **WL. Fields**

1613. To acquire power and cling to power for power's sake is doomed to fail. — **Yahyakhan**

1614 **A.**

Yaksha Prashnalu

(a) Yaksha – Which is the holier than Earth? Dharmaraj – Mother **A=Answer**

(b) Which is the higher than sky? – (A) Father

(c) Which is faster than air? – (A) Mind

(d) What is it which cannot be measured deeper and wider? (A) Worry.

(e) Who is the friend to a man in the clutches of death? (A) Charity.

(f) What are Centres for Dharma, fame, heaven and happiness? (A) Dharma – Ability

Fame – Charity

Heaven – Truth

Happiness – Character

(g) Which is the Atma of a man? (A) Son

(h) Which covers the whole world? (A) Ignorance

(i) What is the delay? (A) Not to follow Dharma

(j) Who is enjoying happiness? (A) One who is not in debts.

(k) What is real bathing? (A) To cleanse the mind from all evil thoughts.

(l) Which is blacker than (Katuke) eye paint? (A) Blame

(m) Which is the most important dharma? (A) Mercy

(n) How do you keep yourself away from unhappiness?(A) By controlling the mind.

(o) Which is the shameful thing? (A) Doing things not socially desirable or acceptable.

(p) Which is Daya? (A) Desiring Happiness for all beings.

(q) Which is equal to death for a country? (A) To be in administration.

(r) What is the standard for becoming brahmin? (A) Caste, education or training, knowledge of shastras, cannot make a brahmin. Only good, and pure character make a brahmin.

(s) What is dharma? (A) Dharma is not (Tharkam) reasoning, Dharma is not what is told by rishis who tell different things. What is in the inner most place of heart (hrudayam) is dharma.

(t) What is the wonder of things in this world? (A) Man knows that death is the end of life. Inspite of it, man behaves as if there is no end or death. That is the most wonderful thing in this world.

1615. We found it increasingly difficult and untenable to continue free power for all categories of farmers.

— Y.S. Rajashekar Reddy, CM, A.P.

1616. The principal yard stick of public life is not justice but success.

1617. Charity once advertised becomes cheap.— **Yash Chopra**

1618. If you cannot bite do not bore your teeth.— **Yiddish Saying**

1619. Speak not much, work not much for they distracts the mind.

— Yogi

1620. One who does not incur debts is indeed a wealthy person.

— Yogi Vemana

1621. You can get old pretty young if you do not take care of yourself. **— Yogi Berra**

1622. If you have not attained true clear vision this causes you to lapse into extremes so that you lose contact with reality.

— Zen Master Yuanwcs

1623. Old, infirm, sick. Parents are economic burden to the children.

1624. Somethings are best left the way they were meant to be.

1625. Ascroll is a thing of the past.

1626. Neil Armstrong, the first man to walk on the moon has got a piece of the moon rock as part of NASA's Ambasador of exploration.

1627. A glimpse of an alluring woman will ruin a man's decision making skills.

1628. We think we are rational beings. It is not so.

1629. People with high testosterone levels are very vulnerable to sexual cues.

1630. The ratio of the index finger to the ring finger indicates testosterone level.

1631. A ring finger longer than index finger is the result of high testosterone is commonly found in men than in women.

1632. People in position of power are most susceptible to the subtle influence of the opposite sex.

1633. I feel young all day long. But when bank refused me loan, or a young lady offered me a seat in a crowded bus or train, I am reminded of my age (an old man in seventies.)

1634. "Do not be under impression that I have lots of money to lend to any body." Son said to his father.

1635. "I am not begging you your money. It is my money. How dare you to keep me silent for years". The father told his on in an angry tone.

1636. Do not give all your property to your children.

1637. Depend not on fortune but on conduct. **– P. Syras**

1638. Honesty may at times be defeated in the battle but ultimately wins the war. **– Ceravents**

1639. On hearing the news that he had a son, the father was crying. On being asked why, he said "There is a 50 percent chance that my son would turn out to be Duryodhana or a naxalite".

1640. "My husband has been suffering from heart disease please lend me some money, that I promise to tetrun" said the sister (weeping) to his brother.

1641. "No, I do not have money not even two thousand. Arrange money any where or let him die" said her brother unmoved by sister's appeals.

1642. Great achievers are born out of small beginnings.

– Subhash Bose.

1643. Books are light houses erected in the great sea of time.

– E.P. W hipple.

1644. The true civilisation is where every man gives every other man right that he claims for him self. **– R.G. Ingersoll**

1645. Conscience is the perfect interpreter of life. **– Karl Barth**

1646. It is better to deserve with out receiving than to receive with out deserving. **– R.G. Inger Soll**

1647. Education is an ornament in prosperty and refuge in adversity. **– Aristotle**

1648. Flattary is a food of fools. **– Swift**

1649. Forgiveness is the attribute of the strong. **– J.S. Mill**

1650. Give love, affection, education and all but not properties to your children.

1651. William Shakespeare [1564 – 1616] is the most outstanding influential figure in the history of English literature.

1652. Something will never change in this world.

1653. When power, money, and status combine to produce a real life court room drama, it can seem a whole way of life.

1654. Family feuds are unavoidable in the world.

1655. Disease knows no age.

1656. After the age of 30 years egos work stronger.

1657. Frictions in family are necessary to release pent-up emotions and tensions.

1658. Friends and relatives may be taken as buffer stock, to absorb family shocks or diffuse tension.

1659. Shakespeare was born probably on April 23, 1554, at Stratford Avon in Warwickshire England. [No recorded evidence of his date of birth].

1660. The first play of Shakespeare was printed first in 1623. The estimated cost of this first edition may be between 2.5

to 3.5 million pounds. The book is to be sold in in May 2006.

1661. Shakespeare would not have been Shakespeare without his plays Macbeth, Julius Caesar Antony and Cleopatra, The Temptest, The taming of the shrew, Henry VIII As You Like It, Measure for Measure, known to the world.

1662. Management is both an art and science.

1663. The Indian Constitution is a torch in our path of democracy.

1664. Nepal king Gyanendra announced on 21-4-2006 Friday, that he would hand over the political power he held 14 months ago, to the leader of the alliance of the seven parties.

1665. One of John Lemon's school books (50 yrs ago), was sold for the equivalent amount of Rs. 1.01 crore at a London auction.

1666. The BBC announced plan to increase the retirement age from 60 to 65, owing to the rising cost of funding staff pensions. (to the workers)

1667. Britain's Queen Elizabeth wanted a nice sunny day" on her 80th birth day on 21-4-2006.

1668. A relationship is a thread if stretched too far it is broken, if tied them together, a tie remains ever after.

— **Feng shui (Chinese Lucky Tips)**

1669. To improve financial luck place bamboo tree in the south east sector.

1670. You can keep itching coins in your wallet or purse or cash box and at the back of main entrance door for continuous income.

1671. The laughing Buddha carrying a money bag behind him is to be placed facing your main door.

1672. Place six rod wind chime and water feature in the north sector.

1673. Have lots of greenery in the east sector for health and luck.

1674. Have two crystal balls, mystic knot in south west sector with mandarin duck.—**Feng Shui (Chinese three Lucks).**

1675. Heaven luck – The luck given as god's gift to every one on the day of birth. It is the opening balance of luck.

1676. Self luck – luck earned by individual effort and it is not fixed, it keeps changing.

1677. Earth luck – Total luck of an individual is earth luck. It is the direct result of our living, or work environment.

1678. A casual is not an affair.

1679. Nature's fury knows no bounds.

1680. Nature's fury caused huge loss in men, money, material.

1681. 26 December 2004, a powerful tsunami killed 250000 people and millions became homeless in south East Asia

1682. On 29 August 2005, a monstrous hurricane hit U.S.A damage estimated at $ 200 billion, third largest, others occurred in 1935, and 1969.

1683. Many parts of India were flooded in 2005 , Mumabi received 944 mm rain in 24 hours on 26 July 2005. Over 1000 died.

1684. 8 October 2005, a powerful earth quake hit the country at 7.6 Richterscale, in Muzaffrakedd and Boramulla and Jammu and Kashmir region, over 45000 were killed.

1685. The growth of high rises in high risk zones of Delhi and Mumabi, is increasingly becoming a cause for concern.

1686. An enormous stress built up all along Himalayan region is released from time to time in the form of earth quakes.

1687. Earth quake prone areas are noted below.

1688. Jammukashmir, Himachal Pradesh, Uttaranchal, U.P and Bihar.

1689. Assam, Meghalaya, Manipur, and Nagaland.

1690. Bhuj region in Gujarath.

1691. Andaman Nichobar islands.

1692. Corals stand out as unique life forms with exquisite beauty.

1693. A cup of hot tea can do wonders.

1694. The scientific study of Algae is called pyretology.

1695. One third of the population in Hyderabad city like other metros lives in pollution.

1696. I do not discuss Judgement but I do not see why a Judgement should not be a matter of fun. — **Mona Lisa**

1697. Knowledge like wealth gets accumulated.

1698. In knowledge accumulation, old things give way to new things. In wealth accumulation, old things and new things exist together.

1699. "Here the tomb suffices a man for whom while living the whole world was not sufficient".

— **(The inscription on the Tomb Stone of Alexander)**

1700. Beneath this stone rest remains of Raja Ram Mohan Roy Bahadur, a conscientious and stead fast believer in the unity of Godhead.

1701. Inscription on Raja Rammohan Roy's tomb in Amo's vate Bristal [U.K].

1702. Here was deposited the mortal part of a man who feared God but not death And maintained Independence.

1703. But sought not riches who thought none below him but base and unjust none above him but the wise and the virtous who loved his parents, kindred, friend, country.

— **[On the epitaph of Sir William James]**

1704. I lived quite glad with out a dame

1705. I wish my father had done the same.

— **[On the Tomb of Dionysius of Jersius]**

1706. When I am dead I hope it may be said His sins were scarlet but his books were read.

— On the tomb of Hillarie Bellock [Famous writer]

1707. Here richly with ridiculus display. The politician's corpse was laid a way while all his acquaintances sneered and slanged. I wept for I longed to see him hanged. Belloc wrote on a contemporary politician.

1708. Who would pray on my behalf or bring a bunch of flowers? Who would light a candle? I am nothing but a gloomy tomb! **—[On the tomb of Bahadurshah jafar, the last Mogul king who participated in the war of Independence 1857 against the British. Sri Abdul Kalam, President of India recited these lines at the tomb, during his vist to Burma]**

1709. The hero goes to the bed room of heroine crossing all the hurdles.

1710. "How did you come? " asked the heroine. But not why did you come?

1711. 1Who the devil was he?

— [on the Tomb of Bernard Shaw]

1712. I shall spend heaven doing good on earth.

— [on the tomb of Theresa]

1713. Sun reader, life and line be thine for ever

— [Browning, on Shelley's Death]

1714. Here let her lie now she is at rest and so am I.

— [a Husband on his Wife's Tomb]

1715. What we may perceive as true may not be true, we see sun rising in the east and setting in west, we see sky blue. But sun does not rise on does not set and sky is not blue.

1716. Truth can be discovered and experienced at various levels.

1717. Change is often triggered by specific issues. But preconditions are usually much more complex.

1718. Thunder storms, cyclones, hurricanes, typhoons are common places – but their formation deserves closer look at clouds

1719. Cassowary are large flightless birds in "Rofile" family. The female cassowary lays 3 to 6 large eggs 5. ½ x 3.1/2 inches. The male cassowary incubates the eggs for about 2 months and takes care of the young ones for seven months until they mature.

1720. Joseph Black developed the concept of latent heat.

1721. I saac Newton has given three laws of universal motion in 1687.

1722. The scientific inventions belong to the world and not to any individual.

1723. John B. Fenn, Koichi Tanaka and Kurt wathrich were Nobel Laureates for Chemistry in 2002.

1724. Uranium is the heaviest naturally occurring element.

1725. Tungsten is the hard metallic element.

1726. Nothing is impossible in this world – said one sage But you can not put released tooth paste back into the tube.

1727. Some are wise some otherwise.

1728. Do not blame darkness, light a candle.

1729. Two mothers and two daughter went to a shopping complex. Each one purchased one pair of sandals. At home it turned out three pairs of sandals. How is it? [Ans. A is the mother of B. and B had one daughter. All counted three. A, B are mothers. (2) B, C are daughters (2) And total there are three women]

1730. National Botanical Research Institute is situated at Dehradun.

1731. Man is the only animal with the largest brain in proportion to body. C.T. brain scan **– Computed topography**

1732. The test involves a series of images of the brain determine if bleeding may be a cause of the stroke. Risk factors.

1733. People who receive first heart stroke will have another stroke with in 5 years.

1734. Factors you cannot control. Age, family background.

1735. Factors you can control. Diet, High B P, smoking, cholesterol, alcohol intake and others.

1736. In some countries regional economy is no longer regulated by planning..

1737. By foul means you cannot achieve success.

1738. Irene curie, the daughter of Marie Curie got Nobel prize in 1935.

1739. Women are advised to take sufficient calcium rich diet during pregnancy.

1740. Astronomy is based on scientific studies, astrology is a belief system.

1741. Heart beats never stop in life.

1742. In newborn baby, the heart beats 120 times per minute. In adult the rate is reduced to 72 per minute.

1743. The Heart lies near the middle of the chest pointing to left side, closer to chest than to back.

1744. Gold inflow in India was around 568 tons during 2003.

1745. Persons found anti national, ought to be killed even if they are sons or friends or relatives.

1746. How to talk with others ?

The subject must be clear

No mistakes in language

Speak in moderate tone.

No confusion in talk.

Talk must relate to the situation

No extra points dealt.

Words flow from heart.

No difficulty in grasping.

Speech directly goes to heart.

No breaks in speech.

Physical body should respond to speech.

Keep some distance from the listeners.

1747. There remains a mismatch between the quality of fomal institutions and existing informal institutions.

1748. The social capital is important for economic, social and political development of a country.

1749. Social capital is trust and cooperative behaviour and net works between groups.

1750. A young Georgian wrestler pulled two Ford mini buses tied to his ear [weight 4.5 tonnes] over a distance of 41 metres 10cm, to enter the Guinness Book of World Records.

1751. Mikhail Kalashnikov is the Russian inventor of A.K. – 47 assault rifle

1752. Empire State Building in New York US, has 102 floors.

1753. A country is not a corporation. It cannot be run like one. Nothing can justify the violation of the fundamental rights of citizens. **– Arundhati Roy**

1754. Rehabilitation in Madhya Pradesh has been disatrous.

– Saifuddin Suz [The Minister for water Resources]

1755. Every meter the dam [Narmada] goes up, an additional 1500 families come under submergence. **– Arundhati Roy**

1756. Why should taking from the rich be called appropriation and taking from the poor be called development?

– Arundhati Roy

1757. Is it right to divert rivers and grow water intensive crops like sugar cane, and wheat in desert ecology ?

– Arundhati Roy

1758. You can either use water for irrigation or power generation.

1759. 36921 families will be affected in 226 villages in Gujarat, M.P, and Maharashtra

– Narmada project – Report by the Ministry

1760. Any Publicity good or bad will do a world of good to sale of a book.

1761. Wealth accumulated gives you diminishing utility but knowledge accumulated gives you increasing returns.

1762. Sex is an eternal subject.

1763. Men Judge generally by the eye than by the hand.

1764. Every one can see but a few can feel.

1765. Every one sees what you appear to be, a few really know what you are. **–Niccolo Machavelli**

1766. We are alone, absolutely alone on this chance planet amid all forms of life that surround 45 not one excepting the dog, has made an alliance with us. **– Maurice maeterinck**

1767. A writer is a person for whom writing is more difficult than it is for other people. **– Thomas Mann**

1768. Work is not always required. There is such a thing as sacred idleness. **— George Macdonald**

1769. Medhapatkar was on indefinite fast against the proposed height increase in Sardar Sarovar Dam, as it will sub merge large number of tribal villages and rehabition was not easy.

1770. Narendra Modi, Gurjarth Chief, Minister went on token fest for water in Gujarath Rajasthan Maharashtra and Madhya Pradesh. Who is right? **– Kush Want Singh**

1771. In Turkey, a seeker after truth, on hearing of Guru in far off east, [India], travelled long distance for days and found his Guru in a small hut to his awe and amazement. Any one who visited him [Guru] was permitted to ask just one question. The traveller from Turkey asked "sir may I ask you Just one question in Turkish?". The Guru rose to leave the place, he said". Your one question is over, you do not need to travel long distances to ask any question. You ask your heart. It is closest, never failing counsellor of all" he went inside and shut the door,

1772. The winds and waves are always on the side of the ablest navigator. **– Edward Gibbon**

1773. A man is not idle because he is absorbed in thought. There is a visible labour and there is invisible labour.

– Victor Hugo

1774. The world is round and the place which may seem like the end may also be the beginning. **– Iry Baker Priest**

1775. If one does not know to which part he is sailing, no wind is favourable. **– Seneca**

1776. When a friend is in trouble, do not annoy him by asking if there is any thing you can do. Think of something appropriate and do it. **– Elgar Watson Hawe**

1777. If I am not worth the wooing. I am surely not worth the winning. **– Henry Words Worth Long fellow**

1778. Friendship marks a life even more deeply than love. Love risks degenerating into obsessions, friendship is never anything but sharing. **– Elfe Wiesel**

1779. Heart is the best, nearest closest, never failing counsellor.

1780. Ideas can be borrowed and not words. Kavya borrowed words. That is a blunder.

1781. When the children of children fight, the parents of parents get disturbed.

1782. The Tailiban has threatened to execute K. Suryanarayana, an engineer, Kidnapped in Afghanistan.

1783. "If India does not pull out all Indians by 19-00 hrs Sunday 30-4-2006, we are going to kill him."

1784. "Our presence in that country [Afghanistan] is to promote the welfare of the people and vast majority of Afghan people have welcomed it".

1785. "We are friends and well wishers of people of Afghanistan"

— **Indian Foreign Secretary**

1786. Freedom of Seas, the world's largest ship 160000 tonnes, 335 metres long can carry 40000 passengers.

1787. The king of Sweden Carl XVI Gust af, celebrated his birth day on Sunday 30-4-2006.

1788. Bill Gates Microsoft Chairman, announced on "Sundays reader" a soft on Sunday 30-4-2006, to facilitate growing number of readers.

1789. The government of Andhrapradesh has made it compulsory, mandatory for all private medical hospitals, clinics, laboratories to register with Health and Medical Department w.e.f. 29-4-2006 for better monitoring.

1790. I see a distinction between work and post as far as post is concerned, I will only take up when I have done adequate work.

— **Rahul Gandhi**

1791. In local and municipal elections candidates matter more than parties.

1792. About 150000 foreign heart patients visit India for Medicare in a year.

1793. Malgudi, R.K. Narayana's fictional town holds an eternal fascination for his millions of fans and readers.

1794. A master and a disciple were on a long journey, in Arabia. "Entrust all your things to God, and He will never abandon His children" said the master using every moment to teach the disciple at the sun set, they stopped at some place. "Tie the horses to that rock for the night" asked the master. At the dawn the horses were not there. On being asked the disciple said. "I entrusted them to God. As you taught me yesterday, He will never abandon His children".

1795. The wise man changes the situation when he is forced to do so. The foolish man does not believe the hand of god in all events. **– Zaochi**

1796. You cannot see your reflection in troubled waters, so also you cannot seek God with troubled mind.

1797. Always move forward with faith.

1798. The leaders in any political party are encouraged to cut each other to size, failing which they cannot hope to rise up the ladder.

1799. Emperor servant fall a sleep in the same way. Brahmin and chandala end up in the same grave yard.

1800. A shopholic is a person addicted to shopping.

1801. To be able to celebrate life is religion. **– Osho**

1802. Consumer Education and Research society Ahmedabad (CERS), has petitioned Gujarath, Electricity Regulatory Commission to return to consumers Rs. 9.72 crores collected by unfair and unjustified method during 2004-2005.

1803. "I did not say a loan "but said" Leave me alone" said the bank manager.

1804. Purchase food items under Agmark only – wheat atta, suji, maida basan, Pulses vegetable, ground nuts spices, ghee, butter, honey, etc.

1805. 20000, anti diabetic tablets have been tested and found 20 national brands, conforming to the standards.

1806. We as a nation epitomise the virtue of tolerance. The extent of compromise corruption, crime in almost all walks of life gives evidence to our tolerance. We tolerate injustice and corruption in day to day life. – **Pritee Shah [editor Insight]**

1807. A researcher in Krishna College of Science Binjnor, in Uttar Pradesh has developed a technique to produce petrol and diesel from discarded plastic toys.

1808. Tomatoes are rich in antioxidant lycompene known to benefit health.

1809. Beta carotenoids in carrot and popayya may help prevent arthritis.

1810. To commit a crime is no less wrong than to endure it.

1811. If a product is malfunctioning during the warranty period and if the repairs are not found satisfactory, it is deficiency of service and the consumer can claim full refund of the cost of the product.

1812. Not all parents are benevolent, some are corrective, and others are punitive.

1813. Sometimes a customer becomes a spoilt child making unreasonable demands, throws tantrum and becomes stubborn or sulk.

1814. Be soft, but firm. What your eyes convey. Your heart abeys. That is the secret of attraction.

1815. Secret laws of attraction.

Beauty appeals.

Definition of attraction is not simple.

May be you turn your mate on.

May be you make your mate laugh.

Sexual attraction is based on a complex series of messages hidden or open.

You may not be aware of these secret messages. The heroin says "you are an idiot".

Attraction depends on likes, position or status, family, or caste, age, life style, hobbies, talent and host of other things including neighbourhood.

Attraction also depends on mutual need.

The eldest or first children are likely to be high achievers. High achievers attract high talent.

Elder children are likely to take greater responsibilities. Elder boys attract elder girls.

The second children are likely to be adventurous, kicking against convention. So rebellious children attract rebellious children.

The youngest children or [last born], are likely to be sunny, funny and easy going. The youngest attract the youngest.

Attraction depends on three important factors, proximity, physical appearance and similarity.

People in similar background are attracted.

Education, religion or caste. Social status, accent, body language, and attitude speaks volumes.

Pheromones, the body's chemical messengers are hidden in flesh, determine attractions between two.

Body symmetry also determines attraction.

Opposites do not attract. Similar facial shapes are attracted.

People with middle fingers exactly corresponding lengths are attracted.

Press your hand against your partner, see if they match. People with similar hands are attracted, and love is lasting.

People who had the misfortune of having bad child childhood are attracted to people with problems, addicts, convicts, and emotionally troubled.

Proximity is an important factor, for attraction. Land owner's daughter is attracted to a tenant or vice versa.

Height is also important. If girls height is greater than boy's height, there would not be any match.

Colour of hair will also determines attraction.

Obese people are attracted to obese people.

In spite of all these rules, there are exceptions, you can not make out any theory for people's attraction.

1816. Hiccups happen because of sudden contraction of breathing muscles.

1817. Buyihg a saree is a big deal and wearing it is an art.

1818. Mr. Suryanarayana, an engineer was murdered. It is obvious that the kidnappers were not interested in negotiating, and real motivation was the act of terror [1-5-2006] — **Shyamsaran [Foreign Secretary]**

1819. Krishna Kumar, a youngster palys 65 roles in 12 hrs, to go into Limca Book of Records.

1820. Freedom Tower 1776 ft high will be financed by New York and New Jersy cost. $ 7.5 billion, and $ 2 billion for the tower alone.

1821. John Kenneth Galbraith economist, the greatest American friend of India 97 died on Saturday 29-4-2006.

1822. Pleasure is dependent on five senses, while happiness independent of them.

1823. Silence beyond thoughts is freedom.

1824. We see things through the eyes of ego, that is the reason for suffering, unhappiness depression, anger, conflict and all other negative feelings.

1825. No emotion is negative. Feelings have a lot of energy in them which can be used as motivational force. Jealousy is when you perceive a threat to one self or something you have, may be taken away, whether it is a relationship or some material thing. Envy is when someone is doing better, making more money, a certain amount of envy is natural. It prompts people to do better. – **Dr. Rajat Mitra**

1826. A violence knows no rules.

1827. A research study from World Bank examined the economic prospects in 2005 for 42 African countries.

1828. Poverty and income inequality remain high and deep rooted in some Asian countries. – **World Bank**

1829. Economic crises prove devastating for the poor.

1830. The poverty rate shot up from 30.8 percent in 1999 to 58 percent in 2002 in Argentina. The poverty rate rose from 26.6 percent in 2002 to 42.2 percent in 2004 in Dominican Republic. — **World Bank**

1831. The poor lack the minimum level of assets to fully benefit from the growth process. – **World Bank**

1832. Latin America often appears to lurch from the success.

– **World Bank**

1833. Successful or not, even the beautiful people have to learn to handle that envious streak.

1834. Envy is perennial. – **Preet Bedi**

1835. Envy is a powerful tool to cash in on.

1836. Advertising uses all the seven deadly sins to play on the consumer mind. Envy of course plays a huge role.

– **Bharat Dhabolkar**

1837. This dark passion makes the world go round as much as love.

1838. The jealousy has provided grist for literature and movies down the ages.

1839. I am envious of people who are good looking and slim of people who are well traveled, of people who are well read and better educated. **– Sandhya**

1840. you are programmed to respond to envy and jealousy swallow your bile and move on.

1841. It was not natural not to feel jealousy **– Freud**

1842. It is the person who did not feel jealousy, who did not show it was pathological. Showing jealousy was the normal thing. **– Freud**

1843. A husband gets inordinately. Jealous if she even calls on her boss or colleagues from office during non-office hours it affects the notion of honour in many families.

– Bonita Baruah Anubha Sawhney

1844. In homicidal attempts between siblings the younger brother/ sister usually carries fantasy of deep humilitation and rage which starts very early and gets steadily more powerful. A stage comes when the fantasy has to be acted out. It leads to violent conflict between them.

– Bonita Baruah Anubha Sawhney

1845. It is not only natural / normal but actually desirable to feel jealous. It is developed to give us dues to what is happening in our lives. **– Freud**

1846. Jealousy helps the body to quickly respond to a problem and give an instant solution.

1847. Jealousy is as necessary as love and sex.

1848. With out passion we would lie listless in bed for there would be no motivation to do anything at all. Passion inspires us to achieve life's goals. **— Freud**

1849. When Dharmaraja went to swarga [Haeaven], he saw Duryodana there.

"I do not want Swarge" said Dharmaraja, Envy in Dharmaraja worked.

1850. Ingratitude is treason to mankind. — **Tomson**

1851. Kindness is the sunshine in which virtue grows.

— **R.G. Ingersoll**

1852. It is easy to drive people what is hard is to lead them.

— **Rabindranath Tagore**

1853. A fool despises good counsel but a wise man takes it to heart. — **Confucius**

1854. Philosophy is thinking about reality speculatively — **Osho**

1855. The only man who never makes mistake is the man who never does anything. — **Theodore Roosevelt**

1856. Responsibilities gravitate to the person who can shoulder them. — **Elbert Hubbard**

1857. The surest way not to fail is to determine to succeed.

— **Sheridon**

1858. An optimist expects his dreams to come true, a pessimist expects his night mares to come true – **Laurence Peter**

1859. Those who want to succeed will find a way, those who do not will find an excuse. – **Leo Anguila**

1860. There is nothing more frightful than ignorance in action.

– **Goeth**

1861. Even if you are on right side some one will knock you down.

1862. Great men are born like us eat the same food, lived the same life like us. Greatness lies in the works they did, words they have written, battles they faught for justice and equity, sacrifice they made for humanity.

1863. Man is born in debt of parents, gods, Rishis, and humanity.

By having children, raising them and serving parents in old age, doing shradhas they clear the debt of paretns.

By performing Yagnas, you clear the debt of gods.

By doing Tapas, by study of vedas, acquiring knowledge, you can clear the debt of Rishis.

1864. By giving arms, by showing mercy and kindness you clear the debt of humanity.

1865. Mantram protects the human beings from all evils.

1866. It is not bad to think of enjoing all pleasures and comforts, and rising to the highest position in life.

1867. It is wrong to enjoy pleasures and comforts by denying others, and by killing others one should not acquire power.

1868. Work hard, use all opportunities, acquire skills and earn power and prospertiy by right means.

1869. Dharmaraj spoke untruth during Mahabharat war. Is it a sin? Is it a crime?

He spoke only half untruth. "Ashwadhama hato hatah naroya Kunjaro" the words uttered by Dharmaraja meaning – "Ashwadhama was killed, a man or an elephant" while uttering these words, he lowered his tone whild speaking "an elephant".

Dharmaraja uttered these words to save men on his side from the cultches of adharma, injustice.

For self defense, speaking untruth is not sin.

Dharmaraja spoke untruth at instance of Lord Krishna. It is not sin to speak a lie when some one has dictated to you.

Dharmaraja spoke untruth for the victory of Dharma whatever may be the reasons for this untruth spoken by Dharmaraja, he has seen naraka (hell) for sometime.

1870. Why was Duryodana a bad man?

From the childhood Duryodana developed negative attitude towards pandavas.

He wanted to kill them and take over all the kingdom.

Bheema was poisoned, tied hands and legs and was thrown into sea. Duryodana thought Bheema was his rival and he could kill all other pandavas.

Duryodana built lac house and asked pandavas to live in it. One night the lac house was burnt, but pandavas escaped from it.

Duryodana played mayajoodam" false dice and won the game. Winning a game by foul means, is not good.

After (13), years, 12 years Vanavasa, 1 year Agnathavasam, Pandavas came back and asked their share in the kingdom. Duryodana refused to give even a small piece of land to them.

Duryodana always wanted to kill pandavas and usurp their half share in the kingdom.

Srikrishna came to Duryodana for negotitations. Duryodana ill treated krishna and tied him to a pole. Any embassodor from enemy camp should be received and treated properly.

Duryodana refused to negotiate peace. He decided to fight and win war to rule the entire kindom.

1871. Man can enjoy worldly pleasures from the comforts earned by right means.

1872. Duryodana and Dharmaraja, are two opposite characters in Mahabharata.

1873. About 190 planets have been discovered orbiting other stars [2006].

1874. A good accountability will lead to a win-win situation in which both politicians and organisations are satisfied.

1875. Vedas.

Not written by any man.

They are passed on from generation to generation by rote method. Pupils heard them from gurus and they in turn taught their pupils. In guru – shishya parampara vedas are handed down to us.

Vedas are called "shrutis" because they are heard from gurus.

The collection of manthras is called "samhita".

Four vedas – Rig Veda, 2. Yajurveda, 3. Samaveda, 4. Atharvanaveda.

All vedas have (4) four parts – 1, Samhitha 2 – Brahmanaa, 3. Aranyaka, 4. Upanishad.

According to patanijali, Rigveda –21, Yajurveda – 101, Samaveda – 1000, Atharvana veda 9 branches are there.

1876. [A] Rigveda –

The oldest of all vedas. It has (8) eight chapters, and 2006 divisions. According to another classfiication (10) ten cantos, 85 anuvakkalu, 1017 rules [Suktas] and (11) suktas are famous. There are 10589 rukkulu 153826 words in Riveda. Total letters are 432000.

1877. [B] Vajurveda

It contains manthras invoking and inviting gods some manthras from Rigveda are repeated here. According to Krishna samhitha there are 86 branches in it but now only 41 are available It contains 7 chapters, 18000 manthras.

Types of yagnas – soma Vajapeya, Rajasuya, Purushamedha, Ashwamedha, etc.

1878. [C] Samaveda.

1879. Sama – means swara music or gana based veda most of the manthras have taken from Rigveda only 75 manthras are independent Total manthras 1875. This veda had 1000 branches, but only 13 are available. In Gandharva veda, there are 16000 ragas [tunes].

1880. [D] Atharvanaveda.

There are 20 branches in it you find treatment details for different diseases. How to react to enemies? This has been noted in Atharvana Veda. Antidote for snake poison has been given in this veda. Pesticides have been explained here in this veda. It contains 760 suktas, 5987 manthras. Rules of administration for kings have been given. The tigers of Bengal have been mentioned in this veda. Emphasis has been given to spiritual practices.

1881. Eating food - Results.

Faching East - you get long life

Faching South - you get fame

Faching West - you get wealth

Faching North - you get truth.

1882. While eating do not leave the place, if you get back do not eat the same food. [already left]

1883. Carotenoids are best known for their ability to be converted into vitamin – A, which is essential for healthy vision reproduction and for maintaining body tissues.

1884. Fighting cholesterol

Increase fibre in your diet

Reduce saturated fat found in beef, pork, lamb, poultry and fish,

Eat more fruits and vegetables.

Add garlic in your meals.

Use olive oil to cook.

Increase the amount of Omega – 3 in your diet.

1885. Heart strokes are responsible for millions of deaths each year.

1886. The biggest killers in order.

Heart disease

Cancer.

Brain attack or stroke

1887. Warnings of brain stroke

A numb or weak feelings

Trouble in speaking or understanding.

Dizziness – not explained

Biurred or poor vision.

Loss of balance or falling on the ground.

Weakness in muscles.

Difficulty in swallowing

Headaches.

Unconsciousness.

1888. CHILD CARE **– HINTS**

Do not give chacolate or candy.

Limit T.V. viewing.

Encourage child to participate in sports and other physical activities.

Give the child fruits, juices fruit salad, sprouts,

Noodles may be given.

No fast foods. – **Chips, and coke etc.**

Give the child buttermilk, mango, vegetable sandwitches, idli, bhelpuri, chapati.

Spend quality time with your child.

Your love, care, support are very important for child's development.

1889. Four techniques to conquer happiness that is with in you.

Asana

Pranayama

Dhyana **– Meditation**

Japa.

1890. In 2006 deaths caused by tobacco consumption are around 5 millions, and the figure is likely to go up to 9 millions by 2020.

1891. Human curiosity and urge to unravel the secrets of the sea dates back to time immemorial.

1892. Oceanography is a multidisciplinary approach to learn all about the biology physics, chemistry, geology engineering and meteorology of the ocean.

1893. Zooplanktons inhabit all regions of the oceans.

1894. Man's hunger has caused dwindling of forests from the beginning.

1895. Essential nutrients have been lost from dairy products, fruits, and vegetables etc over the last 60 years due to factory forming.

1896. In vegetables, a decline of 27% in iron, 46 percent in calcium and 24% in magnesium, have been reported over the last 60 years.

1897. Eat less to live longer.

1898. A ginat tortoise died in kolkata - due to liver failure having lived for about 250 years. The oldest tortoise in the world.

1899. Sea food contains Omega – 3 oil, it cleans out arteries, improves intelligence, concentration and mood, reduces, inflammation.

1900. There are more than 7000 species of sea weeds of which 160 species are commonly used as food in different parts of the world.

1901. Proteins are composed of amino acids.

1902. DNA – protein complexes are chromosomes.

1903. The structure of DNA was discovered by Watson and Crick.

1904. History remembers only those who did something worth while not those who helped others do it.

1905. Hirobito Shibuya, a 58 year old in Tokya lived openly with his 11 wives. He said "I will stop living with these women" and renounced this worldly life.

1906. Trust is the best formula for success.

1907. A girl born to a lower caste family has different opportunities from a boy born to well educated and affluent parents.

1908. A concern with equity is of immense importance for development. — **Finance and Development**

1909. Do not eat while standing.

1910. Six gunas – gnana, bala, Ishwarya, Veera, Shakti and Tejas.

1911. Man should have heart

1912. Man should be wise

1913. Man should put knowledge in practice.

1914. Man should be self reliant. over senses.

1915. Man should not yield to temptations.

1916. The whole world steps aside for the man who knows where he is going. — **Anon**

1917. Doing what is right is not the problem, it is knowing what is right.
— Lyndon B.J ohnson

1918. No body really cares if you are miserable, so you might as well be happy.
— Cynthianims

1919. Life is the art of drawing without an eraser.
— John W. Gardner

1920. The happiest moments of my life have been a few, which I have passed at home in the bosom of my family,
— Thomas Jefferson.

1921. The best to cheer your self up is to try to cheer somebody else up.
– Mark Twain.

1922. I have long come to be lieve that people never mean half of what they say, that it is best to disregard their talk and Judge only their actions.
– Dorothy

1923. Those who cannot remember the past are condemned to repeat it.
– George Santayana

1924. I owe my success to having listened respectfully to the very best advice and then going away and doing the exact opposite.
– G.K. Chesterton

1925. A long habit of not thinking a thing wrong gives it a superficial appearance of being right.
– Thomas Pain.

1926. A piano is the world's most expensive instrument priced at $ 250000. A Piano made in 1707 was auctioned for $ 3.5 million.

1927. Special Economic zone (SEZ) – The area specially designed to attract huge investments by setting up manufacturing, warehousing, trading activities. At present there are 10 SEZS.

1928. Liquid oxygen has been used as a substitute for dynamite in coalmining.

1929. Nuno gomes, 52 year old engineer from south Africa, dived to a depth of 318.25 metres [1044ft], on June 10, 2005, the deepest record sofar.

1930. The social equations can alter relationships at the inclusion of extra digit in your bank account.

1931. The real issue is not money itself, but the power money gives you. — **Delton Conley**

1932. Friendship and money are a two ends of the spectrum.

— **New York Times**

1933. Growing old is not an issue

1934. Age is an issue of mind, if you do not mind, it does not matter. — **Mark Twain**

1935. Everything depends on one's mind and personality. If they are looking and feeling good, why cannot they feel 20?

— **Manipreet Brat**

1936. Love can change lives.

1937. What could I be doing at 64? I am a grandfather now and would not be playing romantic roles any more.

— **Amitabh Bachchan (2006)**

1938. Why Some women get attracted to married men?

People want "forbidden fruit".

A married man represents a certain security she craves.

Getting a married man signifies a triumph of one woman over another woman.

The relationship gives excitement.

The married man is a trophy to catch.

To have a married man means, making impossible possible.

A married man at her beck and call, addes to her value.

Having a married man increases her self esteem.

A married man is a symbol of authority.

A married man makes her extra special.

This relationship is about fun and adventure.

Married men love playing games. Sex for them is a past time.

The woman does not resist the vibes of attraction from a married man.

A married man can give you a great time.

Women love playing power games.

A married man can take you through highs.

Women both single an married love to have married men.

A married man presents wild attraction.

Women are vulnerable to charms of married men.

A married man can meet her emotional and material needs in a better manner.

Men are polygamous by nature.

Men disassociate sex from love.

Women tend to ignore the fact that her partner is married.

A vegetarian eats meat. He continues to do so. A woman continues this relationship in the same manner.

Human beings are fragile.

It is a no-win situation when a woman falls in love with a married man. She lives in a fantasy.

1939. Three meals interspersed with two snacks to prevent long hours of starvation is a ideal brain food.

1940. Certain nutrients in one's diet, go a long way in enhancing our thinking capacity creative out put and memory power, and slows brain's ageing process.

1941. The brain needs 20 percent of oxygen and 50 percent of available glucose to do its job.

1942. The brain comprises only 2 two percent of the total body weight.

1943. Brain uses 20 percent of body's available energy resources.

1944. Brain's 10 billion – plus cells have very high appetite which must be satisfied every minute of our lives for proper functioning. — **Deepti Bansal**

1945. The brain requires 120 gms of complex carbs per day.

1946. Consuming 1 to 2 table spoons of flax seeds or about 2 walnuts per day is beneficial.

1947. The French are the most unfriendly. — **British Poll**

1948. Habib Miyan alias Rahimkhan the oldest man in India celebrated his 137 birth day in Jaipur on Saturday 20-5-206.

1949. The Indian is confused how to behave in board room and bed room.

1950. A powerful earth quack 6.2 on rickter scale struck at 5-54 am on Saturday 27-5-2006. 300 kms east of Jakarta, which flattened homes and buildings and killed more than 3000 people.

1951. A medical student from Cuttak Orissa attempted self immolation on Saturday 27-5-2006 in protest against OBC quota

1952. A doctor patient does not trust other doctor treating him.

1953. The simpler it is the more beautiful it will become.

— **Wilhelm Backhaus**

1954. A cynic is a man who knows the price of everything but the value of nothing. — **Oscar Wilde**

1955. I intend to give her as much attention as I can for she has talent. **— Claraschuman**

1956. An expert is a man who has stopped thinking he knows.

— Frank Lioyol Wright

1957. When people keep telling you that you cannot do a thing, you would not like to try it. **— Margaretchase Smit**

1958. If people never did silly things nothing intelligent would ever get done. **— Ludwing Wittgenstein**

1959. If you love life, life will love you back. **— Norman Vincent**

1960. If liberty means to tell the people, any thing at all, it means the right to tell people what they do not want to hear.

— George Orwell

1961. What we love to do, we find time to do.

— John L. Spaiding

1962. The subject of plagiarism is ancient and modern.

Examples

The literary giants like Shakespeare, Coleridge and Oscar Wilde were accused of plagiarism

Martin Luther King was accused of plagiarising many college papers his doctoral dissertation, and his speeches.

Dan Brown, was acquitted. by the London High Court of alleged plagiarism in all time best seller The Davinci Code.

Ms Kavya Vishwananthan, a 19 year old. was accused of lifting 40 passages from two novels sloppy firsts and second helpings by an author Megan Mc Carfferty for her novel. How Opal Mehta Got kissed, Got wild and Got a Life and the publisher Brown and company had to withdraw 100000 copies of the novel from all countries including India.

1963. Man has (3) three types power or Shakti.

Ichcha Shakti **– Thought Power**

(b) Jnana shakti – **Knowledge Power**

(c) Kriya Shakti - **Work power**

1964. I love the soul inside everyone.

1965. Finding a kind way to speak the truth matters much.

1966. Every thought, word and act is a reflection of how we see and expect the world to be for us. – **Donna K. Devane**

1967. Every one of us has a vision of the world which depends on our experience, beliefs, dreams and expectations . – **Donnak, Devane**

1968. What is defeat? Nothing but education nothing but the first step to something better. — **Wendell Phillips**

1969. Bureaucracy defends the status quo long past the time when the quo has lost its status. — **Laurence J. Peter**

1970. There are two ways to slide esily through life. To believe everything or to doubt everything both ways save us from thinking. — **George Sand**

1971. People find it tough to discard age old tradition, a part of ethos and conscience.

1972. I find spirituality in the work I do. — **Vikram Akula**

1973. We live increasingly in a world of multiple choice. — **Jug Suraiya**

1974. Karakuram, Leh, Ladak regions of Himalayas at 3500 meters high are highest hillstations in India. Other popular hill stations are Ooty, Darjeeling, Shimla and Nainital.

1975. The London Eye is the largest observatory wheel in the world built 1999 on the south bank of river Thames in London, at the height of 135 metres giving one a panoramic view of London for 25 kms in all directions.

1976. Women have based their entire lives on sacrifice.

1977. In Thaittreyi Upanishad, mother is given the place of pride.

Worship your mother, your father, your teacher and your guest. Mother is of paramount importance.

– Advice by teacher to the student on convocation upanishad

1978. Acharya is ten times greater than upadhyaya, father is hundred times greater than Acharya, Mother is thousand times greater than father. – **Goutama Dharma.**

1979. Heaven lies at the feet of Mother. - Quran

1980. The greatness of man lies in the following factors.

The training influence of mother.

The example of father.

The influence of teacher of all the mother' role is the greatest.

1981. Love is more powerful than discipline.

1982. Children cling to the mother for her love, and tenderness.

1983. Many mothers went hungry out of their self sacrificing love and concern for their children, who became ungrateful after marriage neglected them and put them in old age homes.

1984. Salutations to Mother.

1985. [On International Mother's Day]

1986. Let us pay our tributes

To the mothers who spent sleepless nights to serve the sick children.

To the mothers who spent hours and days soothing their crying children.

To the mothers who spent their lives in serving physically, mentally challenged children.

To, the mothers who in school functions to watch the events in which their children participated.

To the mothers who try to discipline their children demanding 'I want this or I want that' beyound their capacities

To the mothers who arrange books and lunch boxes, tie their shoe laces, to prepare them for schools.

To the mothers who go hungry to satisfy the hunger of their children.

To, the mothers who tie their children to a branch to tend others children.

To the mothers who tie and carry their children at their back to work place.

To the mothers who get beaten by the employers for tending their children.

To the mothers who forego all the comforts to make their children comfortable.

To the mothers who sell their bodies to feed their children.

To the mothers who toil in the fields, or who hammer or cut the stones to educate their children.

To the mothers who are put in old age homes by their children.

To, the mothers who keep expecting their grown up children to help them from foreign lands.

To all the mothers, who are not mentioned in these lines.

To my mother (no more to day)

Who was innocent and ignorant, and made me what I am to day.

(Plagiarised I.V. Chalapati Rao)

1987. It is ideas, not vested interests, which are dangerous for good or evil. **– John Meynard Keyness**

1988. Reading is an important skill, and reading ability of students tends to increase with the size of their shoe size.

1989. We often desire acceptance from others. We want to know what others might think about us. In fact, others are not thinking about us.

1990. Doing the right thing from our point of view is enough. We can do nothing more than our best in all circumstances.

– Peter Cajander

1991. It is enough we are honest to our self. **– Peter Cajander**

1992. It is hard to rely on our selves. We continuously worry about how we are perceived by others. **– Peter Cajander**

1993. Attempting to please others is not good policy to pursue

1994. Often we take things for granted and accept everything face value.

– Rene Descartes (one of the Most Famous 17th Century Western Philosophers)

1995. When we get right choices and answers from within there is no need to look for acceptance from others.

1996. Accepting ourselves and being content with our own lives are the first and the important steps in our existence.

– Peter Cajander

1997. The sooner kids understand that you are not perfect, the sooner they will realise they do not have to be perfect.

– Joequen

1998. Misery may love company but not as much as happiness does.

1999. A bad mood diverts attention from performance.

2000. The average person "knows" a lot of people. **– H. Russell Bernard**

2001. Stand for your own rights you be a good friend.

– Dalai Lama

2002. If there is dramatic change then a chaotic situation may develop and that would not be in any one's interst.

– Dalai Lama

2003. Sexual desire and sexual attachment are enjoyable but these actually act as a basis to anger hatred and jealousy.

– Dalai Lama

2004. Monks fast and clothes are limited.

2005. People suffer because of their past lives and past karma

– Dalai Lama

2006. Reducing anger does not mean we give in. **– DalaiLama**

2007. Buddha killed one man to save the lives of 4999 people.

– Dalali Lama

2008. I do not believe in God. I do not believe in the creator. But I have respect. **– Dalai Lama**

2009. We must respect other people.

2010. So long as space remains so long as sentient beings suffering remains I will remain in order to help in order to serve prayer. **– Dalali Lama**

2011. Reservations are now the interest paid on loans borrowed from vote banks. **– Editor. DC**

2012. Types of worship in different Yugas for Moksha

(a) Kritayuga **– Dhyanam Meditation**

(b) Tretayuga **– Yagnas**

(c) Dwaparayuga – **Archana, Pooja**

(d) Kaliyuga – **Japa, Recitation of Lord's Name**

2013. Nine types of BhaktiShrvanam, Keertanam, Smarana, Padasevanam, Archanam, Vandanam, Dasyam, Sakhyam,

– Atma Nivedanam

(a) Shravanam **-Listening**

(b) Keertanam **-Bhajana**

(c) Smaranam **-Repetition of Lord's Name**

(d) Padasevanam **-Worship of Holy Feet**

(e) Archanam **-Worship or Pooja**

2014. (f) Vandanam **-Namaskaram**

2015. (g) Dasyam **-Acting Lord's Slave and doing Service**

(h) Sakhyam

—Treating Lord as Friend. [Sudama – Lord Krishna]

(i) Atma Nivedanma **—Self Surrender**

2016. Spirituality is recognising oneness among human beings and act accordingly. **— Vikram Akula**

2017. Every one deserves respect you should respect every individual. The way you would like to be treated.

— Vikram Akula

2018. By being aware of your thought and actions you can change your vision one step at a time **— Donna K. Devane**

2019. Long life can be a penalty if one is plagued with illness or disability. **— Editor Science Reporter**

2020. There are 70 million people over the age of 60 today in the country [India] (in 2006) and the figure increasing at 15 percent a year.

2021. In India 22 lakh infants and children die every year from preventable diseases and one lakh mothers die at child birth. (2006)

2022. Every living being emits neuro waves all the time, when she is thinking of some one, and these wave are sensed by the one thought.

2023. On 29 July 2003, Mike Brown of the Columbia Institute of Technology, announced the existence of a new planet in the outer solar system, he had discovered along with his colleagues chad Trujillo of Gemini observatory and David Rabinowitz of the Yale University temporarily named as 2003 UB313 farthest object sighted, to make one revolution in 560 Earth Years.

2024. Creating an environment of creative learning for knowledge and an irresistible urge to explore is the need of the hour.

2025. Neurons emit Neuro radiation a special kind of radiation, through this radiation one can communicate with out any phone. [In ancient times – telepathy]

2026. It is difficult to talk ceaselessly to anyone through cell phone.

2027. Neuro communication to day is akin to chemistry.

2028. A new born baby has a brain 1/4th of the adult brain weight.

2029. People clashed in the streets where real and presume problems have led to violent demonstrations and self immolation attempts. – [May 2006]

2030. Trade in counterfeits has grown at eight (8) times the speed of legitimate trade. — **interlope**

2031. Money laundering comprises between 2 percent and 5 percent of the world GDP

2032. The number of slaves in the 21st century is larger than in the previous four centuries combined.

– Moises Naim. In this book "Illicit"

2033. The technical change in globalisation has brought about the reduction of transport or transfer costs for people goods and the exchange of information.

2034. 170 million people live in countries other than those in which they were born. **– Moises Naim**

2035. Hundreds of millions of people cross borders every year as tourists, or workers, or for other reasons. – **Moises Naim.**

2036. The illicit activities in the world include trade in weapons, material for nuclear devices drug trade, trade in people [current version of slavery], stealing, unauthorised use of intellectual property laundering of money, and growing trade in human. **– Organs. – Moises naim**

2037. Hence forth in the event of divorce a woman who gives up her career to bring up children theoretically be entitled to an equal share in the family's assets created during the marriage. **– Hason Suror**

2038. The House of Lords, Britain's highest court, has obliterated the traditional and some what perverse distinction between the home maker and bread winner on the ground that marriage must be regarded as an alliance of "equal partners" and the contribution of the partner who stays home to raise the family is no less important than the one who brings home the bread. **– Hasan Surror**

2039. Divorce settlements incase of stay at home mums centered on maintenance or her "living costs" rather than her right to a share in the family assets. [London – Prior to new ruling]

2040. There should be no bias in favour of the money – earner against the home – maker and the child carer. The length of a marriage is irrelevant in deciding a settlement.

2041. The women who put their career prospects second to the needs of their husbands and children can now expect to be compensated for that sacrifice by this new ruling.

– Hasan Suroor

2042. My advice is "Do not marry". If you do make sure your other half is as wealthy as you are. You do a prenuptial agreement and keep your fingers crossed.

– Mr. Jeremy Levision (a Lowyer)

2043. Paranola is but natural for any concerned parent.

2044. Parents of teen agers (13to 15 year) sneak into their children's room and check their belongings, SMS on cell phones, etc.

2045. Shah Jahan's building projects include places courts and mausoleums in Lahore and Agra, mosques in Ajmer.

2046. If you give something out of your income, it is called, Donations. If you give all, your income, it is called sacrifice and if you give more than your income, it is foolish.

2047. Thomas Edison the inventor of light bulb was afraid of darkness

2048. Scientists are not normal people.

2049. Tiwa tribe people living in Morigaon district of Assam, still practise barter system (2006).

2050. Neither the judiciary nor the legislature knew its limitations.

– Sri. J. Sarabji former Attorney General

2051. None is above law.

2052. It is an every day nightmare for children, senior citizens, physically challenged people to cross the road in busy hours in metropolitan cities.

2053. The litigation in courts takes very long time and often by the time when justice is delivered one of the parties exists no more. **—Dr. Jayaprakash Narayan**

2054. Politics affect every aspect of our lives.

– Dr. Jaya Prakash Narayan

2055. We cannot remain indifferent towards politics any more.

—Dr. Jayaprakash Narayan

2056. We need to be in power long enough to be able to make a visible impact. **– Dr. Manmohan Singh**

2057. India must be rid of chronic poverty and steps to ensure that farmers, workers, minorities and the weaker sections had a bright future. **– Dr. Manmohan Singh**

2058. With hard work, determination selflessness, commitment, we are on the verge of creating a new India.
— Dr. Manmohan Singh

2059. I prefer to listen **— Rahul Gandhi**

2060. January 23, 2006 Monday was to be most dismal of the year. **— Mr. Arnall**

2061. A good circle of friends and neighbours, a happy disposition and a bulging bank account all contribute to a heal their and more active old age.
— A study by city university, Hong Kong

2062. China and India are two of the top markets in terms of mobile handset growth.

2063. A Saudi Arabian Court has pardoned Abdul Lateef Noushad an Indian national whose eye was to be gouged out under the tit for tat laws of the country. **– The Hindu 24-1-2006**

2064. Leaders cannot be created. Youth should reach out to people in the country **— Rahul Gandhi**

2065. Move away from the corridors of power and listen to people and understand because leadership is created by listening and understanding rather than through posts.
– Rahul Gandhi

2066. Assumptions are the termites of relationships

2067. It takes considerable knowledge just to realise the extent of your own ignorance.

2068. Nothing vanishes so irretrievably as the annals of another age. **– David frum**

2069. Stress is an ignorant state. It believes that everything is an emergency. **– Natelie Golderg**

2070. Humour is a rubber sword. It allows you to make a point with out drawing blood. **– Mary Hirsch**

2071. Adversity is like a strong wind. It tears away all things torn so that we see ourselves as we really are. **– Arthur Golden**

2072. The past actually happened but history is only what some one wrote down.

2073. Half of the harm done in the world is due to people who feel important.

2074. Adventure today means finding one's way back to the silence and stillness of a thousand years ago.

2075. Millions of travellers never have trouble, but thieves are there

2076. Prices of rooms in hotel change according to the seasons in different countries, please check web sites.

2077. The beech belongs to every one.

2078. When you are in love, your eyes light up, your face lights up. These love spots are same. When photographs of your sweet hearts are seen, different areas of the brain scan it up. **— indicating Higher Blood flow**

2079. In the absence of relevant material, much less due verification, the report of the Governor has to be treated as the personal ipsedixit (perception or opinion) and extreme action under Article 356 of the constitution cannot be justified on mere ipsedixit, fancies of the Governor.

— Supreme Court. 24-1-2006

2080. The Governor may be the main player but the Council of Ministers (union cabinet) should have verified the facts stated in the report of the Governor before the report of the Governor hurriedly accepting it as a gospel truth as to what the Governor stated has misled the Council of Ministers led to aid and advice being given by the Council of Ministers to the president to the issue of the impunged proclamation.

— Supreme court

2081. The extra ordinary emergency powers of recommending dissolution of legislative Assembly is not a matter of course, to be resorted to for good governance or cleansing of politics for the stated reasons with out any authentic material.

— **Supreme Court**

2082. Create your own identity.

2083. On the South Australian Coast, a family found a piece of whale omit 14.75 Kg worth about $ 20 a gram, making a total of $ 295000.

2084. I transcend the business angle and aim at bringing a total change in one's personal tips on family life and making one lead a purposeful life. – **Yanda moori Veerendranath**

2085. We are not divine, we are fallible. The need of the hour is disciplined action by all citizens.

– **A.P.J. Abdul Kalam. 25-1-2006**

2086. If makes big money for the richest nations while fueling conflict across the world, because they are manufacturers and suppliers of weapons.

2087. Torture, murder, theft and rape all take place at gunpoint.

2088. Women raped at gunpoint, are victims terrorism.

2089. Cinema goers will be shocked this week to see an advertisement selling them AK. 47 machineguns (2006).

2090. Some people are making big money from the spiraling violence. The global arms trade amounted to $ 21 billion.

2091. The armed violence is even more shocking than that pictured on our cinema screens.

2092. Do not use charity for conversion. – **Pope**

2093. When you need help these days you do not need a bugle to call the cavalry. — **John Horrigan**

2094. Today we talk about violence in narrow terms of assault rape, or murder Gandhi brings out the multidimensional violence – economic violence, violence of power and control, the violence of poverty, the violence of status and how they inter act with each other. — **Douglas Allen**

2095. Electoral politics do not change history. — **Douglas Allen**

2096. People empowered themselves, mobilised public strong enough to make politicians listen to them.

— **Douglas Allen**

2097. We have to build such alternative centers of power.

2098. Every family must do research and produce a book on its family tree. – **B.K. Karanjia, [editor of film fare, Indian Express for 28yrs editor of Blitz]**

2099. Government would not be pressured into doing anything that hurt national interest. – **Manmohan Singh**

2100. We will do what is right for our country. India's national interest is our prime concern. Whether it is domestic or international policy, we will not act under pressure on any thing. – **Dr. Manmohan Singh**

2101. My country gives me my right. —**Mr. Al. Armouti**

2102. We are planing to build permanent basics on the moon by 2005 and begin the industrial scale delivery of the rare isotope Helium – 3 by 2020. – **Nikolai Sevatyanov**

2103. President George W. Bush unveiled similar plans tied to the same time frame

2104. "The country which is first to deliver helium –3 to Earth will win the race for global energy leadership". – **Eirk Galmov**

2105. "I was president for 35 years"

— **Mr. Hussein (in the court)**

2106. "I am the judge and you are the defendant"

— **The judge said to Suddam**

2107. According to catholic doctrine remarried divorcees are regarded as being in a permanent state of sin and cannot receive communion.

2108. Mushroom rock at Nizamabad [AP] was 2 billion years old.

2109. Do not expect your children to pay for your funeral.

2110. Little by little misfortune fades.

2111. The teacher should be strict and impartial while imparting education.

— **Brahmasri Gullapalli Anjaneya Salakshana Ganapathi**

2112. Girls are becoming endangered species.

— **Renuka Chowdhry**

2113. Do not bite the bait.

2114. People quit the job for various reasons – money, work hours lack of job satisfaction, or lack of opportunities for promotion

2115. A 6 year old boy in Massachusetts was reportedly sexually harassed a girl in his elementary school.

2116. Just switching to low fat foods is not likely to yield much health benefit in most women. — **Marcia Stefanick**

2117. Just reducing total fat intake does not go far enough.

2118. A fake China's Great Wall was built with 9999 bricks at the cost of $ 1.2 million to satisfy $ 120 visitors.

2119. "Tell me why I have been punished".

— **Dharam Singh, [Chief Minister, Karnataka] 8-2-2006**

2120. Pavuluri Venkata Naga Dheeraj, 4 year old, son of Krishna Mohan, an English Assistant at the Zilla Parishad school in Allaparru Village and Padmavati, a mathematics teacher at Andhrapradesh Social Welfare Residential School, has so far showed his abilities, in 65 shows could answer 500 G.K. bit questions in 30 minutes and likely to enter the Guinness Book soon, and break the record of Rajnath Singh Who could recognise more than 200 names and things blindfolded. The Hindu 9-2-2006.

2121. Right to freedom of expression is not absolute. —**Amnesty**

2122. A Japanese company has made 20 cm tall entertainment humanoid robot weighing 770 gms and named.

2123. Two beautiful Buddha statues have been discovered at Kalapakkam village, 20 Kms from the inscription showed that it was donation by Sri Vijaya Maharaja, the king Sumatra, to Shiva Temple during period of Raja Raja Chola 985 to 1085

2124. The key for healthy living is in fact, a good bout of exercise.

2125. Orgasms even release pain Killers in to the blood stream helping keep mild disease like colds and aches and pains at bay and produce extra estrogen and testosterone. These harmones keep your bones and muscles healthy.

2126. Life is a long song.

2127. Management is doing things right and leadership is doing right things. — **Peter Drucker**

2128. The leader of the team is one who realises that there should not be more than enough space for "I" in the team.

2129. Leader puts his self interest behind for the sake of team.

2130. You never know what you might encounter in your life.

2131. The fossils of 40 million year old "giant" penguin in natural history nuseum in Newzealand is attracting huge crowds.

2132. About 15000 turtles crawled seashore to lay eggs at 2 kms, stretch of beach at Rushikulya river mouth in Drisia.

2133. Depriving children of a loving family environment causes lasting damage to their intelligence, emotional physical state. Lack of care and attention leads to lower IQ.

2134. Temperatures in the Indian sub-continent could rise to three to four degrees Celsius above average by 2100 owing to global warming (The Hindu 19-2-2006)

2135. The temperature rose close to 50 degree Celsius in the year 2003 in Andhra Pradesh and hundreds of people died.

-(The Hindu 19-2-2006)

2136. A 62 year old, grand mother of 20, and great grand mother of three, gave birth a 2.3kg baby boy, her 12th child.

-the Hindu 19-2-06

2137. Vaporetto (water Taxi) in Venice takes you round the city.

2138. In middle class families the young still do not have much of a choice when it comes to choosing their life partner.

2139. Operation Manju [asin Meerut] where the police took it upon themselves to harass and thrash courting of private spaces.

2140. In middle class families the parents do not give their daughters the right to choose their life partners.

2141. "I do not think any one can believe in god any more but to me it seemed need time, superman unfold itself out".

– Upamanyu Chatterjee

2142. Friends cheat not the enemies.

2143. When you are suffering from cold, fast for one day.

2144. Men who ate about 10 grams of chocolate a day had lower blood pressure and a reduced risk of death.

— A Study in the Natherlands

2145. You will never lose or forget ID card to carry with you.

2146. St Hilda — All Women college setup in 1893, will admit men and take male lecturer, according to the students voting. **—[The Hindu 1-3-06]**

2147. Citrus fruits float in salt water.

2148. Beijing is launching a compaign on radio television, the internet and mobile phones to stamp out public spitting and littering, ahead of 2008 Olympics. The fine for public Spitting is 50 Yuan about Rs. 225 [1 Yuan = Rs. 4.5] in March 2006.

2149. Women in Gujarat are offering themselves as surrogate mothers.

2150. Women preferring to become surrogate mothers are told that they will have to hand over the child after delivery.

2151. Women, from middle or lower middle class, preferring to become surrogate mothers. Will get between Rs. 1 lakh and Rs. 2 lakhs for the job. [2006. March]

2152. "We have got a couple of issues that are important that remain unresolved but we are going to keep working it whether or not there is a deal on this trip". U.S. President on Nuclear deal — **in India on 2-3-2006**

2153. Nuclear deal was signed by Bush and Dr. Manmohan Singh on 2-3-2006. Fast breeder programme and about 35 percent of nuclear capacity is out of IAEA safe guards. [IAEA – International Atomic Energy Agency]

2154. In Urban India money makes money, but in rural India failed monsoon means failed crops means disaster and a good monsoon means bumper crop can also mean disaster to the farmer who will have to sell for loss. – **Gopal Krishna Gandhi [Governor West Bengal. 2-3-2006, The Hindu]**

2155. Private lending in rural India has led hundreds of farmers to swallow pesticides they have borrowed.

2156. It takes courage to take ideas upstairs.

2157. Counseling is a cost effective and efficient practice.

2158. The best CEO can create outstanding executive teams even out of ineffective top team leaders.

2159. Mahatma Gandhi was not born the prime minister or leader, but he changed the history of the nation.

2160. Some people do not even aspire to be the best in the world.

2161. Indian society lays great emphasis on young people finishing education at one stretch and then starting their career, unlike in the west.

2162. Nobody has monopoly over knowledge.

2163. If you have invented something then people do use it.

2164. The companies are facing a conflict of meeting the requirements of rural masses and urban elite.

2165. If a company is not making money then it has to revisit its costs.

2166. Only one book out of hundreds will be read from cover to cover.

2167. East or West, home is the best.

2168. Two judges give two different verdicts for the same crime.

2169. Objectivity is lacking in the Judgements pronounced by the Judges.

2170. Time lag between crime and punishment is long enough to make people forget the injuries inflicted by it.

2171. If you breath too deeply or too open you lose too much Carbondioxide, which can cause a panic attack.

2172. Every breath makes a difference to your body.

2173. Breathing correctly can keep you safe from a number of illnesses.

2174. Women are worriers which keep them prone to depression.

2175. Women are prone to depression by nature.

2176. 260000 satellites are currently revolving around the earth. (March 2006)

2177. Katherine Hepburn, has won the most number of [13] Oscars in Academy Awards History.

2178. Judo is a Japanese system of wrestling developed in 19th century.

2179. I never lose faith in myself and God. — **Nanapatekar**

2180. Mother's love is the most unconditional in the world.

2181. 41 percent of people gave more than one small bribe in India, during the last 6 months [March 2006]

2182. Microsoft on Thursday 9-3-2006 displayed an ultra mobile P.C. project origami, running window's XP with a touch screen and wireless connectivity, with a keyboard. It has 17.8 cm touch – sensitive screen and will sell between $ 600 to $1000 weight less than 1.1 kg.

2183. Richard Attain Borough made Gandhi – film to pay homage to the leader of non – violence. But the film failed to tell the western audience that Mrs. Gandhi was not the daughter of Mahatma Gandhi. Reagan said after viewing the picture "Gandhi was an outstanding man like his daughter".

2184. Try to earn more by getting on with the things. **– Advice for the Parsilvio Berlusconi Prime Minister Italy]**

2185. Our prayer are always answered.

2186. India – in nutshell Area – 3287782 sq.kms East to West – 2933 Coast line – 61000 kms. Land frontier – 15200 kms. 15 percent of worlds population 1.1 billion 2.4 percent of world's land.

2187. Virginia Easton Smith, — the woman from Hawaii has grown mango weighing 2.25 kgs, roughly the size of human head, the world's heaviest mango, as recorded in the Guinness Book world Records **– [12-3-2006]**

2188. In the Quiet Land no one can tell If there is some one who is listening for secrets they sell. The informers are paid in the blood of land and no one dare speak what the tyrants would not stand in the quiet land one laughs and Burma no one thinks out land.

– Aung San Suu [Nobel Peace. Prize winner]

2189. "We will become a global manufacturing hub for small cars in the next 3 to 5 years."

– Chidambaram [Finance Minister. 12-3-2006]

2190. Billionaires club with 793 member, total combined wealth stood at $ 2.6 trillion. **– 2006 Forbes Magazine 2006**

2191. Top 10 richest persons Bill Gates, Warren Buffelt [US] Carlos slim [Mexico], Ingavar Kamprad [Sweden], Lakshmi Mittal [India], Paul Allen [U.S] Bernard Arnault [France], Prince Alwaleed Bin Talal [Saudi Arabia], Kenneth Thamson [Canada], Lika Shing [Hong Kong].

– The Hindu 11-3-2006

2192. A successful leader secures power base and lives up to people's expectations.

2193. It is not always propriety that matters in ensuring one's success as capacity to get away with transgressions.

2194. The older sinners mastered the art of survival.

2195. The nature of untruth is the same every where.

2196. We are easily deceived. How to save ourselves?

2197. Raghav Srivasthav, a student III class, from Armoor in Nizamabad, has entered the Guinness Book of World Records for fastest spelling of words in reverse direction. He spelt 50 words back wards in 2 minutes 40 seconds.

2198. If you want to prosper do not tax agriculture.

– Schiff Valdes

2199. According to Kautilya there are (10) ten means of supporting life. Science, Arts working for hire Attendance, cattle tending trades, agriculture, determination, begging usury.

2200. Manava Dharma Sutras – King's functions are (8) eight. Agriculture, Trade, Road forts, bridges, elephant training, taxes, occupation of deserts.

2201. Understanding is better than understood.

2202. Nuclear agreement is not a surrender. **– Manmohan Singh**

2203. Nano technology, the science of incredibly small could be used in healing some of diseases in humans, with in five years.

2204. In the middle of difficulty lies opportunity. – **Albert Einstein**

2205. Promotion means additional burden of responsibilities and possible transfer from comfort one to a new place.

2206. Three ways in which people respond to greater responsibilities.

Some try best to avoid promotion.

Some would allow them to be thrust on them.

Some aggressively seek out additional responsibilities.

2207. Being a go – gotten does not mean grabbing every opportunity that comes your way.

2208. Know your limitations promise to do only what you can accomplish and deliver what you have promised.

2209. Accept what you can accomplish.

2210. Promise what you can do.

2211. Deliver what have promised.

2212. Do not bite more than you can chew. **– a ground rule**

2213. Learn when to say 'No'.

2214. After Independence the Indian Society had undergone a basic change with the advent of new prosperity. However certain inherent weaknesses remained in the society and some divisive forces started taking advantage of these weaknesses to create disturbances.

– [Mrs. Indira Gandhi Prime Minister]

2215. We must temper our satisfaction with a proper measure of caution.

2216. It is not that we do not know what actions need to be taken. It is not that we do not have the instruments to do the job. We have them.

2217. What is lacking is a firm commitment on the part of Government to act. **– G.K. Reddy**

2218. It is not too late to translate that capacity in to a major effort to accelerate growth and reduce poverty.

2219. And reduced population growth would allow resources to be invested in improving productivity and welfare instead of being stretched out to cover more people. – **G.K. Reddy**

2220. Destiny is not a matter of chance but it is a matter of choice. It is not a thing to be waited for it is a thing to be achieved.

– **Mr. Gandhi**

2221. We cannot claim to be the fount of all wisdom.

2222. People continue to struggle with the problems.

2223. Tee-to-taller is a person who does not smoke drink, even tea.

2224. The very first essential for success is a perpetually constant and regular employment of violence. – **Hitler**

2225. Lotus eater is a parasite person, an idle dreamer

2226. In extreme poverty people earn 1/3 of the per capita Income or even less than one third of average income.

2227. The bulk of the population is engaged in perennial struggle to meet the basic needs.

2228. The genius of our people is for standing still.

– **M. Visveshwarayya**

2229. We must love one another or die. – **Auden**

2230. Man will do rational thingking, but only after exploring all other alternatives.

2231. We shall reach out for the years a head with assurance sustained by conviction that this country has a future in its present. – **N.A. Palkwala**

2232. In economics nothing sprouts over night with out the back roots in time.

2233. Faith – those words which have a resonance wider than their original meaning.

2234. Business has only two functions – marketing and innovation" **– Dr. peter Drucker**

2235. The curve of urban prosperity has no place to go except up,

2236. We have not inhertited this earth from our forefathers. We have borrowed it from our children. **– A W. Clawsen**

2237. The fatal Shots that were fired on October 31, 1984. [Mrs Gandhi's association] still echo round the country and will continue to do so for many a long day.

2238. Non violence is the law of our species as violence is the law of the brute.

2239. Secularism is the very heart of our republic. **– Nehru**

2240. The time has come to show our capacity for change and for learning from experience.

2241. There is always a clash of Socialist ideology with obstinate reality

2242. In a free market a product moves forward at the command of the consumer.

2243. We shall support the cause of rural development to the limits of our wisdom and to the limits of our resources we can muster. **– Dr. Manmohan Singh [Prime Minster]**

2244. There was storm of cheering then a storm of cheering when he ended his speech which lasted a minute.

—After Presidents Speech

2245. A cheat who took Rs. 75 lakhs from banks with out security said "Assuming I am a cheat how can the mangers be absolved of their responsibilities?"

2246. The Government has ear marked a 97 acre site to the

Andhra Pradesh Industrial Infrastructure corporation [API IC] for the proposed trade house corporate, star hotels and 7 entertainment theaters. To be constructed at Manchirevula, in the Business District. [16-3-06]

2247. The self perpetuating plight of the poor has tended to cut them off from the economic progress.

— Robert Mc Namara

2248. Growth alone cannot assist the poor unless it reaches them.

— R. Mc Namara

2249. The condition of poor man's life is so limited by malnutrition, disease illiteracy, low life expectancy and high infant mortality as to be beneath any rational definition of human decency.

— Robert Mc Namara

2250. "Sons and daughters of India – be you workers or Kisans business men or industrialists, teachers or students writers or artists in this country. Through your veins runs the blood of heroes and great men. Let difference give way to confidence Let despair give way to hope we have embarked on an exciting venture. We shall face every difficulty with courage and determination."

–Mrs. Indira Gandhi [Prime Minister]

2251. The administration and formulation of guidelines for credit are subject to frequent government interventions.

2252. You should not take the promise of others seriously.

2253. Public expenditure doubled every 4 or 5 years.

– S. Bhootha Lingam

2254. There is a dichotomy in profession and practice.

2255. Land reforms have been distorted to help big landlords.

– S. Bhootha Lingam

2256. Honesty is a luxury and dishonestly is a means to livelihood.

2257. Before work is done a man is prepared to pay much but when completed he may not part with a single rupee. It is human nature. You can verify it from health or Medicare.

2258. The senior positions in an organisation are very few. The bulk of us have to be content spending our lives plain. Many become discontent and frustrated. Getting to the top should not be or cannot be end all of our existence. There are many other things in life as important as being chief executive. You may be good athlete., or a talented musician or table tenni player, a loving father, a devoted husband.

–C. North Cote Parkinson

2259. One of the biggest dangers for the average executive is the yes man type of subordinate. You must be able to see through yes man and shoe licker as quickly as possible other wise, they are bound to land you in trouble.

– M.K. Rusthamji

2260. Being able to enjoy the miseries of life is one of the choicest blessings.

2261. The capacity to enjoy difficulties is rare.

2262. All people have problems or difficulties, there are no exception.

2263. Some people have problems, not to be told or not to be disclosed. For example if one's wife is unfaithful how can he disclose it to others? He can not share his grief with others. But not the other sex.

2264. Some people give instant solutions to other problems but cannot find ways and means to solve their problems.

2265. We assume that our problems are difficult and others problems are easy.

2266. Every one has his own problem he is alone to solve. Others can only give suggestions.

2267. Life is wonderful unexpected things happen.

2268. Character is like a compound of habits, ideas, social background, income, occupation, blood and s oil.

2269. A teacher is not richer with buildings and cars, but he does not lack shelter and food.

2270. There are two sections of people in he world.

Some people wipe out evil in the man.

Some people forgive evil in man.

A teacher belongs to second category.

2271. In love no one gets defeat or success. In any game or play, if one is loser other is winner and vice versa. But in love, if one is winner, other is also winner and vice versa. Two people will be either winners or losers.

2272. Desires are waters, likings are waves, Relations are crocodiles Ignorance is a deep pit. Hope is a big river courage is a big tree.

2273. A good friend does the following.

He turns you away from sin.

He does what is good to you.

He keeps your secrets habits.

He does not leave you alone when you are in trouble

2274. He helps you when you are in need.

2275. He takes you in dharmic ways.

2276. Decisions taken in haste or in emotion become problems later on.

2277. Love is weak as much as it is strong.

2278. Love letter – You do not know how to begin and you started writing. You do not know how to end the letter, and you have completed the letter.

2279. The end of love need not be marriage.

2280. In every one's life there are always unexposed events or relations.

2281. There are moments in life, and you know the value when they are lost.

2282. Man does not realise how much of his life gets lost or wasted.

2283. Husband like, a glass dome, is security to his wife.

2284. Wife like a string to a kite provides stability and balance to her husband.

2285. Sections 309 of Indian Penal Code makes "attempted suicide" a punishable offence.

2286. The supermen Court on 27-4-1994 struck down section 309 of IPC as unconstitutional and it is voiolative of Article 21 of The constitution which deals with the fundamental right to life and property.

2287. Political stress syndrome is an ailment triggered by the country's tense politics **– Thailand**

2288. All arranged marriages involve an element of coercion.

2289. Australian strippers have won the right to take time off after taking their clothes off.

2290. Violence is a betrayal of the sense of one's own humanity.

— Tabish Khair

2291. You do not need to be religious in order to have a sense of the sacred.

2292. Customs like dowry cannot end.

2293. Giving and taking of dowry is illegal.

2294. If committees and laws could solve the problems, [social], India would have been a paradise on earth.

2295. The idols of Lord Vishnu and Buddha were discovered in Tulchanna village in Tripura [21-3-2006]

2296. It is important to enjoy what you cannot avoid doing.

2297. I am better at 48 than at 20 women become the most interesting at 50s. Age enhances woman's appeal.

— Sharon Stone [actress]

2298. Dinosaurs were wiped out 65 million years ago.

2299. Mental cruelty can cause more serious injury than physical harm to married woman **— Supreme Court**

2300. Non consummation of marriage it self would be constituted mental and physical cruelly to a married woman and would be a ground for divorcee under the Hindu Marriages Act 1955. **— Supreme Court**

2301. "Spouses owe rights and duties to each other and in their relationship they must act responsibly" Supreme Court. 22-3-2006.

2302. When cruelty consists of not violent acts, but of injurious reproaches, complaints accusations or taunts. It may be mental frigidity towards wife. Denial of company and abhorrence or physical abstinence from sexual inter course without reasonable cause. **– Supreme Court**

2303. Arthur Winston, a bus maintenance worker retired on Wednesday 22-3-2006, on his 100th birth day, after more than three quarters of a century working for public transit agencies.

2304. I am not going to sit and mope in the house.

–Winston a Centenarian

2305. Mr. Somanth Chaterjee, speaker of Loksabha, speaker, being chairman of Srineketan Shantiniketan Development Corporation, an office of profit, is to be disqualified. His name appeared along with other members. 23-3-06.

2306. Bhakti transcends racial barriers.

2307. There are Job hunters on company' time, who do not bother about their bosses.

2308. A male Aldabra Giant tortoise, estimated to be about 260 years old died at Ali Pore Zoological Garden [The oldest animal in the country] on Wednesday 22-3-2006.

2309. Ms. Sonia Gandhi said she did not step into political and public life for personal gains. It was only to serve the country Indian society and protect secular values.

2310. Though several hundred meteorites hit earth no human being has ever been known to have been killed.

2311. Kuala Lumpur's twin Pertnes Towers are the tallest buildings in the world.

2312. When you close your eyes you hear breathing sound.

2313. Easter Sunday is the first Sunday after 21-March.

2314. Time has come to leave behind animosities, misgivings of the past. It is wrong to link normalisation of relations with Pakistan with Kashmir problem. — **Manmohan Singh**

2315. A modest sustained reduction in cholesterol can lead to a dramatic reduction in the risk of coronary heart disease.

— **US. Study Report**

2316. Half of Green land and vast areas of Antarctica are destined to melt if global warming continues at the same pace until the end of the century.

2317. Carbondioxide levels in the atmosphere stand at around 380 parts per million but many scientists believe that Carbondioxide levels will rise to 550 parts per million by the middle of this century.

2318. Vegetarians have lower rates of heart attacks diabetes cancer and obesity.

2319. **Bharata Ratna Shehanai Maestro Ustad Bismillah Khan cut a 91 kg cake birth day (21-3-2006) to enter birth day celebrations on Saturday (25th March)**

2320. Social problem is not a mathematical problem. Mathematical problem has a single and unique solution, but social problem has multiple solutions.

2321. The children played in the garden while Mum and Dad had coffee in the restaurant.

2322. John Hubers a 47-year old has devoted his life to building a near faithful replica of Noah's Ark in Holland, with an estimated cost of 500000 Euros sofar, spending 10 hours a day, six days a week a small price to pay for salvation.

2323. Burj Dubai, the iconic tower, when completed by 2008, the centre piece in 500 acra area will be the tallest estimiated cost of $ 20 billion with 80000 residential flats 9 hotels, 200 meters recreational facilities, entertainment venues, and an observatory.

2324. We see horses as being achievable business, now that does not have a regulatory process associated with it. – **Mark Walton, [the Chief Executive of Viagebn, a Closing Company]**

2325. Two companies – Via Gen and Encore genetics, are charging $ 150000, for the first clone and $ 90000 for second clone [Champion horses]

2326. Royal Blue Boon, (horse) a champion and big money earner has been cloned. The birth of Royal Blue Boon Too, last month, (5 week old filly runs with the mare] is the start of commercial horse cloning. **—1- 4 - 2006**

2327. I am like a pied piper who brings out troubles out of your body by mixing little bit of Mantra Shastra astrology, and carnatic to create celestial music

— Ganapathi Sachitanand Samiji of Avadhoota Datta Peettam of Mysore — 31-3-2006

2328. Eighty day exploration in Rwanda's southern Nyung forest, has discovered a new source of Nile adding 100 and odd Kilometers to its length 6611 kms. (6718 kms), the longest river in the world.

2329. Restoration work on great Sphinx of Giza, continues to bring it to its original shape.

2330. The direct street action is the result of the conviction that nothing concrete can or will ever be delivered by the political party or business establishment.

2331. The profit levels are such that when company says it is going to reduce staff to day in order to stay competitive two years down the line that is when I see red. Does that mean only the share holders count. Only profits matter? And what about the huge bonuses company managers give themselves – millions of dollars in stock options. Special bonuses and if thing go wrong astronomical sums in the form of severance pay? What about the poor worker toiling for the minimum wage? Can we at least not give the lowest of the low some job security? Or do we have to accept the no holds barred savage capitalism that we call globalisation.

– Rene Leclere [C.G.T. Union member France – 5-4-06]

2332. It may sound corny but we in the health care medical sciences need to get serious about happiness and the lifestyle that produces it, relative to mind. Body and spirit. Laughter is the best medicine for so many years.

- Dr. Berk

2333. You cannot ignore the voice of the poor. – **Medha Patkar fast [Leader of Narmada Bachao Andolan NBA 5-4-06.]**

2334. The world may end in fire or in ice.

2335. Cockroaches make group decisions.

2336. The enemies should be shot on capture and no prosecution.

– Churchill

2337. Saddam Hussein would receive justice, he had his people.

– George Bush

2338. If you are determined to execute a man (a head of the state) in any case there is no occasion for a trial. The world yields no respect to courts that are merely organised to convict.

– Robert Jakson. [The US Prosecutor at Nuremberg]

2339. Our biological clock says work during day, and sleep during night.

2340. Leena was one of the candidates in the race for the job. She was selected. She had no knowledge of soft ware projec, Hiring her was a major faux pas.

2341. Degrees cannot replace actual on field experience.

2342. One of the Students Indian School of Business ISB, received the highest offer Rs. 1.04 crores ($ 232800). The Students of I.S.B. bagged offers crossing $ 20000. The average international salary was $ 120700 (Rs. 53.5 lakhs). [6-4-2006]

2343. Women rate the financial status of a man as being more important than his looks.

2344. People now look at blood types to analyse compatibility with potential romantic partners.

2345. The blood types could not explain everything as environment and parental guidance play key roles in shaping a personality. **— Dr. Nomi**

2346. You cannot get back your money you lent to others without bending your ways as you cannot take ghee with out bending your fingers.

2347. More than 1200 village women in Iran have set to work weaving a giant carpet worth $ 8.5 million about Rs. 38.25 crores.

2348. At first relationships are sweeter, more exciting than normal relationships.

2349. Do not give all.

2350. Bird watching can teach patience and help people achieve peace of mind.

2351. Guru Nanak, the founder of Sikshism, is believed to have taken a holy dip in the river kali Bein.

2352. The world's highest railway lines from China to Tibet Doctors will travel in the train to help passengers survive attitude sickness. Oxygen masks are attached to every seat.

2353. Women find domestic chores. "mentally therapeutic"

– A British Study

2354. The majority of women prefer house cleaning with vacuum cleaner

2355. The average age woman between 18 and 80 spent more than 9 years, two months in cleaning.

2356. A woman said "Cleaning makes me feel that I am in control of my life".

2357. 20 years ago house work was seen as a sign of female subjugation. [2006 year]

2358. Cleaning gives women more satisfaction than sex.

2359. We should learn to live with jealousies and heart burns.

2360. Prince Hussein 32, the second son of the billionaire spiritual leader of Shia Ismaili Muslims is to many American Kristin J.White.

2361. David Blaine 33 the US magician, Starved himself and frozen in ice, now plans to stay submerged in water for week from May 1, 2006.

David Blaine, US magician fasted for 44 days, suspended above London Themes in a glass box.

The world record man held breath for 8 minutes 58 seconds in the past.

2362. Thirumala city will be developed like Vatican City, spread over 27.5 sq. kms.

2363. Setting up a State Reorgnisation Commission is bound to set off vociferous demands agitations for the creation of these many other states. We will therefore be sparking of pockets of unrest in a large number of places. It will not be possible on the other hand to accede to many of the demands on security or practical considerations.

– L.K. Advani[the then Home Minister in 2002]

2364. Internet users send an estimated 60 billion. E- mails every day around the world.

2365. A Japanese researcher in Tokyo on Wednesday 27-4-2006, created robotic legs that can negotiate staris, may be a substitute for wheel chair.

2366. Sir Clire Sinchalir, has made 3-wheeled small car to run on compressed gas, in narrow streets I meter wide 3 m long, height 1.35 m, weight 400 kgs, Max speed 100 km/h. purchase price 50000 Euros 70000 to 14000. – **27-4-2006**

2367. You can kill a man, you cannot save a man.

2368. Guru said "killing is easy but saving is difficult, disciple replied "saving is easy killing is difficult" Who is right?

2369. We would not allow the perpetrators of the attack to succeed in their aim to disturb peace and tranquility. Peace efforts will continue and these attacks will not deter us.

– Shiv Raj Patil, [Union Home Minister on attacks in Jammu 4-5-2006]

2370. Events in the recent past clearly give a signal and point to the larger designs of the country's enemies. The holy city of Varanasi and then Jama Masjid were attacked with the aim of dividing the brothers. Even the Jammu attacks are part of the same process. We have no doubt that a secular country like ours would give a befitting reply to the people who are behind these acts.

– Shivaraj Patil [Union Home Minister]

2371. Muhammad Noor CheMusa, a 33 year old Malaysian married 104 year old Ms Wook Kundor (71 years gap) he said "God's will" and tied the knot with some one old enough to be his great grand mother]. 4-5-2006.

2372. David Blaine, the illusionist, 33 year old American started his latest stunt living in a water filled tank for a week. [3-5-06]

2373. A mother and daughter were allegedly burnt alive. – Where are rakshasas? [Present day Yama dootas]

2374. Male fertility declines with age.

2375. The Central Government on Thursday 4-5-2006. moved the Supreme Court against Gujarath High Court order directing demolition of places of worship. The apex Court, stayed May 2 High Court order and ongoing demolitions.

2376. Friends and relatives of M.S Cruz Hernandez's celebrated his 128th birth day [EL salvador] on 3-5-2006.

2377. Why do people become fatty? we have taste buds for fats and these taste buds prepare the digestive track to receive fats.

2378. SIP – Systematic Investment plan is an investment vehicle that permits an investor to invest fixed amounts of money every month for a continuous predetermined period.

2379. ELSS – Equality Linked Saving Scheme offers a golden opportunity to save income Tax along with enjoying the benefits of equity investment.

2380. The tax rebate would be 20 or 15 percent under section u/s 88 of the Income Tax Act The eligible amount has been increased from Rs. 10000 to Rs. 1 lakh with effect from

Financial year [FY] 2005-06]

2381. People suffer from a crisis of self confidence or self esteem.

Factors

(a) poor confidence

Fear of failure or losses.

Fear of rejection or neglect

Fear of incompetence or unproductive act. How to deal with crisis of confidence ?

Your inability to say "NO". Have courage to say "NO" Do not say "YES".

Ask questions without hesitations.

Be active listener.

Do not be Judgmental. Do not undervalue other's point of view.

Take constructive feed back.

Ask clarifications for all doubts.

Take inspiration from others achievements.

Balanced views help you a lot.

Take risks, related to work.

Smile and smile.

Take 10 deep breaths morning and evening.

Take moderate Veg-food food ácts on mind.

Help others in need this will boost your self confidence.

2382. Laser treatment [1.5 minutes] of your eyes help you do away with the inconvenience of using glasses or contact lenses. A power 1 to 15 can be corrected.

Laser treatment is commonly used to treat myopia. Around

30 P.C of the people in the world are myopic

LASIK – Laser Aided In. Situ Keratomoleusis using the Excimer laser to reshape the cornea permanently.

Eye surgery is not advised during pregnancy.

If the patient is diabetic the blood glucose level must be brought under control.

Both eyes can be treated on the same day [Laser treatment].

After laser treatment 80 P.C of eye sight is recovered on the second day, stability in vision after 2 to 3 weeks.

After laser treatment take care of the eyes for one month. Let soap not enter the eyes. Do not splash the water into the eyes for (3) months.

Success rate in is 94 – 95 percent for patients under 18 to 35 age group.

LASIK – procedure for both eyes costs between Rs. 20000 to Rs. 25000 [2006 prices]

2383. On examination of patient the doctor said. "As per the test you have 1.5 kg of stone 2.03 of sand 3.05 of glass 2.5 of brick powder 4 of chemical etc." – [on adulteration].

2384. Adulteration – As per the prevention of food Adulteration Act 1954. "If any inferior or cheaper substance has been prepared. Packed, or kept under unhygienic conditions and if it contains any filthy or rotten animal or vegetable matter or is insect infested making it unfit for human consumption.

2385. Adulteration is of two kinds.

Intentional adulterants – sand marble chips, stones, mudtak, chalk, powder, water mineral oils, and harmful colours.

Incidental adultorants pesticide, residues, rodent excreta larva lead from water, industrial effluents, and tin from cans.

Food adulteration is deceiving the consumer and it poses serious health hazards.

Adulteration may lead to serious health problems paralysis cancer and brain damage.

2386. You are the creator of your destiny. — **Vivekananda**

2387. Every man commits some mistakes in life, that mistake is a weak point spot it.

2388. Today's poll 8-5-2006, is a Tamilnadu's ciffhanger of an election and a water shed in state politics.

2389. People flockd in large numbers to see Sachin Ramesh Tendulkar, the demi god of Indian Cricket when he came to Sri kshetra along with his family for worship (Srn subramanya temple) in Dakshina Karnataka, on Sunday 7-5-06

2390. The work of Shakespeare is still resonant and relevant.

2391. Sigmund Freud, one of the greatest intellectuals all time was born on May 6, 1856, and his life long struggle touches every one.

Criticize Freud, but do not trash him. He is too good for that.

The repression of our deepest primal sexual urges can be profoundly costly. — **Sigmund Freud**

Sigmund Freud did not believe in God.

Inspiration is a mystery.

2392. You may find me quasi romantic — **Johnson**

2393. The creative urge is like a spider weaving its web and dying in that very web. — **Sheen Kauf Nizam**

Genuine poetry can communicate before it is understood.

– S.K. Nizam

Poetry is an orphan of silence. **– S.K. Nizam**

The words never quite equal the experience behind them.

– S.K. Nizam

Words come from heart to lips, but from where do the words come to heart?

There is no poet like him, no friend like him, no human being like him.

– (Opinion of the People Touched by S.K. Nizam)

The poet is a rich man rich because he has encountered many other selves and transformed into beautiful whole.

A poet is like a child who wants every other toy.

Life is poetry.

We all see the same sunset, yet your sunset is different. We take out different meanings from it.

A language does not belong to any religion.

– S.K. Nizam

We side with the ruler not with the ruled. We start believing in the culture of victory. **– S.K. Nizam**

Aap hain aap, aap sab kuch hain. Aur hain aur, aur kuch bhi nahin.

(You are you, you are every thing. Others are others others are nothing.)

If you have not tasted them you will not know how sweet are sugar, jaggery and honey. **– S.K. Nizam**

2394. Poetry is an echo. **– S.K. Nizam**

2395. Section 16 of the PFA Prevention of Food. Adulteration Act permit, to impose fine verying from Rs. 500 to Rs. 5000, if the adulteration is detected and prosecution may be launched against the concerned manufacturer distributor, wholesaler or retailer.

2396. Environment includes water, air, and land and inter relationship between them.

2397. World Environment Day is 5th June.

2398. Please note your reaction for the following.

When you see a tree being feiled.

You are disturbed by noise pollution.

You see burning of leaves, papers, dry wood on the Road.

You see over flowing of sewage water.

Water tap is leaking on your way.

2399. The contraceptive pill contains both estrogen and progestogen. The Oral contraceptives raise the risk of blood clots and breast cancer.

2400. For women fertility starts to decrease after the age of 35.

2401. Make love and improve your ability to cope with stress.

2402. Vegetable curry may prevent cancer. The incidence of prostate cancer is very low in India where vegetable foods and curry are popular.

2403. George W. Bush says his best moment as president was the time he caught 7.1/2 pound large mouth bass in his lake. The most awful moment was Sept 11th 2001.

2404. Art can only give you ecstasy.

2405. There is no time to simply enjoy an experience for the sake of it.

2406. To day everything is about quantity. How many books have you read or writen? How many marks you got? How many houses / flats have you? And soon.

2407. Mr. Clean does not clean.

2408. I think there is a lot of hypocrisy and a bit of fear involved in sex. **– Bruno, (a Brazilian Prostitute)**

2409. A call girl is called a program girl in Brazil.

2410. People will do anything to get money including selling their bodies to be able to buy cellular phones. – **Maria Clara**

2411. We have always had prostitution, but it was a hidden forbidden thing. Now it is professional option like anything else and that is the truly shocking thing. – **Maria Clara**

2412. We feel sympathy for the poor woman selling her body to feed her children.

2413. A prostitute is a woman seen as a victim of the country's glaring social and economic inequalities.

2414. Only a man has a right to command his own sex life and that control is seen as a basic attribute of masculinity.

– **Roberto da Matta (a Leading Anthropologist)**

2415. When a young attractive intelligent woman appears and says she is a prostitute you have complete inversion of roles, leaving men. Fragile in a terrain where she is the boss not them. – **Roberto da Matta**

2416. Economics examines issues with clinical detachment.

2417. Nora Lusting the noted economist advocated well targeted social policies to help the poor break out of poverty for good.

2418. If you want to reduce poverty more quickly with growth you need policies that have a very profound impact on equalizing opportunities in many respects.

— **Nora Lusting**

2419. Nora Lusting has developed the concept of socially responsible macro economics.

2420. Economics has to do with the need to empower the poor to gain access to economic development.— **Nora Lusing**

2421. Changes in inequality and poverty would through reforms and not revolution.

2422. People opened their minds and accepted that more than a single route to economic development. – **Nore lusting**

2423. The biggest losers in a crime are always the poor.

2424. There are over 2000. Islands in the world.

2425. "To walk away scot-free" It is a seotish term, any one who did not have to pay taxes, walks away scot-free.

2426. Peter Pan – Peter Pan is a fictional character created by scotish novelist cJames Mathws. Peter Pan refuses to grow up spends his never ending childhood on the small is land of Never land.

2427. The water cannon was invented in 19th century originally used for fire boats.

2428. As the Joke goes – One Bengali is a poet, Two Bengalis are a film society three Bengalis are a political party, four Bengalis are two political parties. – **both leftist**

2429. Trade liberalisation affect the poor producers who cannot compete in the short run.

2430. Protecting the poor from equity enhancing. It also promotes growth.

2431. Social programs should be part of the established institutional frame work.

2432. We have not run out of ideas. – **D. Chakravarthy**

2433. As long as people do not ask for refund of their ticket money we are safe

– D. Chakravarthy (Film Director and Producer)

2434. People make stable and long term relationships later in life.

2435. Marriage is on the wane in Europe.

2436. People in Europe are more inclined to move in together or without getting married.

2437. People are less bothered about cementing their union in marriage.

2438. Couples in Europe breakup more readily than they used to.

2439. Co-habitation before marriage is an accepted norm in Europe.

2440. A higher cohabitation rate led to higher divorce rate.

2441. People are traditionally more inclined, in mediterranean region to continue living with their parents.

2442. In Mediterranean countries, the couple does not move in together until after the wedding.

2443. Meiwes, a 44 year old computer technician who killed and ate another man was convicted of murder and Jailed for life on Tuesday 9-5-2006.

2444. Shanghai is set to open a 'human zoo'. Four Australian men will live in a glass box for two weeks in June, with the public able to watch them, sleeping, eating and bathing. [12-5-2006]

2445. Taj Mahal, attracts almost 3 million domestic and foreign tourists per year some 20000 workers toiled for over 20 years to build Taj Mahal, the spectacular tomb.

2446. Great lives inspire you.

2447. In Mahabharath, the last canto is swargarohana, Read this last chapter. It is interesting.

All five brothers, and Draupadi, and a dog were going to Heaven. On the way Sahadev, was dropped.

"Why was he dropped?" Dharmaraja answered. "He was proud that he was alone beautiful man in this world. so he was dropped"

Nakula was dropped.

"Why was he droped?"

Droupadi was dropped "Why was droupadi dropped?"

Dharmaraja answered. "Droupadi favoured Arjuna more than any one else".

After some time Arjuna was dropped why?"

"Arujuna was proud. He thought that he alone faught Mahabharath war." Answered Dharmaraja. Now this time Bheema was droppoed.

"Why?"

"Bheema faught with Duryodana, and won. Bheema kicked Duryodana while he was dying". We should respect the dying man.

2448. We keep doing these things always. There were some under water lights. The electricians changed lines and there was a short circuit. Miraculously I got out of the pool two seconds before. There was accident unit member lost his life. — **Mahesh Babu**

2449. A great performance is captivating, because each and every moment is specific and or iginal rather than general and predictable.

2450. I work really hard and leave the rest to God.

— **Mahesh Babu**

2451. Brahma Kamala, (flower) blossoms only once a year at night.

2452. Andy Green 45, a British inventor spent [2000] over two years created 3 wheel car 3.1 metres long 0.6 m wide, weight 30 kgs, doing 12875 km for one gallon (4.5 litres of petrol). 13-5-2006.

2453. You will see Japanese eating with a pair of disposable wooden chopsticks from China [13-5-2006]

2454. There are always people who support the evil doer. The sycophancy in Ramayana.

Ravana captured Sita and broutht her to Lanka he held darbar and asked the opinion of the ministers and officials and people whether Sita would be given back to Rama.

"No. No, Sita need not be given back" one minister said. Others also said same thing. Except Vibhishana, all others supported Ravana. People supported Ravana as long as he is in power. You can learn one important lesson. The opinion or support of the majority need not be taken for granted. Following their sugestion led to the destruction of Lanka.

2455. The creator of weapons may not use them. Vishwamitra gave weapons to Rama to fight the evildoers.

2456. Angela Merkel the German Chancellor after six months in office is likely to take over EU presidency in Jan 2007.

2457. Duryodana alone could not opt for war. He was supported by Bhishma Drona, Karna, and others, fought and lost. The war Support one gets need not lead to success or Vijayam.

2458. Working hours during nights, was a nightmare in the lives of employees.

2459. The employees start off with lots of enthusiasm but the initial fervor dies as soon as reality sinks in.

A killer called Boss [Burn out stress syndromes]

People lose their sleep and appetite due to abnormal working hours.

The alienation from the family can lead to nervous disorders like memory loss and lack of focus.

The industry or organisation must keep not only its customers but also its employees happy.

The organisation should provide inhouse gymnasium, fun areas weakened parties etc, to combat work related stress.

Provide healthy food to employees.

Organise frequent breaks, give mandatory vacations and provide medical assistance.

Stress management sessions and personal counselling will help employees.

2460. Guidance about physical and mental co-ordination to synchronize body clock and maximize brain body potential to meet the demands of organization or firm is necessary. — **Dr. Jitendra Nagpol (Consultant VIMHANS Vidyasagar Institute of Mental health and Neuroscience)**

2461. Establish forums to voice their concerns and redress their grievances.

2462. Never sacrifice your educational goals for a job.

2463. Do not hurt others, you get hurt, do not harm others you get harmed. Do not criticize others, you get criticized. Do not dig a pit for others, you will get buried there in.

2464. Take a tour of mystical Inca fortress at Machupichu. The legendary features refuge from Spain's 16th century conquest can be seen w.w.w machu pichu 360 com.

2465. Pigmy owl – 15 cm. Long and weighs less than 85 gm.

2466. Nymark, a tiny island, situated at sralbard archipelago in the Arctic by London artist Alex Hartley in 2004.

2467. Children need to stay in touch with their parents.

2468. Mr Karunanidhi, and his 30 – member minority Government was sworn in on Saturday 13-5-2005, for fifth term as C.M.

Mr. Kardnanidhi, CM, T.N announced that rice would be made available through PDS w.e.f 3 – June, 2006, his birth day costing additional burden of Rs. 550 crores a year to the exchequer.

2469. International mother's day 14th May.

2470. Big bricks measuring 70x47x10 cm, dating back 2000 to

4500 years have been found at brahamsar Teeratha about 40kms from Kurukshetra the holy city in Haryana.

2471. Srimati Sridhar a teenage Indian student, a Junior, at Bethesda Chevy Chase High school [B –CC], in Bethesda, Maryland, U.S, has been named Editor – in – chief of the online. Com.].

2472. Pod cast publishing – The process of distributing audio content with web or RSS feed is known as pod casting.

2473. Be smart in your appearance and work.

2474. Something has gone in ink and print, will never bring it back I long for the great days again when the kings in white were back. "The Book Worm" by Water Dela Mare.

2475. Everything West Indians did was idiosyncratic stylish and gilded with their pleasure in playing.

2476. The parents do not claim greatness for their children.

2477. Seattle is beautifully located along a sea inlet on the United States west coast.

2478. Water sports are a popular summer past time.

2479. Psychology in Ramayana-on return from Lanka Hanuman said" I have seen Sita" to waiting anxious crowds and worried Rama. People were expecting some good news from hanuman. Hanuman did not describe the journeys to and fro. First words uttered by Hanuman were "I have seen Sita" that is important.

2480. Psychology in Bhagavatha—

Ms Rukmini sent love letter through an hold brahmin. Rukmini contemplates thus "whether brahmin has gone, or whether he got tired on the way, whether he properly communicated the message, whether Krishna received him properly, whether Krishn received the letter, he read the letter or whether he properly responded so on so forth. ………"

[The Mind set of Rukmini is Clearly Desceribed. The same Mental Moods will be Experienced by any Girl or Boy in First Love Letter]

2481. Parents from around the world, including India are for $ 19000 (about Rs. 8.55 lakhs) for a ground breaking gender selection treatment offered by some U.S. clinics.

2482. Kanuga trees are raised on 43 nurseries in Adilabad Dist for bio-diesel. **– 16-5-2006**

2483. I cannot reply yes or no to the charge [execution of 148 shia villagers in 1980s] A head of state is protected by the constitution. **– Saddam Hussain**

2484. You can board a running bus, but you can not board running boat.

2485. When a passenger boat or passenger ship sinks, it is loss to the owner and the passengers lives.

2486. You can write poetry in prose, and prose in poetry.

2487. Youth and wealth are enemies to a woman.

2488. Mark Inglis, 47 year old Newze Land mountaineer who lost his legs 24 years ago, reached on the top of the world Mount Everest after 40 tough days of climbing on Tuesday 16-5-2006.

2489. It is easier to get people through the eye of needle into the Kingdom of heaven than it is to get people into a bookstore at 7 O'clock at night **– Suzame Balaban**

2490. Americans will spend on average of 106 hours reading books in a year 2004, and 5.66 percent of adults had not read any book during the year.

2491. Listening is an art

2492. The art of listening is fast disappearing in the corporate world.

2493. It is difficult to give a person time and attention.

2494. To day communication talking, speaking, and writing is of paramount importance.

2495. Attentive listening completes the process of effective communication.

2496. Comprehension starts with listening.

2497. Attentive listening leads to better relations.

2498. In effective communication, ideas are generated.

2499. Effective listening requires mental discipline

People want to be heard.

Listen with open mind.

In attentive listening the non-verbal communication a nod, a smile, even a frown is essential.

Use the time gap for better communication.

Be sympathetic to the speaker.

Recapitulate what was said (students), restate the point, ask for clarification if any.

It is immensely satisfying experience to be heard.

Speakers look for support and a positive reaction from the audience.

Attentive listening helps people connect, and create better understanding.

2500. Talent alone is not sufficient for your dream career

2501. Character and work ethics matter more than talent and skills for promotion or a post of power.

2502. For example – the story of Telugu film "Missmma" was based on this theme. The selection of a person for a post of power, MD character is important

2503. The talent could fetch you fancy perks, and an immediate hike in your pay pocket.

2504. You must have strong work ethics, and strength of character if you want a position of power or authority.

2505. Character has to do with top performance.

2506. Some workers not gifted with talent or bursting with creativity but they are good at work, honest, and responsible.

2507. There is no dearth of educated, qualified and skilled employees in the world today. But workers with good character, are not available in sufficient numbers.

2508. You do not have to look too long and hard to find people with a decent level of competence, required for the job. But it is difficult to find people with good character and work ethics.

2509. Every employee affects your organisation's efficiency.

2510. Talent sans character has no real place in an organisation.

2511. Every employee has a unique set of inputs that will contribute to the company's progress.

2512. Unfortunately the existing their pay rises cannot keep up with the rising entry level offers.

2513. Fighting salary compensation is an ongoing battle with no one—time solution.

2514. Most of the employees indulge in boss basting

2515. Students should take examination tour – write features, manage time, repeat, reset your mock tests.

2516. The essence of knowledge having it to apply it, not having it to confess your ignorance. — **Confucius**

2517. I keep six honest men they taught me all I knew their names are what and why and when how where and who"

— **Rudyard Kipling**

2518. "Body exercise when compulsory, does no harm to the body, but knowledge acquired under compulsion obtains no hold on the mind." — **Plato**

2519. If knowledge can create problems, it is not through ignorance that we can solve them. — **Isaac Asimov**

2520. Cramming will not get you the very best of you.

2521. Do not let your children dictate you.

2522. Do not let your friends dictate you.

2523. What is over is over.

2524. Pay attention to deadlines.

2525. Make your own notes for examination.

2526. Results of a study on employee, management relations.

80 percent of the employees quit their jobs because of boss's attitude.

Boss compatibility tops the list of work place conditions.

95 percent of employees indulge in "boss bashing"

3 out of 11 managers have personality disorders. The personality disorders are not common in criminals.

2527. Sins of a managers.

The managers embarrass employees in public with their criticism.

Public criticism hits the employee morale and lowers self repect

The managers think that if they appreciate employees, it will go to their heads.

If managers do not appreciate the work of their employees, it will go to their hearts.

People love to be appreciated.

Recognition and appreciation are the most cost effective ways for retaining their employees.

The biggest mistakes the employers commit is the failure to recognise and appreciate the work on job of employees.

The managers fail to meet the training needs of the employees.

The managers do not care the needs of employees, they are indifferent un sympathetic, insensitive to the employees needs.

The managers ignore the individual differences. Uniformity will not work.

The managers fail to delegate powers and responsibilities when necessary.

The employees should not be over burdened and multiple responsibilities will not promote efficiency.

2528. In hospitality industry there is ample opportunity to meet all types of people, which can be interesting.

2529. Carnivorous plants capture small insects and digest them to obtain nutrients.

2530. Hebron – Hevron, or Alkalil, is an important place for Arabs and Jews where religion dominates life. No mixing between opposite sexes There are no movie halls, no malls, no discos, no bars or pubs in this city.

2531. Tourists in redlight area of Amsterdam watch ladies in the glass cases near church. "Sin all ye want, and atonement is just round the corner".

2532. The simplicity of R.K. Narayan's writing – Nothing too complicated, very few words that assault the brain so much that you need to assault the dictionary.

2533. The Indian stock market recorded its sharpest ever fall by 1111.70 points in Sensex on Monday 22-5-06.

2534. Even if the professional work is not fully satisfactory in certain regards, it is most important that one is some how normally integrated into curious machinery of economics

– Einstein

2535. The Davinci Code, the controversial film, was made with an estimated cost of $ 125 million.

2536. "It is going to be one of the biggest world wide openings ever. We are really crossing the territory that has not been traveled." – **Jeff Blake, (the Vice Chairman Sony Pictures)**

2537. Titanic film, is the biggest gross earner $ 1.8 billion world wide.

2538. "I always dreamed of working for Bollywood. I spent many sleepless nights. Outside studios asking for work.

— Mr Khan, (the Riksha — Driver Turned Film Maker — "Isq na rnana")

2539. Merit and social Justice are multi-dimensional and the pursuit of one does not require us to abandon the other.

2540. An offbeat cellular phone number 6666666 was auctioned off in Quatar to an anonymous bidder for 10 million qatari riyals (about Rs. 12.33 crores)

2541. A 7 year old Arizona boy swam 2.25 kms from Alcancisco in 47 minutes.

2542. Rising use of caesarean delivery in developing countries is linked to greater risk of death and sickness for mother and baby alike.

2543. The Hollywood block buster. 'The Davince Code,' recorded a staggering opening weekend in some $224 million.

2544. Each individual is a combination of several personality traits.

2545. Five personality traits -emotional stability, openness to something new, extraversion, agreeableness, conscientiousness.

2546. Personality tests are poor predictor of job performance or disqualification.

2547. A legislator stands out side the executive and it is there fore necessary that she does not occupy a position that could make her indebted to the executive and create a conflict of interest.

2548. Office of profit – An office that provides a regular salary and the holder of the office can exercise the executive powers and take decisions on distribution of government funds and confer patronage.

2549. Article 102 (1) of the Indian constitution prohibits an elected representative from holding an office of profit.

2550. There is no clear definition of office of profit in law or practice.

The important principle is that there should be no conflict of interest between legislators duty and demands of the office.

2551. The Prevention of Disqualification Act of 1959 that do not disqualify the holders from membership of parliament any office not on the list will disqualify a member of parliament or legislature or if there is any remuneration over and above the expenses for discharging the duties of the office.

2552. Positions in government bodies and quasi state bodies have become compensation for legislators who can not be accommodated as ministers.

2553. Terrorists will be fought **– Man Mohan Singh**

2554. Bob Dylan, singer song writer, is to celebrate his 65th birthday on Wednesday 24-5-06, He was being celebrated as the voice of generation.

2555. Never trust your kidneys.

– Art Buchwald, [the Humourist U.S, Relived to Laugh]

2556. Ploists are perceived to be a problem ever.

2557. The government has not moved quickly to articulate the new policy, to diffuse the students movements on quota issue at different places in India threatening to shake the political landscape. **– 25-5-06**

2558. Popular movements are unseating governments throughout the world.

2559. Change is often triggered by specific issues,

2560. Understanding the episodes of dramatic change in political power requires a wide lens.

2561. Solving the mystery of HIVS Human Immuno Deficiency Virus, ancestry was dirty work.

2562. It is not easy to transfer power from one group to another.

2563. A moderate growth has brought millions above poverty line.
– Eric Berglof

2564. The effectiveness of distribution mechanism varies greatly across the countries.

2565. Attitudes change slowly.

2566. Pro-poor policies can have a negative impact on growth opportunities.

2567. How did gotras come into vogue?

There are sapta rishis Vishwamitra, Jamadagni, Bhardwaja, Goutham, Atri Vashista, Kashyapa, and other three rishis. Agastya Bhrugu, Angeerasa, totoal ten [10], - and disciples and children carry gotras by these names of rishis.

2568. To shed light on the theory of Karma, the following lines are noted.

Sanchitam – The fruits of Karma in the previous births are to be experienced.

Prarabdam – from previous births, whatever is received is known as prarabdam.

Agami – The fruits of Karmas will be experienced in future births.

Mukti – The chain of karma and the effects of Karma lead to births and deaths. The end of this chain or break in the chain is Mukti.

2569. Punyam **– Doing good to others**

2570. Papam **– Harming others**

2571. Why? Sometimes I believed as many as 6 six impossible things before break fast. **– Queen (in Alice in Wonderland)**

2572. The benefits from reservation that might and do accrue to society as a whole are rarely mentioned. **– V.K. Natraj**

2573. We are some how like an amalgam, a mix of bacteria and human cells. There are some estimates that say 90 percent of the cells on our body are actually bacteria. A human adult carries 100 trillion microbes.

2574. The Mizoram Government has chalked out its plan to utilise its bamboo resources before they flower and perish in the current cycle. **– 3-6-06**

2575. Once the credibility is lost, it is difficult to regain it.

2576. World's response to AIDS disease is inadequate.

– UN Report 2-6-06

2577. Twenty five year after the first AIDS cases were reported, there is no sign of half to the pandemic (AIDS) which is likely to spread every corner of the globe.

– AIDS – Agency U.N.

2578. The scientists on Wednesday have discovered a fossil (31-5-06) dating back millions of years near the Israelite of Ramile.

2579. Success reached by foul means will not last.

2580. Anti Tobacco Day 31st May

2581. Men are equal. It is not birth but virtue that makes the difference. **– Voltaire**

2582. Get the facts or the fact will get you. and you get them right or they will get you wrong. **– Dr. Thomas Fuller**

2583. Experience is not what happens to a man, it is what happens to a man that does with what happens to him.

– Aldous Huxley

2584. Sexual morals can not be guided or directed or managed or controlled.

2585. It is your right to get what you deserve.

2586. The state of Maharashtra banned dances in the bars. The Bombay High Court had struck down the ban. (The ban rendered hundreds of dancers [75000] jobless). The question of determining the right to performance and the question of bar dancers sexual morality now is at the door step of the apex court. [The supreme Court reopens the appeal filed by the state of Maharashtra] 2-6-06

2587. The Bombay High Court had struck down the ban order on two grounds.

Exemption given to star hotels and clubs, etc violative of Article 14 of the constitution of India. [The State shall not discriminate]

The ban violates the fundamental freedom of the bar owners and dancers to practice an occupation or profession and is violative of Article 19 (1) (g) of the constitution.

2588. Frank and Anita Milford have become Britains longest married living couple after celebrating their 78th wedding anniversary. [June 2006]

2589. Hard work is not recognised or appreciated in an organisation.

2590. Ramesh with less than two years experience in the company was selected for the team to go to England. It was his luck or gift or the grab that won this opportunity.

2591. The "slogger" is always aggrieved.

2592. Let others speak for you.

2593. Employees need to sell their work in order to get noticed.

2594. Besides hard work, the employees need.

2595. Effective communication.

2596. Excellent presentation skills

2597. Social grace

2598. Position in the society.

2599. When hard work is not recognised, the morale of the employee takes down trend, productivity falls, costs increase, employee is not happy, he loses interest in work, and loyalty decreases.

2600. Assertiveness is the key to success in the corporate world.

2601. Docility and meakness are signs of cowardice and weakness.

2602. Try not to be unduly submissive.

2603. Clarify rather than suffer in silence.

2604. Avoid confrontation with your immediate boss.

2605. You need not be workholic to be recognised.

2606. Most ethnic groups prefer to speak in home languages.

2607. "You stink" said Archimedes spouse. Your odour permeates the house. Go give yourself a through wash so Archimedes took his tub bath then suddenly with whoops about his body's buoyancy he upped and ran through Syracuse still naked and gave out the news "Eureka folks! I can relate water displacement to body weight."

2608. Most people let out whoops of glee when they get bright idea.

2609. The politicians are required to put on a leaden countenance and deal with serious matters seriously.

2610. Illiteracy can be removed only by a people's movement.

2611. In India we have half the world's illiterates among us.

2612. Not all men and women are anxious to do their bit for the poor.

2613. The leader does not want lime light. Limelight wants the leader.

2614. I will sit down today, but time will come when you will be listening to me attentively. **– Benjamine Disraeli**

2615. We do not know as much as we need.

2616. A satisfied middle class is important for markets and democracy. We need to start thinking about social contract in these societies. **– Carol Graham**

2617. I remain convinced that lessons from success can help paint the way forward for others currently facing difficulties.

– Kohler, Managing Director IMF

2618. Good governance ensures that all members are involved in the process.

2619. People are willing to listen but they would like a dialogue.

2620. Getting the guidelines on paper was a big job, but it is much bigger job to get the benefits off the ground. **– Boughton**

2621. The changes cause some people to lose while retaining the benefits for others.

2622. There has always been tension between the need for change and need to provide social safety nets.

2623. When the people and the government work, they can make a difference.

2624. If you help some one it comes back in a better way.

2625. Pythagorus gave mystic meaning for numbers. 2 for a line 3 for surface, 4 for density, 6 for soul 7 for health and light 8 for love.

2626. Shankaracharya organised matts to unite Inida, Sringeri in Karnataka, Dwaraka in Gujarath, Purin in Orissa, Badrinath in Himalayas.

2627. Marcus Junius Brutus, the son of Cervelia Caesor's keep, loved Caesor who loved him. He plunged knife in Caesor's chest. [Son attacking father]

2628. The peaks of success are not far away for those who are willing to live in the dark valleys and yet hold their heads high to see with the inner eye. The universal unity amidst external diversity.

2629. A good Student

A - Always liked by the teacher

G - Greets every one with

O - Obedient to teachers and elders

O - On time for school and college

D - Dress neatly

S - Studies with interest

T - Treats every one with respect.

U - Understands every lecture taught

D - Does daily home work

E - Eager to learn

N - Never misses a class or lecture

T - Talks less

2630. Once a student was asked how many hours he studies. He worked out and gave the following.

2631.

Particulars		**Days**
All Sunday in a year no work	-	52
Summer holidays	-	60
Sleeping hours 8 hrs per day	-	122
Bathing, eating' and dressing	-	30
Talking 1 hr per day	-	15
Examinations	-	27

Public holidays	-	11
Playing 4 hr per day	-	45
My birthday	-	1
Teacher's day	-	1
College day	-	1
Total	=	**365**

Where is the time for study ?

2632. If the students are losers in any competition they will react differently they feel.

The result was fixed

The favourite student got it.

They burst into tears.

They may threaten the winner

They threaten to kill themselves.

2633. Explosive child is easy to identify.

They will not cope up with ups and downs of every day life, or deal with the failures in life.

They expect instant gratification. Other symptoms.

Home work note books are torn

Remote controller is thrown or broken.

Cups, saucers, glasses are broken.

Window pans or car pans are broken

Clothes are torn, TV sets or computer systems are damaged.

2634. Education has been changing over period of time as noted below.

Teacher centered

Curriculum centered

Value centered.

Examination centered.

Child centered

2635. Success is a mile stone and not a destination.

2636. Teacher need not be a task master, he should be a friend, guide and philosopher.

2637. The students in formal education are compelled to put up with a kind of monotonous long spells of dictatorship.

2638. 3 As (i.e. Apathy, Agony and Aversion) are not good in life.

2639. A good student has to put in 4 -6 hrs of regular and effective study in a day. He should have inquisitive. Finest mind scientific temper and large patience.

2640. A working woman has a dual role. House wife and employee.

2641. One philosopher developed nice theory – House wife is not a part time job, but it is a whole time job.

2642. A Greek soldier is a symbol and a combination of beauty, valour and strength. Every teenage girl wants all these qualities in her dream boy.

2643. ABCD of success

A – Ability to learn and ability to recall – ATR will determine success in the examination

B – Be regular, punctual and attentive.

C – Commitment to study. (total)

Conviction concentration and character (4 Cs of success)

D – Determination

Devotion,

Dedication

Discipline

(4 Ds of Success)

2644. The secrete law of nature-the parents are programmed to love and protect their children and not vice versa.

Hen protects her children.

The birds feed and protect their children.

Human beings love and give protection to their children.

2645. You study 300 days and write examination for 3 hours.

2646. When something goes wrong, everybody says that somebody has done it. Who is this some body? Somebody, any body, are hidden in every body, but nobody knows somebody.

2647. It is difficult to assess all emerging problems. We should design some ways to address them.

2648. If you know what you want it is one step to success.

2649. Dust is democratic. It settles down on every one young and old, rich and poor

2650. In very young and very old age people do some crazy things.

2651. His silence was out of respect for Mahatma. – **Sarojini**

2652. All predictions are notoriously unreliable.

2653. God when creating Homo spines under baked his first attempt and burnt the second.

2654. I can give the progress of India in 800yrs time — Most of us would not be around to prove me wrong.

2655. There will be many surprising and unforeseen events in 2103.

2656. Following the foot steps of famous father or mother is tough.

2657. I am laughing with the people and not at the people.

– **Deepa Mehatha**

2658. I want to study as long as I can but if it is between choosing among the two, dance will always come first.

– Yamini Reddy

2659. I often fed the urge to return home to India –Laxmi gill

2660. A bad team with a good leader may be sometimes productive but a good team with a bad leader is always a disaster.

2661. A leader is usually a Jack of all trades but master of none.

2662. Traits of a good leader.

Willingness to assume responsibilities.

Feel accountable for his own performance and also for the performance of the team.

Creates environment that encourages excellence in performance.

Has the capacity to identify the strengths and weaknesses of each and every member of the team.

Try to enhance the strengths and mend the weaknesses of individuals.

He is a good planner, coordinator, and motivator.

He may test the commitment of any member by putting him on Task force.

Has the iron will to keep going.

Grabs hold of the problem like a dog with a bone and would not let go.

2663. Technology has become important for survival.

2664. It is a great time to be in business.

2665. When you are at the top there is no room for mistakes.

2666. The demographics are changing everyday, and we should address cultures of people.

2667. The weak may crumble.

2668. About 3 billion people reside in 9 countries – China, India, Brazil, Morocco, Russia, Indonesia, Turkey, South Africa and Thailand – representing 70 percent of developing world's population – **Group's GDP $ 12.5 trillion [2005]**

2669. The company focuses on providing the right product at the right time, at the right quality and at the right price.

2670. The companies are looking at the low end segment of the economy because it is fast growing.

2671. Emotional Intelligence makes people effective and have positive relationship. It creates positive organisation climate where people want to do the best.

2672. Success for any one is 99/100 anticipation and 1% inspiration.

2673. The achievement is not measured by what you think, but by what you have done.

2674. The minorities enjoy rights under constitution of India but the majority have right s too **– Jaya Lalitha**

2675. You are better off not smoking. **– Martin Broughton**

2676. I may be unpredictably predictable, but I am not harm ful.

– M. Koirala

2677. The writer sat in the court room for hours waiting for his turn, correcting notes.

2678. A woman has to break the barriers of convention and emerge from the shadows of subjugation.

–Supriya, a Feminist

2679. Obstacles are those frightful things you see when you take your eyes off your goal.

2680. There is a kind of smugness that caught up in India, the belief that we have eliminated hunger.

– Amartyasen [Nobel Laureate]

2681. Our ego has grown taller than our physical height. We need to have our feet on the ground and face reality.

– Sharad Power

2682. Bill Gate needs India more than India needs Bill Gates.

2683. My only window through which I have seen the world is cinema. **– Kamal Hassan**

2684. The reality is hard to digest. **– Kamal Hassan**

2685. We need separate adult films that are meant for adults.

– Vijaya Anand

2686. My academic progress report was not good enough to show to my mother. **– Kamal Hassan**

2688. Land grabbing is not just restricted to one city, it is happening in every major city in India. **– Suresh Ambanti**

2689. I wanted to tell people about my bitter experiences in purchasing land in Indian city. – Hyderabad.

– Suresh Ambani

2690. The people of Hyderabad are genuine helpful, and sincere, it is safe city.

2691. There is nothing to be at natural light for its warmth and life giving properties.

2692. The 20th century has brought in auto mobiles, air crafts, information technology and put man on the moon, yet the giant for mankind has not added to the desired level of human happiness.

– Bairan Singh Shekawat Vice – Presiedent

2693. Power is both spiritual and subtle. All revolutions are spiritual at the source. **– Vinoba Bhave**

2694. In separateness lies the world's great misery, in compassion lies world's true strength. **– Buddha**

2695. Democracy does not guarantee equality of conditions, it only guarantees equality of opportunity. – **Irving Kristol**

2696. No body takes a sledge hammer to break eggs.

2697. The wise employer will not take over qualified persons in the organiation.

2698. Every year 3 lakh engineering graduates come out of colleges across the country chasing 13500 jobs (2003). Most of the them remain at home. The same goes with doctors, manager, professionals. They may not be able to service loans taken during their studies

2699. No matter what happens in the industry or economy you can not stop loins from roaring.

2700. A person who performs quick somersault will grab public attention.

2701. The man's expectations invariably oscillate between a cynical pessimism and a hopelessly unjustified optimism

– **Mukund Padmanabhan**

2702. Men do not want to admit that they cannot remember everything. – **Mary Roach**

2703. No matter how unproductive my work has been. I have a sense of accomplishment. – **Jeffy**

2704. The story however old is not unusual. I could tell you countless others. – **Patrick Neat**

2705. If your sexual roles were reverse the man would find himself charged with harassment at best. – **Patrick**

2706. Many women see feminism as an excuse to believe the way men have done for centuries.

2707. The projection of various forms of female sexuality is every where we look.

2708. A kitchen is the heart of home. –**Taria Dalal**

2709. Freedom is when the people can speak and democracy is when government listens. **– Alastair Farrugia**

2710. The Queen (England) says much less and nods a lot.

2711. Pray that god may give me wisdom and strength to carry out the solemn promises I shall be making and that I may faithfully serve Him and you all the days of my life.

– Queen Elizabeth – II

2712. The people spread far and wide through out every continent and ocean in the world were united to support me in the task to which I have been dedicated with such solemnity.

– Queen Elizabeth – II

2713. I do become liege man of life and limb and of earthling worship and faith and truth I will bear unto you to live and die against all manner of folks.

– Duke of Edinburgh to the Queen

2714. Millions outside west Minister Abbey will hear the promises and prayers being offered up with in its walls.

– Queen Elizabeth – II

2715. Women in Australia do not shake hands with women.

2716. Queen Elizabeth II has been Briton's monarch for 50yrs, a remarkable feat achieved by any ruler in the history.

2717. The inventor of Vacuum cleaner was James Dyson who said "People are always copying our ideas".

2718. Let's see what we did wrong yesterday.

– Duke of Edinburgh

2719. You should be aware of the pressures of cut throat competition in cut world of business.

2720. Queen's only job was unveiling plaques, launching new projects. Planting trees and meeting her subjects.

2721. We should be able to know how the media is influencing popular, opinion or it is reflecting popular opinion.

2722. There is now much less time for inherited royal privileges.

2723. There is nothing peculiar about the just opposition of tradition and protocol in the modern 21st century world.

2724. Each event looks effortless and relaxed yet every minute of the day is the product of endless planning.

2725. Women are better at looking after children than stay at home fathers, because they put in tie and attention required to become good at the job.

2726. A history teacher, who turned 40 on April 25, 2005, is not going to set the world on fire.

2727. The easiest job in the world is the surgery on dead people.

2728. She launched into a long list of everything that bothered her about me she dumped me over the phone.

–Lord Wilson

2729. In "Sting operations" hidden cameras are used to expose corruption cases. It is not the invasion on privacy or right to privacy.

2730. Every time I saw her my blood boiled, my heart pounded and I would get tense that I literally felt sick **–Vinod**

2731. My career just started to get off the ground. **– Swamy**

2732. There is no man in the world who has not felt the sting of betrayal or unfair treatment in his life time.

2733. Learning to forgive those who hurt us can have profound benefits.

2734. Forgiving is a new way of managing anger, cut stress and improve health.

2735. Giving up grudges can reduce chronic back pain.

2736. Peace is not a relationship of nations, it is a conditions of mind. Lasting peace can of mind. Lasting peace can come only to peaceful people. **– Jawaharlal Nehru**

2737. An employee is burdened with marital problems and work conflicts.

2738. When the rich and poor compete for th public or private services the rich will get priority.

2739. You cannot sell something when you do not own it.

2740. Anger and resentment are like accidents that do not end, turning hormones into taxins.

2741. Forgiveness is a powerful antidote of anger.

2742. Hanging on to resentment for months or years means making commitment to remain angry.

2743. A woman's fertility is at the high between the ages of 20 and 30yrs

2744. Women are born with finite number of eggs.

2745. Economics is a very difficult subject. I have compared it to trying to learn how to repair a car when the engine is running. **– Bens. Benanke [member Federal Reserve Board of governors]**

2746. Dance is an eternal provider of entertainment.

2747. I spent most of that time sitting in bars getting very drunk, talking about writers and writing and never writing. In two years I have done more than I did in 20 years. **– Jeat Thayil**

2748. People express a desire for more elegant cars, more exotic food, more erotic clothing, more elaborate entertainment.

– John Kenneth Galbraith

2749. I see reservations as a step backwards from the position of meritocracy the reason for Indian education system being held in high esteem all over the world.

2750. If the new reservation policy comes into action, the nation would need to face yet another brain drain.

–Sudhir Jalan

2751. The Union HRD Ministrys proposal of 27 percent reservation of seats for OBC students in Centrally funded universities reignited debate on reservations. People are divided into two groups one favoruing and another opposing.

2752. I am deeply concerned at the proposed retrograde move of implementing extra reservations of 27 percent of seats for OBC students in IITS an IIMS. **– Sudhir jalan**

2753. Reservations are likely to replace excellence by mediocrity.

2754. One need not over rate the mistakes crept into the work when over all performance is fine.

2755. A unique 'Chatra' umbrella belonging to 2nd century Krishna District Andhrapradesh. A cobbler Mula and his wife Bopiya the follower of Buddhism donated the Chatra, a part of stupa.

2756. Working with an enemy at work is not easy.

You can learn about your mistakes, and hot buttons.

Inviting them out for coffee, is an olive branch.

Be careful about engaging some one lower in rank, even if you win or you will lose stature.

Some enemies hang on in their grudge.

Distance will reduce the hasle factor for you both.

2758. You should be comfortable with numbers.

2759. Keep reading books and papers of your interest and choice.

2760. In business success will not come to you, you go to success.

2761. In business or profession [self-occupation], risk charges our attitude and keeps us at our toes.

2762. Hopping does not make nodding off at night It is more difficult and sharpens the mind,

2763. Extra water you drink more than 8 glasses can do more harm than good, it lowers sodium level in the body.

2764. Eating salty snacks during the race may help.

2765. Do not worry about what is happening outside your door.

2766. Spend your birth day with your friends in hotels or bars, no responsibilities, no worry.

2767. Return from picnics fresh and newly inspired.

2768. During the holidays you can try horse-riding, rock climbing, or rowing in a boat or cooking all new dishes.

2769. Leaving a job is almost never easy. Voluntarily or other wise.

2770. When you are leaving job, there are still some loose ends waiting to be tied up.

2771. The dismissal from the job should be just and fair like misconduct, lack of capability, change in company direction or redundancy.

2772. You can not challenge the dismissal unless it is for illegal reasons like discrimination of some kind.

2773. Termination benefits include back pay, any arrears and compensation.

2774. Gross misconduct may lead to summary dismissal.

2775. Severance package on dismissal from service the employee is entitled to one or two weeks pay for every year of service.

2776. Termination package may include, bonuses, commissions expenses, unused vacation pay, accrued sick and personal leave salary etc.

2777. You educate a woman, you educate a family you educate

a teacher you educate a generation. Unemployment insurance some companies pay 4 –6 months pay after dismissal from service.

2778. Out side world is a projection of inside world.

2779. Prostitution is legal in Australia in a limited manner.

2780. Bali is a Hindu resort island.

2781. For better relationships you can be active listener, show interest in your work and friend, guard against harmful activities, tell facts, laugh and make others laugh, take home your friends feelings, invite him or her for parties.

2782. Piles patient is advised to take only butter milk as many times as possible or desirable, no solid food is to be taken for one or two days, Lemon juice may be taken for one or two days. **– Dr. Gayathri**

2783. Lemon juice with salt may be taken for preventing loose motions **–Dr. Gayathri a doctor**

2784. Growth is life and life is growth.

2785. I am delighted it happened I am elated really I am.

– Zadie Smith

2786. British author Zadie Smith has won orange prize 30,0000 pounds for her 3rd novel "On Beauty"

2787. Swans are in fact cheating philanders who regularly flee the nest for extra marital sex.

2788. Most organisms have two kinds of sex chromosomes namely X and Y. Which determine the sex of the organism? The XX / XY sex determination system is the well known for all mammals including humans.

2789. The female has two of the same kind of sex chromosomes [XX while male has two of the different kind of sex chromosorles [XY]

2790. To day competition is severe, intense in every field.

2791. Seek, know, prepare – **Dr. Gopal [Director placement]**

2792. Dubai has been able to achieve compounded Annual Growth Rate [CAGR], of 12 percent and per capita income of $ 22 400, higher than some of the developed countries. [June 2006]

2793. You do not have luxury of time to settle down in life.

2794. Time is of essence.

2795. Understand the key success factors.

2796. Courage will give you strong launch.

2797. Lure of interest ruins a man

2798. Lure of sex destroyed Lanka

2799. Like wine I get better with age.

– Shilpa Shetty, [on her 30th birth day]

2800. Illicit relationships are sweeter, more exciting than normal relationships.

2801. Your attitudes, skills and knowledge determine your chances for the job you applied.

2802. Operate from your strength and not from weakness, what ever field you choose will become interesting and of high potential.

2803. You do not need to force fit now or conform, in 21st century.

2804. Research takes time and effort.

2805. Often non-exciting and routine activities contribute to success.

2806. Understanding any field is not easy.

2807. It is not that we have idle money by selling petrol.

— A Spokes.Person from Dubai Investment Group

2808. Excellence in education enables us to grow better and become consistently successful.

2809. The educational markets are affected by the entry of new colleges or exit of weak institutions.

2810. Creative destruction re allocation of resources among existing firms – entry of new firms and exit of obsolete firms – It plays an important role in transition economies.

2811. In developing countries 20 percent of firms enter the existing markets or exist from the markets every year.

2812. Times endless process

– future ⟶ present⟶ past, [no Reversal in this one Direction Process]

2813. French adventure Raphaela le Gouvella, 46 on Thursday became the world' first person to wind surf across the Indian ocean. She reached the island of Reunion after 60 day odyssey. 10-6-06

2814. President George Bush, turned 60 on July 6, said six decades is not that old".

2815. J.K. Rowling –the author of the record selling Harry potter, series, was named the greatest living British author on Thursday 8-9-06.

2816. Anger is an emotional disorder Anger is not losing your temper. It is intermittent explosive disorder, **[IED]**

2817. Anger **— Tim Dowling**

We all get angry some times.

Some of us have anger as disease

Anger is a condition characterised by "a failure to resist aggressive impulses."

Anger is another way of devolving responsibility for one's bad behaviour.

Sometimes anger is recognised as "Intermittent Emotional Disorder" **— IED**

IED – It involves several discrete episodes of failure to resist aggressive impulses that result in the serious acts of assault or destruction of property and the degree of aggressiveness expressed during the episodes is grossly out of proportion to any precipitating psychological stress.

IED encompasses such common societal ills – road rage, air rage, trolley rage, and phone rage incidients triggered by the pressures of modern life.

IED sufferers commit on an average of 43 outbursts over a life resulting in property damage worth $ 1359.

2818. Explosive personality disorder EPD — **[symptom]**

2819. Attention Deficient Disorder. [ADD]

2820. NO man (how ever Mahtma or Rishi), in a lifetime has gone berserk for no good reason less than (3) three times.

2821. A man suffers from IED from 14 to 40 to end of life.

2822. Life can be more painlessly cruel than fiction.

– Dang Thuy Tram a Doctor

2823. Man writes to release his feelings.

2824. War neer cares about any one.

2825. Forget all the thoughts of love buring in your heart and pay attention to your job. **– Dang Thuy Tram**

2826. We in India pay Rs. 100 extra to get to see first day first show movie, but bargain with vegetable man over the price of cabbage. **– Sathya Saran**

2827. Find your self in traffic Jam where´there are cars trucks, buses, bullock carts, two wheelers, cycles and rickshaws.

2829. In India we are told that there is a ban on cow slaughter; but bullocks horses, camels, bears, monkeys dogs etc, are abused with out a thought.

2830. We take on television how we as women have come into our own and then surrender to a sex determination process/ procedure.

2831. We find a brainy guy to find the biggest loophole in every law made to ensure discipline. **– Sathya Saran**

2832. We in India speak / write English better than the rest of the English speaking world. **– Sahya Saran**

2833. We have great tolerance even for intolerance.

2834. We are happy with almost nothing.

2835. Comets and eclipses are always thought harbingers or calamity.

2836. When beggars die, no comets are seen, the heavens themselves blaze forth the death of kings [now leaders]

2837. The transit of Venus across the solar disc on June 8 is an excitement. It will have another on June 6, 2012. [eight years gap]

2838. To be sure rational thinking and careful measurement belong to the scientist's work just as the hammer and chisel belong to the work of the sculptor. But in both cases they are merely the tools and not the content of the work.

2839. The notion of many infinities was given by George Cantor.

2840. An infinite set is one which is not finite.

2841. He was first of all spontaneous person. Following that scientific genius, next to an artist close to the creative spark and only in the last instance, out of a feeling of duty a homo politics. **– [On Werner Hossen Berg.]**

2842. We are to some extent bound by tradition in the selection of our problems.

2843. We apparently have little freedom in the selection of our problems. We are bound up with the historical process and our choice seems to be restricted to the decision whether or not we want to participate in a development that takes place in our time with or without our contribution.

2844. Problems are given that we need not invent them.

– Werner Heisen Berg

2845. The greatest effort in the development of any subject is necessary at those points where one has to abandon old concepts.

2846. Every progress in science has been paid for by a sacrifice.

2847. The increases in knowledge and insight diminishes continually [the scientist's claim on understanding nature.]

– Werner Helsen Berg

2848. Prasad Bidappa, the fashion guru was arrested in Dubai for carrying marijauna.

2849. Earth –

2850. Inner core – radius 12900 km,

2851. Outer core thickness – 2200 kms.

2852. Crust – 5 to 40 kms. Inner core temperature estimated 2500 °C, the pressure 4 million atmospheres density. 13.5 gm cc.

2853. The energy released during the 2001 Bhuj Gujarath, India, earth quake is about 400 times or more that relased by the 1945 Atom Bomb dropped on Hiroshima.

2854. Rekha is India's Greta Garbo, her mantra has always been a zest for life.

2855. Choosing my life partner does not mean, I am betraying my parents, **- Kumud 26 year old**

2856. There is a god up there watching over us and balancing our lives in one way or the other. **– Nalini Gandhi 28**

2857. If a man is not loyal, a man is not worth it.

2858. Other woman / man factor can throw over – health wise too. Insecurity and anxiety triggers off a whole lot of stress, that your body is un prepared to handle. Your blood pressure rises. Your heart rate accelerates stress causes chaos with the entire nervous system cause intense headaches backaches, a feeling of general nausea and discomfort, you feel threatened.

2859. The Manas National Park in Assam has 40 newly hatched pythons. [2006]

2860. Sex is to be treated like a hand shake in 21st century there is no sin from skin to skin.

2861. Some people think football is life and death. I do not like that attitude. I can like that attitude. I can assure them it is much more serious than that. **– Bill Shankly**

2862. We are always more anxious to be distinguished for a talent which we do not possess than to be praised for the talent which we do possess. **– Mark Twain**

2863. Of course there is no formula for success except perhaps an unconditional acceptance of life and what it brings. **– Arthur Rubinstein**

2864. The trouble with our times is that the future is not what it used to be. **– Paul Valery**

2865. Do not teach yourself into heavy quilts during winter months.

2866. To day kick-ass professional, confident ambitious, caring and progressive women are emerging from a new India.

2867. I want to have fun in life no waiting for things to happen for me and the whole point living is about you getting what you want. **– Sathyasaran**

2868. Money fame and success make you happy.

2869. I can live happily without ever getting married.

–My Mother Did the Same, Sathya

2870. Women in mini and major metros are beginning to have converging attitudes and beliefs.

2871. I see youngsters getting everything they want to day.

– Nisha Jamwal

2872. Some celebrities, the regular drug – pedders come and deliver cocaine even at 3 am the morning. – **Bobby Darling**

2873. Flamenco music is marked by influences from jazz, and Afro Arabic rythms.

2874. Unfortunately, it has long been fashionable in some intellectual circles to discuss concepts to which no very clear definition can be given. – **Anthony Daniels**

2875. The patterns of love have also been altered by a host of new or intensified variables – feminism gay and lesbian rights, longevity late marriages, and single mothers, plastic surgery fashion, falling birth rates advertising immigration and unemployment.

2876. There is always non-stop marketing of sex, and love.

2877. Love has been radically transformed.

2878. Love inside or outside marriage is now exposed to new challenges.

2879. Now people expect the images of physical contact and beauty.

2880. Now here does love exist in a vacuum? It confronts problems, freedom and expectations.

2881. Money cannot buy your love but love is rarely helped by economic hardship.

2882. You have to do away with "yes people" because they are sweet to your face. – **Manishakoirala**

2883. However cautious I am I will never be able to escape the bad time. – **Manishakoirala**

2884. There are good people and bad people, good times and bad times. – **Manishakoirala**

2885. The conviction of Kenneth Lay and Jeffrey skilling from bosses of defunct Enon in 2001 became one of the corporate America's biggest scandles, wiping out $ 31.8 billion debt.

2886. For most young male virgins sex is a desperate need.

2887. Every new experience (sex) is a notch in the belt. In most cases the first time may be the last time.

2888. First time sex – 180 high speed, it must be done other wise you lose face. **– Jerry Pinto**

2889. First time sex myths.

That it is unforgettable

That it is an explosion of your senses.

That it is a of passage. [The last one is true]

The first time you actually had sex with some one you want to forget.

In the old days nobody worried much about the first time.

2890. The young people finally get to make the beast with two backs, they find it a let down.

2891. Men generally had their first sexual experience with

2892. Older women in the family.

2893. Commerical sex workers.

2894. Imagin ary fingeres. **– Jerry Pinto**

2895. A young man told that the first time he had sex with was Swedish girl who was amazed by the size of his doodad.

– Jerry Pinto

2896. The first time sex was a let down. The people were embarrassed abut it after wards, because they had been lousy lovers.

2897. Sex is one part of the whole relationship.

2898. Come rain or shine, a growing number of people in London are jumping on their bike to enjoy the dual benefits of saving money on transport and keeping fit. [13-06-06]

2899. Build intimacy before having sex with somebody.

2900. A girl over 14 years of age physically readies for sex.

– Ruchira Bose

2901. Whatever others say, it is your body, your decision to have sex or not to have sex.

2902. Waiting to become sexually involved with a lover is a sign of your virtue. **– Ruchira Bose**

2903. Sexuality is a natural and healthy part of being human and expressing that part of your self is perfectly Okay

– Ruchira Bose

2904. Your sexuality belongs to you, you have the right and responsibility to choose when and how to express it or whether to express it or not. **– Ruchira Bose**

2905. If you are unsure, your mind, body and heart will give your signals to slow down. **– Ruchira Bose**

2906. Each day 16000 people are newly infected with HIV. India has almost 5 five million cases of HIV the highest in the world.

2907. The risks of having sex first time.

Heart break, regret, pregnancy, STDS and HIV (AIDS) can all happen.

You cannot get pregnant through oral or anal sex but you can get STDS. **— Ruchira Bose**

2908. Some sexual risks are emotional.

2909. Sex is not bad, dirty or wrong.

2910. No sex on the first date.

2911. Talk before you make love.

2912. Dual morality – A sexually active unmarried woman is a slut, but a sexually active unmarried man is not.

2913. Making love with some one is for many women an expression of commitment and getting married to the man you have sexual relationship is important. —**Ruchira Bose**

2914. Be self aware and honest with your self.

2915. Having sex does not guarantee that your relationship will last.

2916. For the best results write often

2917. Writing is an investment it helps you live a more intense life.

2918. Do not make a long face if you fail in your first attempt laugh it away.

2919. An incredible 75 percent of Indian women said they had never musterbated but 100 percent of men do.

—**Sheila Kumar**

2920. All women do not bleed when their hymen is torn.

—**Dr. Pratima**

2921. Men are fascinated by loobs, but breasts seem to have mesmerised men through the ages acreos all cultures, and they have been turn on for men. It is very important to have the right size, shape and pointed ness. – **Dr. Parul R Sheth**

2922. An ideal woman –

2923. A woman haring catherine Zeta Jone's face Jennifer Aniston's hair Liz Hurley's bust, Elle Macpherson's legs and Jennifer Lopez's bottom.

– **American Survey quoted by BBC**

2924. Fitness programme – **Nawaz Modi Singhania**

2925. Swimming, cycling, walking, jumping, rope walking, skating, and are all considered aerobic exercises.

2926. Stretching, strengthening exercises under expert supervision.

2927. Eat less or moderate caloric food.

2928. Dance – **Get on the Floor.**

Eat to live. Consume moderate food items.

Oil, chocolates and sweets cream, whole milk, cheese must be avoided partly or wholly.

Determine goals, for exercise, food, and duration etc.

Drink water, do not over eat. Keep sufficient gap between meals.

2929. Be careful get treatment for injuries happened during exercises.

2930. Large varieties of exercises.

Karate, and Kick boxing are good ways of keeping fit.

Learn a new skill in dancing.

2931. Yoga will hit the shape. Attend stress management workshops.

2932. Transcendental meditation [TM] has now been found to help with a cluster of symptoms which can lead to heart attacks.

2933. TM may modulate response to the physiological impact of exercise conditioning.

2934. Perils of intercaste marriage – In a mandal a girl stripped naked, made to dip in three tanks and three well and her tongue sorced with a heated iron rod. [Satanic act] 14-6-06]

2935. All communication between you and your juniors or your seniors is of most important in a workplace, it sets direction to all relationships.

2936. All of us write something or the other nearly every day.

2937. A good oil massage can strengthen your skin and your hair's roots.

2938. A regular oil massage nourishes the hair roots, making it silky and shiny.

2939. A girl in typical Indian village knows nothing but to cut grass, fetch water and fire wood, help her mother cook and clean, be baby sitter.

2940. Lack of milk to the children will lead to poor dental health, scanty hair, knocked knees and bow legs and other spinal problems. — **Lisa Sarah John**

2941. The average calcium requirement is 500 mq per day for women of all ages.

2942. A glass of milk at break fast another in the evening (or Lassi) and curd for lunch and dinner constitutes an ideal diet.

2943. Cereals like rice, ragiajra, wheat Jowar, and corn are the main source of energy for most of us. They contain 70-80 per cent carbs, 10 percent protein.

2944. Include whole wheat products in at least one meal daily.

2945. Low iron in take will lead to anemia.

2946. It is ideal to eat two three rotis or slicers of whole wheat bread at dinner daily.

2947. Pulses are an excellent source of protein, a good source of vitamin B and iron. So pulses should be eaten both at lunch and dinner.

2948. Eat a fruit at 11 am and 6 pm. add salad to both lunch and dinner menu.

2949. Fruits make a great snack, they contain no fats.

2950. The glucose and fructose sugars in fruits are digested easily in about 20 minutes.

2951. An apple has 50-60 calories per 100 g and a banana has 100-120 calories for 100g.

2952. Tomato is the most nutritious contains vitamin A, B and C high fibre and a few calories.

2953. Rishikesh is situated a 292 m, above sea level.

2954. Men are supermen outside, chicken inside.

2955. Men hate commitment.

2956. Men think that they are smart but they are dumb.

2957. Men love bitch women. — **Arshad Warsi**

2958. Women will always rule the mirror space.

2959. You can never completely understand a woman not even after marriage.

2960. Porn is a force of life. Even married men are porn freaks.

2961. Girls grow up to be women and boys grow up to be boys.

2962. For rainy days men can have bubble wrap and cellophane.

2963. The adolescent, disturbed often become aggressive diverting anger on the available parent.

2964. Oil massage will slow down reduce blood pressure and calm the nerves, soothe the body, mind and soul.

2965. There is no such thing as a perfect relationship.

2966. Like waves crashing against the seashore, hearts break every day.

2967. Sometimes there is no right or wrong point of view. – People just think differently – **Shubrakishan**

2968. Flings – purely physical relationships between men and women.

2969. I expect that bygones will stay bygones. I will not tolerate it if the past spills into the present. **– Ankit Joshi**

2970. It is not possible to introduce new ideas even in the most exact sciences without sometimes taking a risk.– **Planck**

2971. Historians will have to face the fact that natural selection determined the evolution of cultures in the same manner as it did that of species. **– Konrad Zachurias Lorenz**

2972. A human being is a part of a whole "Universe" an art limited in time and space. He experiences himself, his thoughts, and feelings as something separated from the rest.

– Albert Einstein

2973. Hymn of breaking strain. The careful text-book measure [Let all who build beware]. The load, the shock, the pressure material can bear.

2974. So when the buckled girder lets down grinding span The blame of loss or murder is laid upon the man.

– Rudyard Kipling

2975. Generations to come, it may be, will scarce believe that such one as this [Gandhi], in flesh and blood walked up on this earh **– Einstein [about Gandhi in 1939]**

2976. In my opinion there is the correct path and – it is in our power to find it. **– Einstein**

2977. Just as some one who knows sanskrit can savour Kalidasa and those at home with English can delight in Shakespear and those with some musical training can lose themselves in classics. **– N. Mukunda**

2978. We constantly wonder how could one person (Einstein) have accomplished so much? **– N. Mukund**

2979. Einstein was amazed at Yehudi Menuhin's debut in 1929 at age 13 with the Berlin philharmonic, playing Bachms concerts in one programme. Einstein was so moved that he took Menuhin in his arms and exclaimed "Now I know that there is a God in heaven" **– N. Mukund**

2980. Human existence is based upon two pillars – compassion and knowledge compassion with out knowledge is ineffective and knowledge with out compassion is inhuman.

– Einstein

2981. The theory yields much, but it hardly brings us close to the secrets of the old one. In any case. I am convinced He does not dice. **— Einstein**

2982. Our task must be to free ourselves from this prison (delusion), widening circles of compassion to embrace all living creatures and the whole of nature in its beauty.

— Albert Einstein

2983. The Einstein Archives contain about 43000 documents collected papers of Einstein up to 1917 With 8 volumes in English and 32 volumes remain to be produced. He was scientifically active for more than 3 three decades from 1902 up to 1935.

2984. Albert Einstein – His doctoral thesis Just 18 pages long and titled. A new determination of molecular dimensions was submitted on July 20, 1905.

2985. Light energy consists of a finite number of energy quanta that are localized in points in space move without diving and can be absorbed or generated only as a whole.

— Albert Einstein

2986. What are light quanta? Of course today every rascal thinks he knows the answer but he is deluding himself.

—Einstein

2987. Your writing skills can create a good impression on your reader.

2988. If you are less qualified or totally untalented, take comfort in the fact that you are not in minority.— **Padma Ramesh**

2989. Writing is the most valued skill in an organisation.

2990. Employees spend 30 percent of their working time in writing.

Some writing may be peppered with Jargon, uninteresting tedious gibberish for the layman.

The ways in which ideas are expressed are as important as ideas themselves.

Writing should be brief, organised, accurate and conclusive.

The writing should be brief, organised, accurate and conclusive.

In writing, get to your point fast, support your reasoning and conclude rapidly.

In writing organising your material becomes difficult, if you have too much of it or too little of it. An overload of information will defeat your purpose.

Readability is another important factor in writing.

Think of readers you are writing Tailor your message writing to your reader.

The main principle in writing is clarity. If you have clarity in your writing you have the makings of a writer in you some where.

2991. Milk is a colloidal suspension of "Brownlan" particles.

–T.V Ramakrishnan [president IAS Indian Academy of Sciences]

2992. Engage yourself in any physical activity like washing your clothes, fetching water once in a week.

2993. Distant stars in the universe.

Virgo – 76 million light years

Ursa major – 1000m.Lys

Corona – 1400m.Lys

Boodies – 2500m.Lys

Hydra – 3960m.Lys

(Resonance. Dec. 2005]

2994. Corruption often is underdiagnosed or overdiagnosed.

2995. Kurinji plants flower once in 12 years.

2996. I took some tutions and got my first taste of independence.

– Monika Sachdev

2997. My trip to Malaysia gave me assurance and courage to explore. **– Monika Sachdev**

2998. While indulging in oral sex, avoid swallowing semen

– Tina Matheran

2999. Three rights of a young woman.

3000. You have the right to say "NO"s to what ever, whenever, and wherever"

3001. There are no rights with out responsibilities.

3002. Advice to woman.

3003. How you lead your life is how you lead your sexual life.

3004. How do you go about teaching something new? By mixing what they know with what they do not know.

– Pablo Picasso

3005. Scientists like every one else have opinions and preferences in their work as in their lives. These preferences must not influence the interpretations of data, but they are definitely influence on their choice of approaches.

– S.E. Luria

3006. In science the credit goes to the man who convinces the world and not to the man to whom the idea first occurs.

– Sir William Osler

3007. An important question we must consider is whether it is possible to transform the economy of a country to one based on modern technology developed else where with out at the same time establishing modern science in the country as a live and vital force the problem of establishing science as a live and vital force in society is an inseparable part of the problem of transforming an industrially under developed to a developed country.

— Homi J. Bhabha, Jan 6 1966

3008. Relativity teaches us the connection between the different descriptions of one and the same reality. —**Albert Einstein**

3009. Our experiences justifies us in believing that nature is the relaisation of the simplest conceivable mathematical ideas.

— Einstein

3010. Conquering matter is to understand it and understanding matter is necessary to understanding the universe and our selves. **— Primodevi**

3011. India remains a source that does development once the actual technological incubation and relaisation process is achieved.

3012. Causes of failure in business.

Unrealistic goals, Inadequate infrastructure inept planing, inability to break the goals, lack of focus on action, lack of implementation, lack of participatory decision making, inability to bring in commitment, lack of attention, indifference to environmental changes.

Execution is a discipline, our ability to get things done with quality on time and with in the cost makes all the difference in our success.

3013. Suggestions to mangers.

Do not recruit those people who will be the most difficult to retain.

Adapt to market forces.

Focus on what you can change not an what you cannot

Sometimes you need not recruit the high powered skill.

Simplify and standardize jobs.

Focus on retaining intellectual capital.

Keep electronic or computer records.

Participate in associations and clubs.

Work with local school, raise talent there. **– AIMS**

3014. Key attrition factors. In ability to use one's competence, lack of challenge, management style, lack of scope for growth, lack of role clarity, job stress, lack of independence, lack of excitement and innovation in job. **– AIMA**

3015. I have measured my life with coffee spoons.

– T.S. Eliot

3016. Emotional relation to life.

Feeling of difference.

Feeling of likeness or agreement.

Feeling of association. **– T.S. Eliot**

3017. But our lot crawls between dry ribs to keep our metaphysics warm.

3018. They are dead, but we are dying.

3019. T.S. Eliot makes distinction between lower love and higher love.

3020. Sex is seen as both origin and frustration of life.

3021. You find lust rivers every where.

3022. I yearn to die. — **Sibal**

3023. When lovely woman stoops to folly.

3024. What you get married for if you do not want children?

3025. The wheel of fortune moves on.

3026. T.S. Eliot wants to see permanent in the temporary and timeless in time.

3027. Speech without words and word of no speech.

3028. DNA has self repair capacity to arrest ageing.

— **S. Rama Subramanium**

3029. When you are an actor, you are putting in loads of hard work. So if you act a little nice, It is still makes a sense.

— **Uma Goswami**

3030. The stops and steps of mind are difficult to explain.

3031. We are partially aware of the divine. We are both ignorant and aware of the eternal sorrow.

3032. The time of tension differs from the brief transit of life, the birth and death.

3033. The poet's mind is a medium rather than personality.

3034. Poetry is an experience rather than meaning.

3035. Types of poets.

A poet borrows.

Immature poet imitates.

Mature poet steals.

3036. Bad poet steals.

3037. Bad poet defaces what he borrowed.

3038. A good poet makes it something better or different.

3039. The original poet goes directly to life.

3040. Derivative poet goes to literature and mistakes literature to life.

3041. To write poetry in prose and prose in poetry is one of the difficult arts to achieve.

3042. How to fuse wisdom with wit?

3043. Woman and man are alike. Sex is a complicated moral feeling, the attraction and repulsion of sex are common.

3044. O! maiden how many times I recall thee?

3045. Birth – copulation – death are the most eternal facts of life.

3046. Three discontinuous orders of morality.

The order of nature.

The order of mind.

The order of chastity.

3047. The sexual act as sin is more dignified and less boring.

3048. The end precedes the beginning, and beginning comes as an end.

3049. I mould the time of my youth.

— In from Ritual to Romance

3050. Three conditions.

Attachment to self thing or persons.

Detachment from them.

Indifference to them.

3051. While we live our sols are dead with in us, but when die our souls are restored to life.

3052. How can we know the dancer from dance? Humankind cannot bear very much reality. **– W.B. Yeats**

3053. MY rule is to remember that I understood nobody.

3054. There is a lot I do not understand about my wife.

3055. Time works wonders a quiet hour a day is most essential.

3056. If you have no strength to impose own terms, upon life you must accept the terms it offers you.

3057. Accept the terms that life have imposed.

3058. It is a great mistake I do believe for married people to take things for granted.

3059. It is not with in our power to impose terms on life.

[Cocktail party] – T.S. Eliot

3060. The one thing to do is to do nothing.

3061. You will find that you will survive humiliation and that's an experience of calculable value.

3062. What is the experience between two unreal people.

3063. The misery does not feed on the ruin of loveliness.

3064. I have half a mind to change my mind now.

3065. To show you that I am free to change it.

3066. There are certainly things I should like to forget that is hard to bear.

3067. An honest mind, that is one of the causes of their suffering.

3068. For the first time in his life fell in love with some one of whom you had reason to be jealous.

3069. A man who finds himself incapable of loving. And woman who finds that no man can love her.

3070. We must make the best of bad job.

3071. The lover and beloved are equally unreal.

3072. And dreamer is no more real than his dreams.

3073. Half the harm is done by the people who feel important and harm does not interest them or they justify their deeds, because they are busy in making themselves happy.

3074. Do not pluck flowers with wet clothes.

3075. No sex with Rudraksha mala on.

3076. Macbeth is not metphor it conveys moral darkness.

3077. The witches in Macbeth play upon man's innate propensity to be self tempted and self deceived.

3078. Out of the evil men pain will come to not only themselves but also to others. For example in Mahabharath, Duryodhana did all evils, but in Mahabharath war, not only Kaurvas but others also ware killed.

3079. When we are born we cry that we are come to this great stage of fools. — **King Lear**

3080. The evil has power to exact justice in this world.

3081. Then kill Kill Kill Kill Kill Kill — **King Lear**

3082. Killing appears to be only solution to all social or human problems. Political rivalry, adultery opposition, violation of rules etc.

3083. Virtue ought to be seen triumphant at the end, we see in all dramas, or pictures, or stories the hero wins at the end and evil is punished.

3084. No body likes to be on losing side the loser has very few supporters.

3085. All friends shall taste the wages of their virtues and all foes shall have the cups of their deserving. — **King Lear**

3086. When the good is hanged what is the good of good? It is the deepest question of all.

And my poor fool is hanged. No no no life why should a dog a horse a rat have life?

And thou no breath at all? Thou will not come no more
Never, never, never, never. — **King Lear cries**

3087. The child is dear to father and not always father is dear to his son or daughter.

3088. No body does return after death.

3089. Nearer the relation of a person dead, greater would be the sorrow and pain.

3090. Good my lord you have got me bred me loved me, Return those duties back as are fit Obey you, love you, most honour you.

3091. The Lord whose hand must take my plight shall carry.

Half my love with him half my care and duty,

Sure I shall never marry like my sisters, to love my father all.

3092. King Lear had 3 three daughters, Gonerl, Regan and Cordelia. Two elder daughters said that they loved father all. But Cordelia replied that after marriage she will love her husband and she will not marry like her sisters to love her father all.

3093. Speeches of fool are gems of wisdom.

Have more than thou showest speak less than thou knowest Lend less than thou ownest. Ride more than thou goest learn more than thou showest. Set less than thou throwest, Leave thy drink and thy whore.

3094. Fathers that wear rags do make their children blind. [It is true even today, fathers are not well treatd by the son. Son goes in a car and father goes in auto]

3095. Fortune the errant whore. Never turns the key to the poor. [Luck does not favour the poor]

3096. Edmund loved two daughters. (sisters, Goneril and Regan. He says.)

3097. To both these sisters have I sworn my love Each Jealous of the others as the stung, Are of they adhere? which of them shall I take? Both? One? Neither? Neither can be enjoyed.

If both remain alive. [If two sisters are alive, neither can be enjoyed, each jealous of the other.]

3098. It has been an unprecedented seventh. Consecutive electoral victory for the left front [LF], in West Bengal. It has won 235 seats out of 273 in 2006 elections.

— **Economic and Political Weekly** — **May 20, 06**

3099. The L.F has been able to gain and maintain support base in the state for over 5 five decades.

3100. Better to have died than to live like this.

— **a Woman in Slums on the Banks of Yamuna**

3101. In January 2004, the tourism department unveiled a plan to develop 100 acres of land on the banks of river Yamuna occupied by 3500 families about 150000 people uncouth in Yamuna Pushta for over 3 decades.

3102. Just a few months after pioneering partial face transplants in China and France, London a head for a surgeon to conduct the world's first full face transplant. — **19-6-06**

3103. What can I say, the referee is always right even when he is not.

— **Vince Grella World** — **Cup** — **Foot ball 19-6-2006**

3104. Let sensuous moods embrace you, indulge in a lot of face play, watch erotic movies. — **Dr. Prakash Kothari**

3105. Oral Sex is a normal variation, and has been recommended since the time immemorial. Even sage vatsyayana, the author of Kamasutra 1600 years ago recommended oral sex. — **Dr. Prakash Kothari**

3106. Why oral sex?

The nerve supply is the same as in the genitals

There is a great similarity in sensation.

The grip is firmer as compared to vagina.

There is the feature novelty.

A man in this position can also simultaneously stimulate the breasts and clitoris.

The arousal level is considerably enhanced.

— **Dr. Prakash Kothari**

3107 You are at liberty to knock at any door provided you are welcomed.

3108. There are more germs in an individual's mouth than on the penis or vagina so kissing should be prohibited.

— **Dr. Prakash Kothari**

3109. Oral sex is more pleasurable than sexual intercourse.

– **Dr. Prakash Kothari**

3110. The concern about penile size is as old as the human race.

– **Dr. Prakash Kothari**

3111. The width, length and erection of penis vary from one individual to another. – **Dr. Prakash**

3112. Two (2) inches of the outer vagina has the maximum never endings. – **Dr. Prakash**

3113. It is not what you do but how you do it that matters.

3114. Rani worked non-stop 12 hour shift to keep home fires burning.

3115. The vagina has a tremendous capacity as per the size of peris. During the delivery, it expnads to the size of child's head. – **Dr. Prakash Kothari**

3116. Viagra needs to be taken 1.1/2 hours before the anticipated sex act. It increases the rigidity of the penis. – **Dr. Prakash**

3117. One needs to do anything with the consent of the partner.

3118. How do you know you are in love?

3119. You have a feeling, but you do not name it, you have feeling you do not name it, you have like, fond and Love to explain your feeling.

3120. After a burst of claustrophobia a why me period. You get used to the feeling. **– Jerry Pinto**

3121. Men will say things they do not mean.

Men will say 'I love you' because.

Men say it because women expect it.

Some men say out of politeness.

Some men say it because women will bewiling to go to bed.

Some say it just like. "I love music".

Some say it because you are (woman) there and they want to please.

It is easy for men to say I never said "I love you" to be safe.

3122. Does a man love you (woman)?

3123. Answer all the following questions.

3124. Does the man seem in love?

3125. Does the man appear passionate?

3126. Did the man ask you to marry?

3127. Are you willing to trust him?

3128. Did he (man) write you any love letter?

3129. Does he (man) take care of you? (outside).

3130. Does he take pains to keep you happy?

3131. Does he sacrifice his comforts for you?

3132. Performance equals winning.

3133. Iron is vital in cognitive function, it improves concentration, and mental performance, improved memory, increased problem solving ability, enhanced verbal fluency.

3134. The percentage of female literacy in the country has increased from 8.86 p.c in 1951 to 54.16 p.c in 2001 increasing @ 3.15 p.c.a year

3135. Advice to parents — **Children's Reading Habits**

3136. Set time aside for reading aloud to children 30 minutes to 1 hour in a day.

3137. Start reading to them at an early age.

3138. Children want to read the same story or poem.

3139. Children may be encouraged to read on their own.

3140. Never tear pages from the book.

3141. Limited time for watching. T.V

3142. Children may be encouraged to Join library. Reading is an asset for life time.

3143. A smart dealer make you buy what he wants to sell and sells only what he has.

3144. Home truths on men.

Men are suckers.

A man slips easier than a woman.

It is easier for a woman to get a man she desires rather than vice versa

3145. We need attention. For the first 20 years, we get it from mothers.

3146. We have our PMS cycle. In terms of mood swings.

3147. Women are scared of getting married and losing freedom.

3148. Men stray period.

3149. Women want sex more than men.

3150. Questions are important in relationship, but not 500 questions a day.

3151. Men are more possessive than women.

3152. The surest way to man's heart is through his chest with a blade.

3153. Men watch pornography only to get back to women.

— Dabboo Ratnan

3154. Women who suffer from disabilities, are sexually active, enjoy a good sex life in marriage or out side marriage.

— Ruchira Bose

3155 We define sex as physical contact for the purpose of sharing intimacy and pleasure.

3156. Satisfactions are more important than actual inter course.

— Dr. Prakash Kothari

3157. Women who have autonomy and are free to make their choice are happier than men because their choices have been fought for and won. Women are happy to be out at work, and cope with responsibilities at home and work.

— Purabi Shridhar

3158. Hoarding is costly. Some hints.

Do not buy things you do not need.

Do not buy things out of your budget.

Do not buy things to be indebts.

Do not buy things on credit.

Shopping should not become a habit.

Do not fight with your family for purchases.

Do not hide things from your family.

Spending habits should be under control.

Get approval for your plans.

Do not shop alone.

3159. Avoid mail or e-mail, or on line purchases.

3160. Get counseling from experts or from experienced colleague.

3161. Disorder in shopping is not common.

3162. Do not use credit cards.

3163. Prepare a survival budget in times of crisis.

3164. Art speaks an international language a language that audiences find it easy to understand. **– Arun Chandraju**

3165. Sebastian Bergne invested children's cutlery with human qualities so that the cup has a nose and plates has ears and so on

3166. Healthy food habits.

Eat whole some foods

Do not snack at home

Avoid processed foods

Eat fruits and vegetables.

3167. Nutraceuticals - a groups of vitamins and minerals and other natural ingredients, is the buzz word in the beauty industry. **– Ruchira Bose**

3168. If you are eating a healthy diet with a lot of vegetable fruits, and whole grains plus omega – 3 from foods like fish, then you should not have to take supplements. **– Ruchira Bose**

3169. The top of the line—multivitamin may not include ingredients such as lycopene, prime rose oil, green tea extract, pycnogenols alpha lipolic acid, co Q1.0 and high levels of vitamins such C and E. **– Ruchira Bose**

3170. Replace you mascara every three months.

3171. June 22, is the longest day in northern hemisphere.

3172. It people want to look alluring, they wear something to bed and go naked. Nudity is not about sex, it is more about being comfortable with your body. When you are sleeping with some body nakedness about intimacy and warmth rather than sex. **– Poojasrivatsav**

3173. You never know when you will have magical voice- Ranjeet Barot.

3174. Colours – night shades soft blue, sheer silver, violet and rose.

3175. Do not let your friendship fall in to replacement boy friend / girl friend territory it is for disaster.

3176. When you fall in love make friends time in your schedule.

3177. Have communication with your friend at distant place once in 15 days to renew or maintain friendship.

3178. After 30 years of married life, you are less likely to fall out of wed lack.

3179. Change is inevitable in friendship as we move in life.

3180. Friends are important to each other.

3181. Living different lives should not affect the friendship.

3182. A good predictor of friendship, longevity is shared values and not shared paths. **– Dr. Yeger**

3183. I stand before you half the person I was yesterday.

– Mr.s Sauders, [whose husband was killed yesterday]

3184. The owner of a car has forgotten the number. It is four-digit figure. The first two digits taken together is one less than the last two digits taken together. The second digit is

3 times the first digit. No number is repeated. Can you help him? How? [Ans 3940]

3185. Ms Sonia is adnouseam a foreigner, but a woman makes her path stony, but she walks, and stones are turned in to flowers. — **Sathya Saran**

3186. Men are a complicated lot, women can not live with them, and cannot live with out them. — **Namrata**

3187. I am perfectly happy being a woman.

— **Namrat Shirodkar**

3188. You never know what others think about you, they may change their opinoon.

3189. The factors that are important about the partner are understanding. Compromise. Unconditional love and trust.

— **Namrata Shirodkar**

3190. Hate is a strong word to be kept in the book of emotions.

3191. "Oligospermic" means reduced quantity of sperms. The normal sperm count needs to be 20 million per CC.

—**Dr. Prakash**

3192. Retrograde ejaculation is a condition where an individual reaches orgasm but there is no ejaculation. — **Dr. Prakash**

3193. Do not give these gifts to your boy friends. Deodorant, T-shirts, diffuse wear, Kurtas, Shorts, Belt, Wallet Sports Cap, mugs, DVDS pen CD soft toys flowers, balloons, cards, Books, Tickets for show or plays. — **Shobha**

3194. Gifts to men – a watch, sunglasses Indian wear (suit), Digital camera, CD Player, DVD Player, Laptop, latest handset [mobile] — **Shobha**

3195. Bride seeing ritual. [first meeting arranged]

Appropriate dressing and make up.

Artificial conversation leading no where.

Meeting arranged at specific 'muharat'

Relatives of bride and groom assemble.

3196. Agora phobia – anxiety disorder, stepping out side the front door is a terrifying prospect. A person experiences anxiety in a situation from which escape may be difficult, symptoms. Palpitations sweating and shaky hands – It starts in late 30s or early 40s.

3197. Brisk walking is one of the easiest ways to lose weight burning up 130 calories in 30 minutes. **– K. Williamson**

3198. Time together is vital.

3199. News is one of the most common every day stress triggers, and being cut off from world events helps you relax.

3200. You really need a two week break to cut off from everything and give you time to reflect on your life and work.

-Dr. Stephen

3201. Women have vision, spirit and drive to make films.

3202. Wheat grass has the power to keep you young and beautiful. Inside out for years. **– Mita Banergee**

3203. Wheat grass juice like nectar will treat most health problems. **– M. Banerjee**

3204. The basic constituent of wheat grass is chlorophyll and wheat grass is considered the best source.

– Mita Banergee

3205. Wheat grass juice is also called "Green Blood", and it is quickly absorbed in the blood.

3206. Chlorophyll is a potent germicide and purifies blood, boosts functioning of heart, improves blood vessel, intestine lung, and kidney functions. **– M. Banerjee**

3207. Wheat grass contains vitamins E.A. and C, acts as antioxidant, retards ageing of cells in the body.

3208. Wheat grass is an effective tonic beneficial to arthritis and skin allergies, Kidney stones etc.

3209. The wheat grass juice should be drunk fresh as the nutritive quality reduces the longer it is left to stand.

3210. Wheat grass juice preparation.

3211. Soak and sprout wheat seeds.

3212. Use 100 gm sprouted seeds per flower pot, 6 cm. Depth and 24 cm square.

3213. Wheat grass will be cut after 8 or 9 days, 14 to 16 cm. Height.

3214. After through washing, cut grass, grind it in a mixie.

3215. Strain the Juice through muslim cloth and drink it fresh.

3216. Use natural manure organic mixture, and no chemical fertilisers.

3217. Avoid heavy dals, sour foods, and many dairy products and fruits for dinner an ideal diet programme for ageing people.

3218. Fibre has many benefits it regulates blood in the body responsible for digestion of carbohydrates, and helps avoid constipation, reduce cholesterol levels.

– Dr. Shikha Sharma

3219. Fibre rich foods whole wheat breads brown rice, dals with chilka, green leafy vegetables saag, alak, bathua, and methi and fruits. 40 – 80 gm per day.

3220. Avoid foods – naan, noodles and processed eatables like chips, and biscuits etc.

3221. Milk can be problematic for those who are lactose instolerant. tea can cause acidity, gas, flatulence for them. Such people should avoid milk and supplement their body's requirements for calcium from vegetables to fruits and soya milk **—Dr. Shikha Sharama**

3222. Avoid fried snacks, you opt for roasted goodies chana masala, mung chatpata, Roasted goodies are easier on the stomach and high on taste. You can take bhelpuri dhokla, khandvi, idli etc. —**Dr. Shikha Sharma**

3223. Every one likes to look his or her best at any age.

3224. Your teeth will age and at 40 you need dentures.

3225. Teeth wear down almost 30 percent between the ager of 18 to 40.

3226. Beauty enhancing menu-Aloe Vera, apple, wheat, carrot, coconut, cucumber, figs, hemp seeds, nuts olives Popaya, tomato – etc.

3227. All cars are right hand drive in Newzeland.

3228. Mental health and nutrition go hand in hand.

3229. B. Vitamins enhance the functioning of brain neurotransmitters and improve the ability to think reason, learn and imagine.

3230. An affair is most common where the focus is on compensating for unsatisfying marital sex by seeking outside the marriage.

3231. Polygamy is no longer the nature of the human beast.

3232. An affair is easier to prevent than deal with it.

3233. Being attracted to opposite sex is normal.

3234. If you are unfulfilled in marriage do something about it.

3235. Personality wrongs.

Trip fall – trip fall a manager who does not learn from his mistakes tends to commit them again and again.

[me, myself-] one of the most common mistakes a manager makes is to think of himself when taking decisions.

Authoritarian leadership is neither required nor appreciated.

A democratic setup is more suitable in today's corporate climate.

Forever – for always. Mangers must not take their leadership for granted.

Once a leader for ever leader concept is wrong.

True power does not lie with the leader, but it lies with the followers or employees.

3236. Golden rule.

3237. As long as managers treat employees well, they are also treated well.

3238. There are lots of Grey shades and Judging every one by one's individual standards is not the best thing to do.

3239. Every person has distinct individual characteristics.

3240. Considering one self above is indeed the biggest fallacy.

3241. We must know there is still a lot to learn.

3242. Sorry — **No Sorry**

3243. Accepting of healthy self — **Esteem**

3244. Leaders unreceptive to change will find it difficult to survive in this dynamic world.

3245. Old habits die hard.

3246. The person who keeps close relationship with the leader, minister, or officer shall be deemed to possess power or authority to some extent.

3247. When firmness is sufficient rashness is un necessary.

– Napoleon

3248. A lie has speed, but truth has endurance. – **Edgar j. Mohan**

3249. Most troubles only come because we go half way to meet them. —**Due de Levis**

3250. It is not the strongest of the species that survive, nor most intelligent but the one most responsive to change.

– Charles Darwin

3251. Only those who risk going too far can possibly find out how far one can go. **– T.S. Eliot**

3252. To be conscious that you are ignorant is a great step to knowledge. **– Disraeli**

3253. There is a big difference between showing interest and really taking interest. **– Michael Nicholson**

3254. Genius is only the power of making continuos efforts. **– Albert Hubbard**

3255. Pleasure in the job puts perfection in the work. **– Aristotle**

3256. In theory there is no difference between theory and practice. But in practice there is. **– Snepscheut**

3257. Never interrupt your enemy when he is making a mistake. **– Napoleon**

3258. In great attempts it is glorious even to fall. **– Longinus**

3259. A belligerent state permits it self every such misc deed every such act of violence as would disgrace the individuals. **– Sigmund Freud**

3260. All experience is an arch where through gleams that an untravelled world whose margin fades for ever and for ever when I move. **—Alfred Tennyson**

3261. Any poet if he is to survive beyond his 25th year must alter he must seek new literary influences, he will have different emotions to express. **– T.S. Eliot**

3262. If you do not like something change it; if you cannot change it; change your attitude. Do not complain. **– Maya Angelu**

3263. All of us failed to match our dreams of perfection. So I rate us on the basis of our splendid failure to do the impossible. **– William Fallkner**

3264. It is the will, without the will there will never come the power. **– M.J. Akbar**

3265. Sport in India is ruled by non-professionals who believe that sports should serve them not the other way round.

– M.J. Akbar

3266. Life must be understood backward, but it must be lived forward. **– Sorenklerkegaard**

3267. You do not drown by falling in the water you drown by staying there. **– Lindsay**

3268. A good plan to day is better than a perfect plan tomorrow.

– General George. S. Patton

3269. Look for the good in every person and every situation. You will almost always find it. **– Brain Tracy**

3270. To love and be loved is the greatest happiness of existence.

– Sydney Smith

3271. Tomorrow's life is too late. Live to day.

– Marcus Vaterlus Martlalls

3272. We are not creatures of circumstance. We are creators of circumstance. **– Benjamin Disraeli**

3273. Three may keep a secret, if two of them are dead.

– Benjamin Franklin

3274. Prostitution is one such a situation, courtship another certain men seem to consider an expensive dinner a prudent investment in pursuit of a sexual dividend.

3275. Scandals may stain reputations, but the stain is not indelible.

– Nonawalia

3276. Honesty is the best way to counter a scandal. **– Nonawalia**

3277. Every one loves a good scandal. There is some in it for every one.

3278. Despite bigamy being banned in India after the emergence of the Hindu Marriage Act, Several Prominent personalities continue to maintain two homes. **– Nayare Ali**

3279. Long life dependent on medicines and relatives (sons or daughters), can be a penalty. **– Hasan Javed**

3280. Pray that I have a healthy life rather than a long life. **– Prayer of every body**

3281. There are 70 million people over the age of 60 to day [2006] in the country and this number is increasing by 15 percent every year.

3282. The stunning pace of change in medical sciences, molecular biology genetics, cellular therapy and biotechnology have provided new opportunities for health.

3283. New developments such as non-invasive bloodless surgery, reconstructive and regenerative medicines, rehabilitation therapy successful organ transplantation's have added years to life.

3284. There is still a long way to go. In India 22 lakh infants and children die from preventable illnesses (2006)

3285. One lakh mothers die during child birth 5 million people die from HIV/AIDS.

3286. Long life should not become a penalty or curse, and adding years to life and not other way round.

3287. It is the moment when World Cup dreams are realised or cruelly shattered, in a split second you are either hero or villain. (June 2006).

3288. The biggest marine animal is the Blue whale with a recorded length of 31 meters.

3289. The largest fish is whale shark which grows to more than 15 meters.

3290. Life on earth originated in the seas.

3291. Without change something sleeps inside us and seldom awakes. The sleeper must be awaken. **– Frank Herbert**

3292. It is all most as difficult to keep a first class person in a fourth class job, as it is to keep a fourth class person in a first class job. **— Alexander Dumas**

3293. It is impossible to over look the extent to which civilisation is put upon a renunciation of instinct. **– Sigmund Freud**

3294. Be in the world, but not out of it. **– Osho**

3295. Life has no short cuts.

3296. Only he who can see the invisible can do the impossible.

– Frank. L. Galnes

3297. When you cease to dream you cease to live.

– Malcolm Forbes

3298. Experience teaches slowly and at the cost of mistakes.

– James a Froude

3299. At the touch of love, every one becomes a poet. **– Plato**

3300. Do not wait to strike until the iron is hot, but make it hot by striking. **– William B. Sprague**

3301. If you leave the smallest corner of your head vacant for a moment, other people's opinions will rush in from all quarters. **– Geore Bernard Shaw**

3302. Perseverance is failing 9 times and succeeding the 10th

3303. Success is never final and failure never fatal, its courage that counts. **— George F. Tilton**

3304. An businessman is not trusted because we often encounter dishonesty in business circles.

3305. The Svalbard Global Seed Vault in Norway is designed to store about 3 million crop seeds from around the world, located near Longyarbyen about 620 miles from North pole, as a repository of seeds in case a catastrophe sweeps across the world. **— It is New Age Noah's Ark**

3306. Television serials are called soap operas as these companies produced them.

3307. Andorra is a small nation of 453 sq.kms, located on the French Spanish border, famous for tourism and tobacco, French and Spanish currencies are valid.

3308. The word "talko;" is referred to various Japanese drums.

3309. According to rebirth theory, the end of one learning cycle (or life cycle) is the beginning of the next.

3310. Like love by pure accident, I found my wife by accident.

3311. Scientists need to make themselves understood by the rest of the society, they have to be communicators, other wise the society may stop investing in their activities, that are so important for mankind.

3312. God and science are not mutually opposed beliefs.

3313. Chikungunya fever is characterised by sudden chills, and fever, headache, nausea, vomiting and arthralgia or arthritis and rash.

3314. Liver is the world horse of the body.

3315. Life is an echo point whatever you do with others you are doing with yourself, because from every where things will come back a 1000 fold. — **Osho**

3316. You have three layers, child, parent adult, and you are none. You are something beyond, something eternal.

3317. Reason and rationality are monotonous

3318. Be in the world, but do not let the world enter you. — **Osho**

3319. Life is a continuous journey full of tiny halts— Ravishanker

3320. There is nothing to be taught or learnt about life. We have to realise the sphere of life. The theme behind the Art of living is to propagate love. — **Ravishnker**

3321. I follow my heart — **Ravishanker**

3322. My first guru is my mother. — **Ravihanker**

3323. Where there is peace, there is prosperity.

3324. Woman's neck deserves to be seen.

3325. Where ever and when ever we are tired in London, we would hop into a bus.

3326. For every minute of T.V Watch take 100 steps (walking for 1 minute for ordinary people). Your walking should correspond to T.V watching time.

3327. Dynamics of purchasing activity (Saries or dress) people are classified into 3 groups.

People with income of Rs.1000 or set budget of Rs.1000.

People with the income of Rs. 5000 or set budget.

People with the income of Rs. 10000 or over. No budget set.

OL is the scale line

PQ = budget line 1000

RS = budget line Rs. 5000

For group A the purchases will fall below OM.

For group B, the purchases cannot exceed OM_1

For people C, group, there is no limit, may go beyond OM_2

In general, purchases can not exceed budget line for any group.

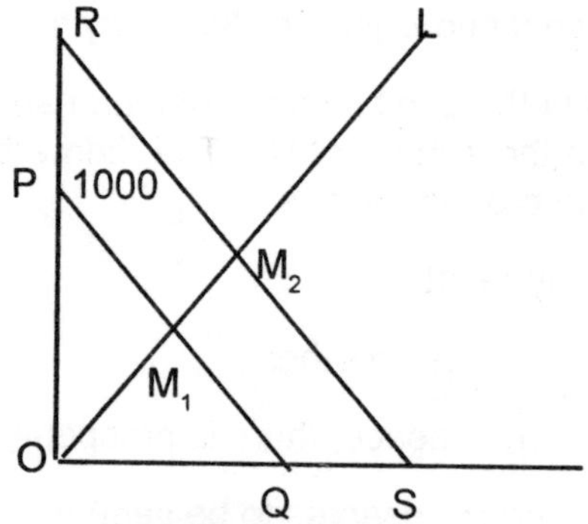

3328. Another explanation.

People are classified into 2 groups.

People with strong preference.

People with neutral preference. Zero preference,

Given the budget or income why do some people take long time for selections?.

People with strong preference take less time in decision making or selection.

These people take the support of others in making decision or selection. Take longer time.

These people are not able to make independent decisions. They depend up on others for their purchases. They may ask others for selections.

3329. Life is like playing a violin solo in public and learning the instrument as one goes on. **–Samuel Butler Yeats**

3330. Few people even scratch the surface much less exhaust the contemplation of their own experience.

– Randolph Bourne

3331. An insincere and evil friend is more to be feared than a wild beast a wild beast may wound your body but an evil friend will wound your mind. **– Lord Buddha**

3332. It is not so much our friends help that helps us as the confidence of their help. **– Epicurus**

3333. Friendship is a single soul dwelling in two bodies.

– Aristotle

3334. A couple applied for a divorce. The judge asked "How will you divide your three children? The couple replied "we will apply next year."

3335. Only in India a very small cabinet committee commits the country to international agreements that go against our national interests. **– AB. Bardhan**

3336. We are satisfied with the progress made in the peace talks between the PCG [Peoples Consultative Group] and the Government of India.

– Arabinda Raj Khowa [Ulfa Chairman]

3337. I am willing to negotiate commerce, but subsistence livelihood and security I will not be willing to negotiate.

– Kamalnath [Commerce Minister. 8-7-06]

3338. 32.5 billion will be watching final Foot Ball match for FIFA trophy today 9-7-2006, between France and Italy. 150 million Italians will be watching a great game of Foot Ball.

3339. You cannot attempt to create a new and different future based on the limitations of your past [Karmas].

– Shitra Hendrie, [Sunday Times 9-7-2006.]

3340. Small opportunities are aften the beginning of great enterprises. **– Demosthenes**

3341. I have witnessed the softening of the hardest of hearts by a simple smile. **– Goldie Hawn**

3342. My motto is; connected with little yet wishing more.

– Charles Lamb

3343. The most important thing is to be whatever you are with out shame. **– Rod Stelger**

3344. Love is the triumph of imagination over intelligence.

– H.L. Menckan

3345. The only thing that overcomes hard luck is hard work.

– Harry Golden

3346. Just because you love someone does not mean you have to be involved with them. Love is not a bandage to cover wounds. **– High Elliott**

3347. It is your choice and not chance that determines your destiny. **– Jean Nidetch**

3348. I believe in natural ways of healing. **– Deepak**

3349. Healing involves much more than an analysis of the old traumas. It is important to actively encourage the unfoldment of one's spiritual potential. **– Deepak**

3350. Over enthusiasm in helping other is also not good.

3351. Most people never really change, sad but true. Some people never even try. **– Shitra Hendrie**

3352. In 2000, De Beers and the steinmetz Group unveiled a 203.4 carat D – colour internally and externally flawless pear shaped diamond, the most valuable diamond in the world in London, "The Millennium star" quoted for 100 million pounds, believed to be a fraction of its price.

– Sunday Times 9-7-06

3353. Hiccups occur when the diaphragm and muscles between the ribs suddenly contract.

3354. I play with my head, my heart and my legs.
– Del Piero, [Player, World Cup Final ready to lift World Cup. 9-7-06]

3355. I will eat humble pie as I am also human and have every chance of going wrong.**– an astrologer [who predicated that Brazil would win a World cup – Berlın 2006 – July]**

3356. Thorium fuel cycle technologies have potential for limitless energy in the future. **– Bharat Karnad**

3357. Stalin was only 5-4- tall.

3358. Love is not lust, but it is not with out lust. Love is lotus and lust is mud love comes out of lust. **– Osho**

3359. The life of a man happily married cannot fail to be influenced by the character and conduct of his wife.

– Julian Hawthorne

3360. Life of a man was (with out wife) "sun with out heat and day with out sun" **– Julian**

3362. Elections and the corruption, injustice and the power and tyranny of wealth and in efficiency of administration will make hell of life as soon as freedom is given to us.

— **C. Rajagopalachary wrote in his prison dairy 24-1-1922**

3362. There is enough to meet the legitimate needs of every one but not greed of every one in the country.

— **Mahatma Gandhi**

3363. Girt and determination are the marks of true survivors.

3364. Part of the thrill of sex is usually having both people in the nude.

3365. Men get their hands on a pair of breasts. Breasts are beautiful works of art. Caress them, cup them in both hands and softly embrace them. Rubbing naked chest against them is always acceptable.

3366. Nipples are not gummy bears, men are looking to make contact with.

3367. Men expect women to be Rambheshari from 'Japanese Kamasutra'. The wonder woman from 'Nights of passion'. Despite all that Pilate's and Thaichi, women might do, women are not Olympic gymnasts from Russia or Porn version of Gemini circus in bed.

3368. A man starts to drown out the traffic noise below the window or "who can wake up the Neighbours?" A litle growl is sexy, and screaming oh Baby 3286 times is not. Men do on Beer-on the Top Radeo in Texas not in bed.

3369. There is more to women than just the hilly area on top and the tunnel down south. Men should not just attack the sexual organs treat women as human beings. Men like when women cutting foreplay, go straight to the main course Groping breasts and panting at the dawn is good only when men are paying by the hour. Men may be surprised to discover different women's erogenous zones. Some women love it when the backs of their knees are licked, others love it when their men gently bite their backs or inside of their thighs. The idea is to be creative and touch women all over because that is the only way to discover what makes them hot and bothered. — **Ruchira Bose**

3370. Coleoptra capered and Lepidoptera leapt in a choppy sea of gastric Juices. — **Aparna Kartikeyan**

3371. Many brains are better than (n)one.

3372. Genius is nothing but a great aptitude for patience.

— **Louis De Buffon**

3373. The future continues one day at a time. — **Dean Acheson**

3374. Let him who would enjoy a good future waste none of his present. — **Roger Babson**

3375. Alas after a certain age every man is responsible for his face. — **Alber Camus**

3376. Man becomes man only by his intelligence but he is man only by his heart. — **Henry Frederic Amiel**

3377. To me old age is always ten years older than I am.

— **John Burroughs**

3378. The employees of an organisation do not pursue the 'eye for eye' dogma but prefer 'tooth for tooth".

3379. Train to Tibet – 5072 metres high – The project is not only a magnificent feat in China's history of railway construction, it is also great miracle for the world.

– President Hu Jintao – China

3380. The bride and groom (frogs) are dressed sprinkled with turmeric and vermilion and taken in procession to the nearest pond for their "honey moon" with fervent prayers for rain 2-7-06.

3381. In Germany, the prostitution is legal.

3382. Different things make different people happy.

3383. Man should earn enough to be able to afford a grand education, and provide a decent living for the entire family.

3384. A woman sometimes takes daring plunge into an affair.

3385. There is security in a fixed job, a small salary is better than the uncertainty of winding one's way through the ups, and downs of being one's own master. (independent profession)

3386. Having a fixed income is good for one's peace of mind.

3387. Fixed income is easy to budget.

3388. Regular, fixed income will make you feel free from anxiety and worries.

3389. The first years in any business are tough.

3390. There is an excitement in the new venture or new way of life.

3391. Fulfilled mamas make good mothers.

3392. Does one need more from life?

3393. Advice to expectant mothers – Drink milk mixed with haldi so that the child will be born fair complexioned.

3394. Fear limits possiblities. Once you over come your fears, anything is possible.

3395. Politics and relationships need not get in the way of one another. Personal and professional lives are kept apart and we shared close relationship despite political differences. **– Vasundhara Raje Scindia**

3396. Politics is accused of being dirty and no place for women.

3397. Understanding and communication is the key to all roles in life. **– Vasundhara Raje Scindia**

3398. Keep your client happy in order to secure your own place.

3399. Accept compliments gracefully.

3400. A compliment is not an insult. "You look great today" does not mean "you looked bad yesterday".

3401. If you get a compliment it does, it does and it does.

3402. Men are not verbally inventive as women. Men may not use words seductive, exquisite, collipygean. "You look good" generally means wow.

3403. Do not expect man to notice everything, (Advice to woman)

3404. Men have healthy recongition of their own plus points.

3405. Crystal therapy helps solve problem relating to health, wealth marriage, education stress, career, and relationships. "It helps restore balance and reduce physical, emotional and mental ailments. – **Sameera Moledina**

3406. Crystals have healing properties and help develop the mystical healing powers within. They are physically good for heart and the spirit, repeat negativity at every level.

3407. Healthy adults should consume at least 26 to 30 gms of fibre on daily basis.

3408. Soyabeans have all the essential amino acids our body requires.

3409. Crystals for treatment of [Chart].

3410. **Amethyst**-Good for headaches, vision scalp, blood sugar, psychic problems, anger, impatience and night mares.

3411. **Aquarnarin**-heart problems, reduces anxiety and fear.

3412. Carnelian – works on circulatory system menstrual problems gall bladder, pancreas, kidneys sexuality and physical energy.

3413. Citrine – Good for acidity indigestion and allergies, kidneys, liver urinary problems, improves memory and will power.

3414. Coral – works on your muscles blood, heart reproductive system, spine, tissue not to use for BP. Patients.

3415. Diamond – Improves clarity and trust and confidence denotes property generosity, love spirituality.

3416. Emerald – good for respiratory system, heart attacks, growth, peace patience, love, honesty.

3417. Jade – Good for heart, kidney, nervous system, wealth and longevity.

3418. Lapus – works on anxiety, restlessness, insomnia, nervous system, speech, hearing improves intuition and creativity.

3419. Malchite – works on vision, stomach, heart, liver, kidneys.

3420. Rose Quartz – Helps emotional balance love beauty, self esteem, stress and anger.

3421. Ruby – Best for infections cholesterol, blood clots, etc.

3422. Saphire – Reduces inflammation fever, burns, and TB, depression.

3423. A headache can be the result of tension and a reaction to hunger, coffein, withdrawl, sleeplessness stuffy rooms, noise, allergies, sinusitis, low blood sugar level, and weather changes.

3424. For a man its very exciting knowing what his woman wants and exactly how he can give it to her. – **Dr. Malvika Bishnoi**

3425. Dirty names for sex and love.

3426. Penis – Wiener, Lover Hammer, Lucky chukie.

– Dr. Bishnoi

3427. Advice to ladies.

3428. "Do not describe long dinner, red roses or long wait, soft candle light, and flower garland in the bed. – **Dr. Bishnoi**

3429. Do not borrow pre fab sex scenes.

3430. Plagiarise, plagiarise, plagiarise.

3431. We are not born with sexual vocabulary.

3432. Telephones are ultimate toy. **– Meenakshi Nair**

3433. Some people are at first more comfortable confiding over the phone.

3434. "Men were constantly to call to discuss their stories with girl friends"

3435. Let us examine the market demand for this extra marital, extra – dimensional service. **– Sriram**

3436. When we get home I am going to undo your shirt button by button. **– Dr. Bisnoi**

3437. Children put a strong damper on erotic expression.

3438. I went to make love on the floor. **–Ritu**

3439. Kids become an excuse not to deal with each other as sexual adults.

3440. You can use words like "luck" or "suck".

3441. Pack your kids off for a night once in a weak or 15 days or a month.

3442. Talking to your lover pays the way for intimacy.

3443. I want you now or you can say 'I want you incide me',

3444. If you can not talk dirty, you can certainly moan dirty.

— Dr. Bishnoi

3445. Public speaking is one of the best marketing tools we have today. **— Pallavijha**

3446. Public speaking costs nothing and gives you a platform to market and sell your products.

3447. To conquer the fear of public speaking.

3448. You are what think

3449. Think and write out your speech.

3450. Practice makes permanent.

3451. The more you do it the better your skill becomes.

3452. Take every opportunity you can speak.

3453. Please remember that every one is a person like you.

3454. Prepare good out of time, and follow it.

3455. Know your audience.

3456. Be your self.

3457. Get to the meeting early. **— Abraham Lincoln**

3458. Practice your presentation well beforehand.

3459. Get to know some of the participants.

3460. True love does not exist any where.

3461. Attractive and talented person counts for something.

3462. We all have to wisen up and toughen up or we will miss the train.

3463. How to fish the biggest fish? Bigger is the better.

3464. Dating game has given a way to "hunting". Bigger is always the better.

3465. Love clouds our judgement, fades away quickly.

3466. We choose to love with our heads and not with our fragile hearts.

3467. You can opt for waxing or laser, or a pulselite treatment for body hair removal. **– Dr. Jamuna**

3468. Cellulite –

3469. A girl of 15 could have as much cellulite as a woman of 50. Cellulite consists of clumps of fat that are deposited under the skin on your thighs, hips, legs and arms.

– Meher, Castelino

3470. Choose one of the following exercises to keep your body young. Power walking, stretches, yoga, aerobics, dances and kick boxing.

3471. Cinnamon not only helps you water retention, but it also works at conditioning the skin with anti ageing benefits.

3472. Take a spoonful cinnamon with a spot of honey at night.

– Doctor

3473. It is never too late to acquire new skills and up grade existing ones.

3474. One of the worst feelings in the world is to be left hanging – not knowing whether your man is reciprocates or not.

– Nitya Alwani Satyani

3475. To know whether your boy friend is in love with you.

3476. These are tell tale sings.

When you are a part of his daily plans.

He consults you in making any decisions.

When he wants to meet your parents.

When he does not enjoy your absence.

When he makes dinner plans for both of you.

When he asks you "where should we party? Or "which play school did you attend?"

When he tells you that his class mates called him "pansy" when he was 18.

When he comes home early or he cuts the class to meet you.

When he tells you his future plans.

When he does not get annoyed to leave the party for you.

When he allows you to shop for him.

When he is not embarrassed to cry in your presence

When he discusses his relationships with you.

When he phones to his parents in your presence and tells them about you.

When he confides in you when there is crisis in his family

When he tries to develop a rapport with your siblings.

When he watches all chick flicks with you.

When he goes shopping with you.

When he calls you in the middle of a busy day.

When he lets you drive his car,

When he confesses his past sins.

[We get to see the worst side when men love us. Woman says.]

When he helps you pack for your trips

When he asks you to select a gift for his friend's birth day.

When he calls you every night before he goes to sleep.

When he goes o bath room with door open in your presence. — **Nitya Alwani — Satyani**

3477. Some people intimidate you the moment you look at them.

— **Hazira Shaheen**

3478. Intimidating qualities.

3479. "I am busy" common technique of intimidating others.

3480. It is easy to be intimidated by some one who is busy 24x7 throughout the year.

3481. Another technique is they rush through conversation, when they talk,

3482. Or they use speakerphone or they pretend to have a zillion things to do.

3483. Personal space – Every one has some space zone and others are not allowed. The radius of this zone is not uniform for all individuals.

3484. The intimidator encroaches this zone intentionally and disturbs your peace of mind.

3485. Privacy encroachment.

3486. The intimidator stands behind you and peers into everything. You have a feeling of your privacy being invaded. Your secret regions are exposed.

3487. You are sorry –

3488. Some people commit mistakes regularly. There is no point in correcting them repeatedly, because they continue to make the same mistakes that hurt you.

3489. People feel important.

3490. The intimidator wants you to lose your cool.

3491. To get your emotions under control.

3492. True leaders can inspire executives.

3493. Boomerang – It is the term coined to identify top performing former employees who are brought back into organisation. Boomerang recruiting keeps the door open for talented ex-employees. **– Bindu Sridhar**

3494. Some candidates are kept "in the loop" so that you can employ them when the time is right.

3495. Our work is our identify.

3496. Managing creative people is frustrating, but also intensely rewarding.

3497. At some point in your lives you will contemplate a career change. Some of us find courage to make it and others prefer to stick it out till the end. **– Hema Gopal Krishna**

3498. Hero always wins at the end.

3499. Most mosquito repellents contain prallethrin or allethrin potent in pesticides, which are injurious to health. So restrict the use of mats, coils and vaporizers.

– Insight, July/Aug 2006

3500. The consumption of soft drinks is on the decline world wide as they cause obesity and tooth decay. Carcinogen Benzene was found in soft drinks.

– Insight, July/Aug 2006

3501. Lifts are a means of vertical transport.

3502. The percentage of accidents in lifts is very small compared to other means of transport. **– Mr. N.K Panchal. [The Chief Inspector of lifts and Escalators Govt. of Gujarath.]**

3503. I embarked on the 200 km drive, all alone just for my friend.

– Usha Mani

3504. Do you know your friend is just a friend or something more?

3505. Keep your ears and eyes open and grab those subtle hints.

3506. Listen to your friends they say something you do not see.

3507. Not every one is slow as you think more than a friend.

3508. To know he or she in love

3509. When he asks you to give up some bad habit.

3510. He or she does little acts of kindness such as waiting in long queue to buy tickets offering out of the way to drop someone home, He or she is admired with a word of appreciation, He or she may purchase a burger for a hungry friend. He or she has a spark of jealousy.

3511. He or she gets offended when other friends poke fun at you, [once he was art of the group making fun of you]. He or she may have a tinge of possessiveness.

3512. Suddenly, his or her conversation may turn to your family members sister, brother, mom dad, grandpa, uncle etc.

3513. He or she may attend classical music you are practicing.

3514. When he or she in the audience, you dance wildly.

3515. He or she may have meal with you.

3516. You get agitated when you hear of his or her casual flings, he or she had.

3517. Any one of the events or all of them are true then it is certain you are falling in love, and a relationship is sure to develop. – **Usha Mani**

3518. Never ever show fear. Stalking stems from Narcism, they think that women should be attracted to them.

3519. We must establish first all the facts, if stalking is coincidental accidentally or voluntary. When stalking is voluntary, it becomes strong suspicion.

3520. Two types of offence.

3521. Cognisable offence.

3522. Non-cognisable offence where he has caused no offence or harm.

3523. Stalker mind set –

3524. "I am concerned about you. I know what is good for you and can help you lead your life in better manner".

3525. One does not know when the line between flirtation and obsession has been crossed.

3526. It is an instinctive feeling or a nagging doubt that everything is not fine.

3527. The talent cannot reach the utmost heights.

3528. I have more character than brains, more brains than talent or specific gifts. – **Maugham**

3529. Value of culture is character.

3530. It is not beauty but goodness that is important.

3531. You must not pursue success. **– Maugham**

3532. There is no more merit in having read a thousand books. **– Maugham**

3533. The writer who wrote for money did not write for him. If his books do not sell the fault lies with the public, not with him.

3534. One must take literature one's life's work.

3535. Writing should become habit. You cannot write well unless you write much and form a habit. **– Maugham**

3536. Success spoils people. Success destroyed Arnold, the author.

3537. Artist should be indifferent to praise or blame.

3538. Pains of production are like pains of childbirth Unlike mothers, the authors lose interest very soon in the child born. [work published]. **– Maugham**

3539. The artist is a freeman people think he is cynical because he does not attach importance to virtues. **– Maugham**

3540. Failure makes people better.

3541. It takes two to make love, and man's meat is woman's poison.

3542. Literature is one of the man's most important pursuits.

3543. The writer does not feel with but feels in, he has no sympathy but empathy.

3544. Not the whole of life is long enough to learn to write well.

3545. The end of an artist is production, but the end of other men is right action. **— Maugham**

3546. We do not write because we want, we write because we must. **— Maugham**

3547. So long as man is man he must be prepared to face all the woes that he can bear.

3548. Hypocrisy is the most difficult vice, cannot be practiced at spare time like adultery it is a whole time job. — **Maugham**

3549. Adultery needs unceasing vigilance, a hopeless passion for a married woman. — **Maugham**

3550. Art goes full circle indeed.

3551. Guidelines to better life.

Do not smoke

Watch your body weight. Lose extra weight.

Moderate exercise for 15 to 30 minutes

Eat at least 700 gm of vegetables fruits.

Eat at least 400 gm of whole wheat.

No alcohol.

Limit your meat 100 gm. Per day.

Avoid fatty foods.

Use less of salt

Annual medical checkups after 60 age.

3552. Do not fold your suit or keep it in a plastic cover.

3553. Time is money. We think twice before squandering with How do you spend your time?

3554. Speed is the order of the day.

3555. One must learn time management. Some hints.

List all tasks in order of priorities.

Delegate some tasks to your subordinates.

Avoid duplication.

Be precise.

Take quick timely decisions.

Avoid mistakes.

Allocate time for each task.

Personal interaction with lunch or snacks.

Save time.

Arrange things in order.

Do not take other's work and avoid obligation.

Avoid distractions to do justice to your work

Make use of wait time productively.

Organise you table in such a way that you need not spend time looking for even a stapler or an envelope. Keep things required handy.

Others are prone to eat your time. So avoid unnecessary meetings you can give time slot for friend's and also keep them informed.

Every body has his own way of working and manage time. One size does not fit all.

You cannot hold the time back, you can only go along. The time is slipping away from your hands.

3556. Most people go ahead during the time others waste.

3557. Organistion is as strong as top performers.

3558. Talent comes at a price.

3559. Talented employees are worth their weight in gold, it is only fair to pay them well.

3560. The very best come at a high cost.

3561. O! life no life, but lively form of death. **– King Lear**

3562. Romeo and Juiliet is an unfortunate pair. In Indian History you have tragic love story Anarkali who was buried alive by father king of her lover Love story, in which lovers meet at their end. Devdas is a love story, but hero gets drunk and dies of TB at the door of his beloved and heroine was a helpless victim in marriage.

3563. The rivalry between two families of Romeo and Juliet is extended to servants and dogs. The servants of enemies fight.

3564. The enmity percolates from top to bottom not other way round.

3565. The children fight and parents continue to fight even after children become friends.

3566. He Jests at scars that never felt a wound.

3567. She speaks yet she says nothing what of that?

3568. "He eyes discourse, I will answer it". **– Romeo**

3569. Romeo – "Lady I swear by the moon................"

3570. Juliet – "O, swear not by the moon, it is not constant, it changes ...."

3571. After 1969, young man "My darling I swear by the moon".

Young woman "Do not swear by the moon it is only rocks and dust ....."

3572. Swearing in love is a common feature.

Romeo – " What shall I swear?"

Juliet – "Do not swear if you want you can do so by your self".

Juliet –

3573. At 9'O clock — I sent the nurse she promised to return with in half an hour. She did not come. Did she meet him? O! no, no that is not. My thoughts go fast ten times that of sun light.

[You read similar thoughts in Rukmini. Rukmini loved

Krishna. She sent a brahmin with a love letter. He did not return soon. She says "Did the brahmin go to him? Was Krishna there? Perhaps he did not see him? Perhaps he (old man) got tired on the way? Did Krisna read the letter what did he think? Did he take it seriously? Did he think I was in haste? Why did not the old brahmin come back?"

3574. Juliet says

"What is in a name? That which we all rose by any other name would smell as sweet.

3575. Capulet – angry father says.

3576. "Hang thee, young baggage. .....dis obedient.

I tell thee what, writh get thee to church on Thursday or never after look me in the face speak not reply not do not answer me."

3577. What did angry father say?

We have one that is too much, and we have curse in having this daughter.

"I will not answer you I will not love you. I will give you to my friend. If you do not agree, hang, beg or die in the streets. I will never say you are my child".

3578. A girl or boy meets an angry father some time or other.

3579. A father has a trump card. He says that he will not give any portion of his property and a girl is dependent on father.

3580. Choose one of the girls.

Cordelia

Juliet

Desdimona

Cordelia–She speaks against the will of father, foregoes her share in Kingdom and gets happily married.

Desdemona: She elopes with her lover incurs father's wrath.

Juliet : She is a timid girl, only pleads for her love. He goes to her lover and kill herself.

3581. Attitudes refuse to change. Dowry continues to remain a reality and therefore girls continued to be viewed as a burden. **– Kalpana Sharma**

3582. Girls refuse to marry a man her parents have chosen for her, **- Kalpana Sharma**

3583. The problem of sex selection is not easy one to tackle. The law alone will not suffice to implement it.

3584. Juliet takes sleeping drug. She thinks of all those horrors of death, grave yard coffins, ghosts and spirits, she thinks whether the drug will work and awakes before Romeo comes.

3585. [Thoughts at the time of self willed death are strange]

3586. Romeo says "Here is to my love (drinks poison) O true apothem carry

3587. The drugs are quick – Thus with a kiss I die.

3588. Juliet says "Poison I see has been his timeless end."

3589. Lovers die un natural deaths.

3590. The genius has a way of cropping up in un expected places.

Shakespeare was born on April 23, 1564 and dies on April 23, 1616, [at 52 age] He married Anne Hathaway, 8yrs older on Nov 23, 1552

3591. Namrata is some one you would not regret knowing

3592. – sleep storage, study and safety for kids.

3593. 3 bs – Beautiful, bright, brilliant for young girls.

3594. Desiviagra – Edegra, penegra, caverta, silagra etc. – as effective as foreign brands, to be taken on an empty stomach one hour to the anticipated act, starting with 25mg going to 100mg, a prescription drug to be taken under doctor's supervision. **– Dr. Prakash Kothari**

3595. Erection once lost is not lost forever. **– Dr. Prakash**

3596. Nine to five [time] jobs are common in all the states.

3597. Men can do certain things well and women other things. Men and women are complementary to each other. One need not prove ones strength.

3598. Every body commits mistakes and sensitive people suffer a lot.

3599. Affection, openness and appreciation are qualities that build long lasting relationship.

3600. As for as that event [Rajiv association] is concerned I would sway it is a great tragedy a movemental, historical tragedy for which we deeply regret. – Anton balasingham Ltte's chief negotiator.

3601. Men need women and women need men.

3602. Not every one can carry off everything Guys gossip, it is harmless fun, they do not bitch.

3603. When men stray, something is wrong with the relationship.

3604. A smile is greatest turn on.

3605. Beauty has little to do with the way a woman looks.

3606. Jealousy and secrets are something that one grows out of.

3607. Men do not talk about work troubles at home.

3608. Men at home with the wife.

3609. You need more space with each other.

3610. Affairs happen un announced and get discovered at the most aackward of times leave in them emotional suffering and scarring. **— Dr. Vijay Nagaswami**

3611. The Ten commandments found it necessary to exhort people, not to covet the neighbours wife.

— **Dr. Vijay Nagaswamy**

3612. Today women are rapidly becoming active initiators of affairs. — **Dr. Vijay Nagaswamy**

3613. An affair is a dynamic relationship, not a static one, it requires nourishment in terms of love, time and energy which are infinite supply. — **Dr. Vijay Nagaswamy**

3614. Sooner or later, the affair is going to demand more. No inamorato is going to be perennially satisfied with a few stolen moments. When the demands increase the person is at a crossroads whom to choose spouse or paramour? Not an easy choice.

3615. It is natural to feel attracted to a perfect stranger.

3616. Your fate and quality of you marriage determine the way you respond to the feeling of attraction.

3617. Affairs happen only when gaps exist in marriage.

3618. Affairs can be survived and forgotten.

3619. Types of Affairs

Sex seeking affairs compensating for unsatisfying marital sex.

The fulfillment seeking affairs – Either one or both partners feel unsatisfied in marriage.

The legimisation or pattern – repetition affairs.

When parents indulge in affairs, the children repeated.

The peer-pressure affairs when one belongs to peer group, that encourages extra marital affairs.

The revenge affairs – The person takes revenge and indulge in affairs.

The good friends affair – It starts as platonic friendship and end up as an affair.

Affairs that happen – The affairs, happen for no good reason. Suddenly it happens.

3620. Foot Ball mad Thais are spending millions of dollars more on electricity this month (June 2006), as they stay up through the night to watch world cup matches (at Berlin).

3621. On an average we make 15000 facial movements daily.

– Shubhrakishan

3622. Wheat grass juice prevents tooth decay and stops hair greying. 15ml of wheat grass juice has as many vitamins as ½kg of broccoli.

3623. Banana has high dose of potassium.

3624. Wipe down the phone you use at work at least every other day.

3625. Since 2002, sex workers have been granted the same rights as people in other profession. Industry in Germanys

3626. About 400000 people work in sex trade every year.

3627. About 40000 sex workers travelled Germany from Eastern Europe, Asia, and Africa during the Olympic Games.

3628. Germany is a source transit and destination country for sex workers. **– U.S. State Department**

3629. Most of the regular sex workers come from Russia Ukraine, Poland, Tatiana, and Croatia. **– 2-7-2006**

3630. Girl power is not just limited to shopping sprees and is fast translating into a passion for this so called “man game” football.

3631. Football beer and women are in irresistible combination.

3632. Football in the 21st century is an industry where managers have the technology to know the exact distance a player has covered in a match, the speed in which he strikes the ball and a forensic break down of passes, shots tackles and runs. **– Daniel Taylor**

3633. Sometimes, some where some one just made money.

3634. Where you go tomorrow depends on where you are to day.

3635. The secret of getting ahead is getting started.

3636. A German scientist has created the smallest soccer pitch 20000 of them could fit on the top of a human hair. Created using nano technology, it is 500 by 380 nano metres.

— **6-7-06**

3637. Hamelin – [German] Once upon a time, the pied piper had the medieval city (Hamelin) spell bound. The city wass full of rats. The pied piper drew all the rats away with the lure of his pipe from the city of bouo the irresistible lure of the World Cup drew thousands of fans to city squares despite Germany's 0-2 loss to Italy in the Semifinals. — **6-7-2006**

3638. I like Germany but my heart booms for Italy.

— **Luderitz a [German Fan]**

3639. The ability to make fuel efficiently from any kind of plant is with in reach. — **A Federal US report**

3640. Fossil fuels are plant matter that has been subjected to heat and pressure over millions of yers. Ethanol production turns plant material directly into fuel by breaking it into alcohol. — **6-7-06**

3641. Thunder and only a lightning bolt always generates lighting Thunder. The bolt 1 to 5cm in diameter could cause the air temperature to rise up to 30000 degrees C. Such a studden rise of air temperature causes explosive expansion of the bolt area to produce compression or shock waves that are heard up to 20-to 30kms away. As thunder or thunder rumblings. The time lapse between the two in seconds multiplied by 330 gives roughing the distance of lighting in metres.

3642. Love of learning – Is the ability to learn a natural instinct? Is the ability to learn acquired?

3643. These two questions are asked in schools at home and work places. The answer is both. The ability to learn is partly natural instinct passed through genes from parents and partly it is acquired. — **The Hindu 6-7-06**

3644. All of us may not be blessed with this natural instinct, but we can make effort and master learning cycle.

3645. Learners are not afraid to make mistakes.

3646. Sex sells far and wide for eternity.

3647. Experience takes years but expertise just 30 minutes.

3648. Four days before the World Cup final tickets in Berlin on the black market went for 10 times their face value. "It is going for 1500 Euros" — **a dealer in Munich [Germany]**

3649. The World Cup final is between Italy and France on Sunday — **9-7-06**

3650. People get drawn to sex objects.

3651. For Miss India, along with the crown comes a whole round of eyes with a good-looking neighbour.

3652. Behind those eyes lies a trust fund.

3653. There is not time for sentimentality. We are all chasing money.

3654. Asha Bhonsle started her career at 14 age, she has more than 30 thousand songs to her credit duty her 54 year long career.

3655. Keep your insides clean with a regular colonic irrigation.

— **Mehercastelino**

3656. Malaysia – Maly National language rainy season November to January currency – **Malaysian Ringitt = Rs. 12,**

3657. For a woman, it is difficult to choose between beauty and brains.

3658. Sometimes friendships at work can cause more grief than joy. So maintain a low level of intimacy.

3659. You cannot change the past.

3660. Cholesterol and coronary heart diseases go hand in hand,

3661. ABCDE – Annual (World) Bank Conference on Development Economics held in January – **2006**

3662. One fundamental challenge shared by developing and transition countries is how to reduce poverty and inequality.

– Erik Berglog

3663. Germany scores much higher than any other country on honesty followed by Greece, Ireland, Estonia, Spain, and Turkey.

– James Anderson [Senior Economist, World Bank]

3664. Victoria Beckham wife of David Beckham has ordered a pounds 10000 belt for the English soccer captain which expands if you have had a little too much to eat.

– 12-7-2006

3665. German Chancellor Anela Merkel congratulated Italy on winning the World Cup on 9-7-2006. But said the German side was the "Champion of our hearts".

3666. The victorious team World Cup 2006, was given rapturous welcome in Rome (the solid gold trophy).

3667. There are senseless acts of violence designed to strike at those innocent people who were just going about their daily lives.

– United States [after Bombay blasts in trains on 11-07-2006.]

3668. It is proposed partially replaces diesel with pongamia (kanuga in Telugu) oil as fuel for good vehicles in Krishna Dist (12-7-06)

3669. TRAI – The Telecom Regulatory Authority of India has issued a regulation on code of practice for metering and Billing Accuracy.

3670. 5 Five percent of electricity can be saved by avoiding the use of the stand by mode, when they are not in use.

3671. Law and business as usual cannot go together.

3672. Life of test tube light of 40w is around 3500 hours. [2000 hrs minimum]

3673. People with a BMI (Body Mass Index), weight (in kgs) Height in meters (square of the height in meters), of more than 30 are considered obese.

3674. Once I lose 50 kgs, I want to propose to somebody

— **Smitha**

3675. The payment of principal a mount EM1 towards housing loan is to be dedicated under section 80C and interest part of EmI up to Rs. 150000 is to be deduced in a financial year.

3676. Do not drink fluids while eating.

3677. Avoid milk shakes and cold drinks.

3678. Limit snacks between meals.

3679. Eat proteins first then vegetables.

3680. Penny wise pound wise (Investment policy)

3681. Vegetables slow ageing.

3682. Mobile Phone radiation damages DNA.

3683. More than a million people now in their 30s (2006-July) could live to be 100 years old and beyound.

3684. The 'ear wax' consists of dead skin and dirt.

3685. The complete Manual of suicide by Wataru Tsurumi published in 1993, sold one million copies is the complete guide to killing one self. The author says "Killing one self not a crime. It is not a right to criticise those who killed themselves because we all have the freedom".

3686. Only a man can commit rape

– Section 375 of the IPC states that rape

3687. Making a woman guilty of committing rape is conceptually inconceivable.

3688. The Bureau of Energy Efficiency BEE has developed an energy labeling programme which will be used to rate tube light brands under the light brands under the programme tube lights would be rated on the scale of 1 to 5 stars with the most efficient product carrying a 5-star rating B.E.E, tabled products are likely to start coming into the market in July 2006. **– INSIGHT – August – 06**

3689. 9 out of 10 women diet. As non-surgical means include diet exercise weight loss, medicines and electro muscle stimulation (EMS).

3690. Liposuction – It is a technique used world world.

3691. For removal 10 CC to 30 CC of fat, liposuction takes 15-20 minutes costing 6 to 8 thousand only.

3692. It is safe and bloodless. Small incisions [4 mm] are made in the target region and a liquid is introduced to liquify and loosen fat which is then sucked out with a metal tube called canula. Fat can be removed from any area of the body - tummy. Buttocks, hips, thighs, legs arms, breast, back, chin neck, and even face. (A). **– INSIGHT – August 2006**

3693. Housing loan, availed, may include stamp duty and registration fees as part of cost of Purchasing a house (Home loans] **– INSIGHT – August – 2006**

3694. Goitre – An enlargement of the thyroid gland is goitre. A person may have goitre when his or her thyroid gland is over active. Under active or normally active.

– INSIGHT – August – 2006

3695. Obesity – It is a Chronic disease where people have too much of body fat as a result of consuming too much of high caloric food. There are 1.2 billion obese people in the world and 35 p.c of them are in India ranking one among the top 10 obese nations. Obesity related diseases include cardiac disease, diabetes, hyper tension. High cholesterol, stroke, certain types of cancers, digestive disorders, respiratory diseases, arthritis, depression, sleep apnea menstrual irregularity fertility related problems. And obese people have 50 to 100 percent increased risk of premature death. — **INSIGHT — August 2006**

3696. "To this day, many stories about Bruce Lee continue to be told and many of which are fabricated or exaggerated."

— **Robert Lee [brother of Bruce Lee]**

3697. Children need to exercise 90 minutes of moderate physical activity 22-7-2006

3698. A judge in North Carolina has ruled unconstitutional a 201-year-old law banning cohabitation of unmarried couples.

— **22-07-06**